D1546214

The Struggle
over Reform in
Rabbinic Literature

The Struggle over Reform in Rabbinic Literature

During the Last Century and a Half

ALEXANDER GUTTMANN

Professor of Talmud and Rabbinics

Hebrew Union College–Jewish Institute of Religion

Foreword by Rabbi Solomon B. Freehof

THE WORLD UNION FOR PROGRESSIVE JUDAISM
JERUSALEM   NEW YORK

Library of Congress Cataloging in Publication Data

Guttmann, Alexander.
  The struggle over reform in Rabbinic literature during the last
century and a half.

  "Hebrew sources": p.
  Bibliography: p.
  Includes index.
  1. Reform Judaism—Controversial literature—History
and criticism. 2. Responsa—1800— —History and
criticism. I. Title.
BM197.G86   296.8'346   75-45046
ISBN 0-8074-0005-X

Copyright, 1977

by The World Union For Progressive Judaism
838 Fifth Avenue
New York, N.Y.

MANUFACTURED IN THE UNITED STATES OF AMERICA

To my children

Ari
Naomi
Esther
Judy

Contents

Part Two: SOURCES

A Word of Thanks

I AM SINCERELY indebted to Rabbi Solomon B. Freehof for calling attention to the need for and importance of a scholarly book on our topic; to Rabbi William A. Rosenthall for proceeding vigorously with the realization of the project and for his encouragement which persuaded me to write this book.

Warm thanks are due Rabbi Alexander M. Schindler, president, Union of American Hebrew Congregations and Rabbi Richard G. Hirsch, executive director, World Union for Progressive Judaism who, by their wholehearted and decisive actions, brought to fruition the publication of this volume; to Rabbi Uri D. Herscher, executive vice president, Hebrew Union College–Jewish Institute of Religion, for his personal interest and indefatiguable labor in clearing the obstacles that delayed the publication time and again.

To Rabbi Lewis R. Bornstein I am very grateful for his excellent textual scrutiny of the entire manuscript; to Nancy Friedman, wife of Rabbi Barry Friedman; to Deborah Kaplan, wife of Rabbi Steven B. Kaplan for their thorough linguistic examination of the text; and, with respect to the final chapters, to Rabbi Gary A. Glickstein and to his wife Joan, for their meticulous reading.

My profound gratitude goes to Mr. Ralph Davis, Director of Publications, Union of American Hebrew Congregations, ably assisted by Ms. Frances Gizerian, for his superb design and production work.

The staff of the Library of the Hebrew Union College–Jewish Institute of Religion was very helpful. Credit for the careful preparation of the typescript goes to Miss Yetta Gershune, Mrs. Edith Goffin and Mrs. Shirley Kaplan.

My loving thanks go to my son Ari and my daughters Naomi, Esther and Judy for lifting my spirit with their constant expressions of confidence in me and my work. I am also grateful to my brother, Professor Henry Guttmann, for many helpful suggestions.

It is with greatest reverence, gratitude and love that I acknowledge here the decisive influence of my late father and teacher, Professor Michael Guttmann, of blessed memory, who first introduced me to the modern scholarly methods of interpreting and evaluating talmudic and rabbinic sources.

My acknowledgments would be lacking without remembering my eminent teachers who taught me the fundamentals of genuine scholarship. Among them were: Professors Ludwig Blau, Ignaz Goldziher, Michael Guttmann, Eduard Mahler, Budapest; Michael Guttmann, Isaac Heinemann, Albert Lewkowitz, Israel Rabin, Gotthelf Bergsträsser, Carl Brockelmann, Franz Praetorius, Hans Heinrich Schaeder, Artur Ungnad, Breslau; Eugen Mittwoch, Berlin.

In the years that followed I had very rewarding and frequent contact and exchange of ideas with many distinguished colleagues, among them Rabbis Leo Baeck, Jakob Freimann; Professors Ismar Elbogen, Eugen Taeubler, Max Wiener, Jacob Z. Lauterbach, Jacob Mann, Jechiel J. Weinberg and Chaim Tchernowitz.

My appreciation goes to the Hebrew Union College–Jewish Institute of Religion and its Presidents Dr. Julian Morgenstern, Dr. Nelson Glueck of blessed memory, and Dr. Alfred Gottschalk. My warmest thanks to Dr. Jacob R. Marcus for his never failing friendship throughout the years.

Most stimulating to me in writing this book was the constant probing interest of my students in the classroom, as well as in the pulpits and universities.

However, my deepest gratitude, more than I can express in words, goes to my beloved wife and disciple Manya who, as in the past, has been most helpful and supportive, and a constant source of encouragement to me in persevering whenever obstacles threatened to impede my work.

Foreword

THE GRAND dynamic of Jewish history remains unexplained. This is partly due to the fact that it has been consciously concealed by a doctrine. The doctrine is expressed in the classical words: "Moses received the Law on Sinai, handed it to Joshua, Joshua to the Elders," etc., etc. This states firmly and almost defiantly that Judaism, from the time of Mount Sinai, has remained the same. There have been no real changes.

The psychological value of this firm doctrine is obvious. It has served to unite the generations, yet its weakness is that it conceals the truth about the extraordinary changefulness of Jewish history which certainly is as significant a fact as its consistency. Actually, it is doubtful whether any historical unit has gone through as many drastic revolutions as has Judaism. It changed from a tribal economy to a royal state, from a royal state to a world-scattered statelessness, from a religion rooted in agriculture to one totally divorced from the soil, from a central religious authority to one of independent study and judgment, etc., etc. The curious thing about Judaism is this consciously concealed dynamic which explains the changes as interpretations of what was always inherent in the tradition. This explanation is surely not factual and certainly fails to do justice to the remarkable power of Judaism and Jewry to live through drastic changes and yet retain a

strong sense of consistent personality. It is this co-existence
of change and consistency which needs explanation if the
miracle of Jewish endurance is to be explained in human terms.

Perhaps the most important period for studies in search of
this explanation is the rise of Reform Judaism, because here, for
the first time, changes were made not as a slow growth of
custom or by careful interpretation of texts but by conscious,
radical action seeking to adjust Judaism to a new environment.
How this conscious change confronted the doctrinal tradition
of changelessness, how it justified itself, why it was attacked
and how the battle cries slowly died down and a sort of peace
was achieved: all this should throw light on how in other
epochs Jewish history confronted drastic changes and somehow
embodied them into the total tradition.

In spite of the fact that there is a large amount of source
material available, the Reform movement hitherto has not
been adequately studied as a sample phenomenon in Jewish
history but as if it were isolated and unprecedented phenomenon. This is because the histories of the movement were based
mostly upon newspaper, magazine articles and reports of conventions.

But the true confrontation with tradition took place not in
modern language reports but in the historic rabbinic literature
found chiefly in the Responsa of the time. These rabbinic
sources were of course always available to specialist-scholars,
but now they are made accessible to all interested in the true
social biography of Judaism. Alexander Guttmann in the
present volume has supplied what was lacking in the literature
of this modern variation in Jewish history. He has given the
chief texts of all the relevant Responsa debates and made them
available to all historians. The material ranges from the Responsa
of the greatest early nineteenth century authorities marshalled
in Eleh Divre Ha-bris (1819) to Moshe Feinstein, the leading

modern Orthodox authority in America (Igros Moshe) who doubts the validity of certain Reform marriages.

Dr. Guttmann himself comes to some important conclusions about the nature of this on-going rabbinic debate: why it calmed down finally and how Reform, Conservatism, Reconstructionism, Secular Nationalism have slowly arrived, if not at a peace, at least at an armistice with the old tradition of unchanging consistency.

The material which this book provides will be a mine for the historian who will wish to arrive at some understanding of the great miracle in the history of a small people which enabled it to face tremendous changes more drastic perhaps than those faced by any other historic group and has given it the power to remain itself, deeply conscious of its unity with the past and its comradeship with its brothers all over the world.

Solomon B. Freehof

Introduction

AS LIFE itself constantly changes, so does religious life. The changes in religious life are necessitated by a variety of exigencies—both evolutionary and revolutionary developments, external and internal pressures. These changes may represent natural growth (evolutionary development) or necessary adjustment to new situations. So far as Jewish religious life is concerned, they may also be the result of new spiritual, cultural, and material developments within the host-nations in the diaspora, or the product of legislative activities of the Jewish leadership. In some instances gentile governments compelled the Jewish communities under their control concerning certain changes. Such changes were often of local character and varied according to place and time.

Changes accepted by large segments of Jewry are often introduced by outstanding, recognized leaders and endorsed by synods. Exceptionally, as in the case of the Napoleonic "Sanhedrin," the gentile authorities may request the convening of a synod. In such instances the decisions of the synod are binding upon the entire Jewish community living in the country concerned. Some examples from the Pharisaic-Rabbinic period of antiquity and from the Middle Ages and later follow.

The Sanhedrin, or *Bet Din Hagadol*, of the Hasmonean period was able to introduce changes in Jewish law and custom because of the authority vested in it by the Hasmonean rulers. During Herod's time, the followers of the Pharisaic leadership —that is, mainstream Judaism—voluntarily recognized the authority of the Sanhedrin, then a private academy, because of the prestige of its members. Their decisions, many of which constituted changes, were accepted even though the Sanhedrin was not backed by the political government.

Since the authority of the Pharisaic-Rabbinic leadership was based on voluntary recognition, naturally there were groups that would not join the mainstream. The major dissenting groups before the destruction of the Temple in 70 C.E. were the Sadducees, the Essenes, and the Dead Sea Covenanters, who are generally considered an Essenian group. Among the sectarian groups, the Judeo-Christians were the most important.

Adjustments were made continually throughout antiquity. Whenever circumstances necessitated, a change was made. Often it was done hesitatingly and with delay, but it was done. Groups that opposed changes or wanted more radical changes remained peripheral. In the course of time, they either returned to, and were absorbed by, the mainstream, as was the case with the Sadducees and many Essenes; or they became a sect, as did, for example, the Karaites; or they went a step further and laid the foundation for another religion—that is, for Christianity.

Changes of consequence, whether sudden or revolutionary or of an evolutionary nature, whether of foreign origin or introduced by a rabbi or group of rabbis, required the consent, explicit or implicit, of a central, or at least major, recognized authoritative body. Occasionally, the endorsement of an outstanding personality sufficed. Such authoritative bodies often instigated the changes by issuing ordinances, which could be new laws, practices, observances, or prohibitions.

This process of making changes of consequence binding for mainstream Judaism, or for one of its major components, was the rule throughout antiquity and continued during much of the Middle Ages. In the talmudic period, the center of religious leadership, embracing most of the Jewish people, shifted from Palestine to Babylonia and remained there for eight hundred years, until the end of the geonic period in 1040 C.E.

Throughout the talmudic and geonic periods, fairly uniform changes in major issues, binding for mainstream Judaism, were ordained or endorsed by centrally recognized leaderships. In Palestine the recognized leadership was the Sanhedrin, or Great Court (Academy), headed by the *Nasi*. In Babylonia changes were introduced by the two great academies of Sura and Pumbedita, headed in talmudic times by the *rashe yeshivah*, heads of the academy, and in geonic times by the *Geonim* (*gaon*="glory" or "pride" of Israel), under the unifying leadership of the exilarch. After 200 C.E. Palestinian Jewry and its leadership played a secondary role.

The most important tie unifying the academies of Palestine and Babylonia was the Mishnah, recognized by both as the basis of postbiblical Judaism. The Mishnah was the point of departure for all further developments and changes. The frequent journeys of sages from Palestine to Babylonia and vice versa served to strengthen the ties between the two Jewries and to harmonize as much as possible their views and practices. This exchange was of crucial importance, since it prevented schisms, and helped to maintain a fairly uniform mainstream Judaism. This uniformity, however, applied to law but not to custom. In fact, tannaitic law by this time already required that local customs be respected and observed.

The methods of making changes, of adjusting the law to the prevailing needs and circumstances, were manifold and changed throughout the ages. Nevertheless, all changes were made with the doctrine in mind that the Torah is divine, and therefore its precepts could not be changed. Changes, however, were unavoidable, due to the fact that internal and external conditions were constantly changing. Old laws, though biblical, had to be abolished, and new ones had to be introduced in order to keep religion in consonance with the realities of life.

The most effective method of changing the law without appearing to do so—that is, without violating the doctrine of the divinity of the biblical laws—was through interpretation of the law. No law of the Torah was ever abrogated by traditional Judaism. However, more than half the laws were suspended entirely by suitable interpretation, or were reinterpreted. The largest category of suspended laws was that of the sacrificial cult. With the destruction of the Temple it was not too difficult to suspend these laws by suitable interpretation, though in former times the sacrificial cult had been continued even after the destruction of the Sanctuary (see Alexander Guttmann, "The End of the Jewish Sacrificial Cult," *HUC Annual*, 1967, pp. 137–48).

Creating a legal fiction was another way to change or circumvent a law. Among the laws of the Torah suspended even before the fall of the Temple was the *sotah* law (Num. 5:11–31). A major category of inoperative biblical laws in the Diaspora is that of "any commandment that depends on the land [of Israel]" (*M. Kiddushin* 1:9). Among these are laws pertaining to tithe, sabbatical year, "dough-offering" (for the priest), and so forth.

Interpretation sometimes completely changed the original meaning of the law. Thus the majority principle was established as torahitic by reading it into Exodus 23:2: "*Thou shalt* not *follow* a multitude to do evil; neither shalt thou bear witness in a cause to turn aside *after a multitude* to pervert justice." The italicized words were read as a syntactical unit and accepted as a principle of the Torah (e.g., *B. Chullin* 11a).

Equity played an important role in the endeavor of the

rabbis to change or abolish certain laws, or to introduce new laws. In the realm of civil law, the principle הפקר בית דין הפקר "Decision (declaration) of the court that certain property is ownerless has legal validity," is a significant example of equity jurisprudence. This principle permitted the court to settle a case involving propery in an equitable manner, even if to do so would be at variance with a law of the Torah or an established traditional law or practice. The successful introduction of this principle was justified by suitable interpretation of biblical passages (B. *Yevamot* 89b).

Talmudic-rabbinic laws giving women a greater role in religious life than was accorded them in the Torah or under the older Halachah also fall into the category of equity jurisprudence. Ordaining that, as a rule, women kindle the Sabbath and holiday lights is an obvious instance. Other examples include the right of the woman to initiate the divorce procedure in certain instances though no such provision is found in the Bible (see particularly B. *Ketuvot* 77a–77b; *Shulchan Aruch, Even Ha'ezer* 154); her participation in the celebration of Passover (e.g., she has to drink four cups of wine just as the men are required to do, B. *Pesachim* 108a); and her partcipation in the celebration of Chanukah and Purim (B. *Shabbat* 23a; B. *Megillah* 4a, etc.).

The purpose of some of the new rulings was to further friendly, or at least tolerable, relations with the controlling authorities of the diaspora. Such a ruling was דינא דמלכותא דינא "The law of the [non-Jewish] rulers is valid law" (B. *Gittin* 10b), that is, it must be observed even if Jewish law has no corresponding ruling at all in a certain instance. This principle, however, is not all-encompassing; it has its limitations.

Over the centuries a number of new laws and practices had been introduced long after the Torah was concluded. Some of these commemorated historical events, such as Purim and Chanukah. Others were adjustments to the non-Jewish surroundings, such as certain practices of the *seder*, the Passover meal. Some of these practices were justified by elaborate interpretation, as was the introduction of Chanukah (B. *Shabbat* 21a ff., especially 23a). Others, such as some of the *seder* ceremonies, were first accepted tacitly as general practices of the surroundings, and then were later given religious sanction.

All these methods of changing, abolishing, and introducing laws, including the *takkanot* (ordinances) and *gezerot* (prohibitive ordinances), were employed most extensively in the talmudic period (see Alexander Guttmann, *Rabbinic Judaism in the Making* p. 257 n. 4). Their application declined, so far as fundamental changes are concerned, during the gaonic period.

They continued to decline throughout the later Middle Ages. The Jews of the medieval ghettos had only limited relations with the outside world, and therefore the need to initiate changes was not as urgent as previously. As a result, changes during the medieval period were relatively less fundamental in nature. Aside from regulating certain aspects of business life, the changes introduced during this period were concerned mostly with religious customs pertaining to prayers and the life-cycle. The changes were generally limited to a segment of the people—a community, a group of communities, or a country—and only rarely did they embrace all of Ashkenazic or Sefardic Jewry. This local limitation resulted from the lack of an authoritative, centrally recognized leadership. Occasional synods coped with urgent problems, but made no continual adjustments on a large scale. The influence of these synods was limited to certain areas.

Limited changes and slow adjustments resulted in a growing discrepancy between the Jewish ways inside the ghettos and gentile life outside them. Where ghettoization was not the rule, as in Spain, Jews were better able to adjust to the culture of the general society, although at a later time, it would nonetheless reject them for racial and theological reasons.

When the Jews of Central Europe left the ghettos and became part of the general society, many of them felt an urgent need for major adjustments. This feeling was shared by the gentile community. The gentile rulers often felt that the Jews, in addition to practicing a different religion, were not well adjusted to society as a whole. Enlightenment and emancipation made the Jews in various countries of Europe keenly aware of social and cultural tensions, and of discrepancies between themselves and their host nations which they had not felt while they were isolated in ghettos or ghettolike communities.

Following the emancipation of the Jews, the struggle over reform, which had existed at all times, though usually only on a latent and minor scale, became the central and crucial problem of Judaism. Leaving the ghettos and being integrated into the general society resulted almost immediately in the division of Jewry into two groups: the Liberals and the Orthodox. This schism was only the beginning; struggles on three fronts followed:

1. Struggles among the Liberals
2. Struggles among the Orthodox
3. Struggles between the Liberals and the Orthodox

The struggle over reform within the Orthodox branch of Judaism was, and still is, different from the struggle within Liberal Judaism. The Orthodox often adopted reforms to which they had vehemently objected in the past—for instance, permitting the sermon to be delivered in the vernacular—but they usually did so quietly, pointing out the necessity of the reforms without calling attention to the strong opposition offered by their great authorities in the past. Occasionally the Orthodox borrowed a reform from Liberal-Reform Judaism with minor modifications; for instance, they accepted the Bat Mitzvah, but observed it on a weekday (usually Sunday) instead of Saturday. In some instances the struggle over reform within Orthodoxy was fought with greater ardor, and with more venom, than any struggle among the reformers.

However, the most crucial struggle over reform was the one fought between Orthodoxy and Reform, or Liberal, Judaism. This struggle was of paramount importance because it threatened the unity of Judaism and the Jewish people. It did not result in a schism mainly because of the fact that, in spite of the fundamental differences between Orthodox Jews and Reform Jews in the realm of theology, the overwhelming weight of the struggle was focused on observances, that is, on law, ceremonies, and customs. Theology played a minor role, particularly from the view point of the average Jew.

In earlier times, Reform justified the changes it made by citing talmudic and rabbinic sources and precedents. Later, however, especially after the Pittsburgh Conference (1885), where the principal validity of the Oral Law had been openly denied, changes were introduced to conform to the spirit of the time. Laws and observances were discarded or modernized in order to harmonize with the cultures outside the ghettos, to make Jewish practice more palatable and acceptable in a Christian environment, and to stem the tide of mass conversion to Christianity.

The struggle over reform was not an exclusively Jewish affair. The secular authorities, sometimes even heads of state (e.g., Napoleon, who strongly interfered in matters pertaining to the Jewish religion), entered the struggle on their own initiative, since they had questions regarding the loyalty and acceptability of the Jews as an integral part of their nation. In most instances, however, one of the feuding Jewish parties asked the gentile authorities to interfere and to take steps against their Jewish adversaries.

Since the struggle over reforms within Reform Judaism has been treated extensively (see Bibliography), we shall not discuss this part of the struggle in great detail here. We shall concentrate, rather, on the struggle between Reform and Orthodox Judaism, particularly as it has been conducted and related in Hebrew, primarily in the responsa literature. Non-Hebrew literature will be considered only on a minor scale because the modern scholarly literature pertaining to the struggle over reform is based mainly on German and English sources, and is, therefore, easily accessible. The Hebrew responsa literature, though very significant, has been neglected. An examination of the Hebrew responsa literature will serve to provide a new perspective and a deeper insight into the struggle over reform in the past and the present.

In order to substantiate our observations and findings, we include in this book original English translations of Hebrew sources, mainly responsa, much of the material hitherto unknown or inaccessible to people working in the field of Jewish history. Because of the abundance of the Hebrew source literature, we include here only the most important parts of it. Lengthy passages are given in abbreviated form or in paraphrase, without blurring their essential contents.

Part One

THE STRUGGLE

I

Public Worship Service

The Minyan

THE QUESTION whether a nonobservant Jew may or or may not be counted as a member of the *minyan* in an Orthodox synagogue will be discussed later. Here we shall cite the views of two noted Reform rabbis concerning the *minyan*.

Rabbi Aaron Chorin of Arad, in his responsum *Kinat Ha'emet* (The zeal of truth), maintains that praying with a *minyan* is not a daily obligation, and is not even considered a *mitzvah*. He cites as the source of his opinion *Maharil*, who speaks about praying individually at home and going to the synagogue on the Sabbath and holidays. After quoting a statement by Rabbi Yochanan, "When God comes to the synagogue and does not find ten men there, He immediately gets angry" (B. *Berachot* 6b), which seems to contradict his opinion, he says, "In our time there is no anger. On the contrary, He says: 'Who has required this at your hand to trample my courts?' (Isa. 1:12). This is so because the holiness of the synagogue had been desecrated by those attending it without the fear of God."

Most interesting is Chorin's subsequent reasoning that what he had just said refers to the Orthodox, who pray without reverence and decorum. However, this is not true of the

3

reformers, and therefore he states, "You, who are praying with reverence and decorum . . . why should you cause, God forbid, God's anger saying: 'Why did I come and there is nobody?' Listen to me: If you are able to appoint ten men to pray daily in your synagogue, do it." [p. 197]*

The implication is clear. In our time, God does not get angry with the Orthodox Jews if they have no *minyan*, since they pray without reverence and decorum. Therefore, it is better for them to pray at home without a *minyan*. However, God does get angry with the reformers if they pray without a *minyan*, since they pray with reverence and decorum and should, therefore, pray in the synagogue with a *minyan*.

Today, Chorin's somewhat perplexing position is disregarded by Reform Judaism, but it continues to be a serious problem for the Orthodox. (See David Hoffmann, *Melamed Leho'il, Orach Chayin* resp. 1, pp. 28–29 and see below pp. 52, 57, 90). Some Conservative congregations count women as members of the *minyan*. In some (Orthodox) congregations, a Torah Scroll, placed on the *bimah*, is counted as the tenth man.

Rabbi Moshe Kunitz writes in a letter published in *Nogah Hatsedek* (pp. 27–28): "I advise you to open the synagogue every morning and evening, and ten idle men be appointed to pray there. . . . The houses of worship of the nations are open twice every day . . . following the ancient Jewish way. . . . Now observe the law . . ." [p. 200]. Needless to say, Rabbi Kunitz was one of the earliest Reform rabbis.

---

* Except where otherwise indicated, page numbers in brackets refer to the sources in Part II of this volume.

Text and Language
of the Prayers

THE STRUGGLE over reform manifested itself in the responsa and related literature most extensively and conspicuously in the realm of the prayers and other parts of the worship service in the synagogue. The Orthodox were opposed to any changes in the worship service; liberal Jewish leaders were eager to introduce reforms in this area.

The early reformers did not intend to replace Hebrew completely with the vernacular. They suggested, instead, some sort of compromise. Quite interesting in this respect is Rabbi Aaron Chorin's detailed discussion of the problem of the language of the prayers (Responsum *Kinat Ha'emet*). He quotes Mishnah *Sotah* 7:10 and other traditional sources which permit certain prayers to be said in any language and says: The Men of the Great Synagogue arranged the "prayer" (the Eighteen Benedictions) to be recited in Hebrew, on condition that the people would learn the Hebrew. For a person who does not understand Hebrew, it is better to pray in a language that he understands, as pointed out in *Sefer Chasidim*.

Then he suggests a compromise: the Eighteen Benedictions, the *Shema* and the prayers pertaining to it should be read in Hebrew. He maintains that they are written in easy Hebrew and can be learned without difficulty. The Men of the Great Synagogue wrote them in pure, simple Hebrew because

5

this was the distinguished language God used in speaking to our fathers and His prophets and in giving us the Torah. However, other prayers, which only very few men understand, should not be said in Hebrew. [pp. 192–93]

Eliezer Libermann also suggests a compromise, but an entirely different one (in *Or Nogah*, First Part). The "prayer" must be understood, and, therefore, it may be said in the vernacular. Libermann points out that the situation in Germany is quite different from that in Poland. The Jews in Germany speak German well and only a few know Hebrew; therefore they should pray in German. However, in Poland the Jews speak a faulty German (Yiddish), but they know Hebrew. Therefore, it is better for the Jews in Poland to pray in Hebrew, as ordained by the Men of the Great Synagogue, than to pray in a corrupt German, or in a good German which they do not understand. [p. 202]

Libermann has additional suggestions in the matter. Though prayers may be said in any language the worshipper understands, nonetheless it is proper to say some of the prayers in Hebrew. Children should be taught Hebrew, "the most important of all the languages." He suggests further that everyone in the synagogue should have a prayerbook. It is easier to follow the cantor if one has a prayerbook. A person who does not know Hebrew should use a prayerbook with German translation and follow every prayer with the reader. [p. 205]

We have examined the highlights of the positions of early Reform authorities concerning the use of Hebrew in the liturgy of the synagogue, as presented in Hebrew responsa. The Orthodox position is, of course, quite different. Characteristic views follow.

The first of the three prohibitions given on the title page of *Eleh Divre Haberit* is the one prohibiting any change in the traditional "order" (i. e., text, etc.) of the prayers. [p. 209] "The liberals . . . arbitrarily added some prayers and omitted others. . . . the silent prayer was abolished, the reading of the prophetic portion on Sabbath was omitted" (ibid., introduction).

Moses Sofer (*Chatam Sofer*) ibid., (pp. 6–11) declares that an authoritatively established *takkanah*, Jewish institution or ordinance, retains its validity even after the reason for it becomes invalid. This applies particularly to the texts of the prayers. However, the reason for the traditional prayers did not become invalid; therefore not even Prophet Elijah can abolish them (see *B. Yevamot* 102b). [p. 212]

Sofer's subsequent attack on reforms is directed against the omission of prayers for the coming of the Messiah, the return to the Land of Israel, and the reestablishment of the Temple service, that is, the sacrificial cult. Sofer also objects to the omission of the prophetic readings (*haftarah*), citing traditional sources (Mishnah *Megillah* 4:2, etc.) [pp. 213–14]

The reformers, however, do not believe the words of the prophets and sages with regard to these matters (see *Mishneh Torah, Mamrim*, chap. 3). [p. 213]

Rabbi Mordechai Benet of Nikolsburg likewise attacks the reformers, among others, for their omissions and changes of prayers (*Eleh Divre Haberit*, pp. 11–16). His first attack is directed against the new Reform prayerbook because it differs from all preceding prayerbooks as a result of omissions and other changes. Most important among the omissions are those concerning faith, redemption, and our hope for resurrection (ibid., pp. 41–42).

Rabbi Hirz Scheuer of Mainz claims that Mishnah *Sotah* 7:1, which permits the worshipper to pray in any language, applied only to the women of former times, since they did not understand Hebrew at all. This permission does not apply today, for today both men and women know some Hebrew, which they learn in childhood. The Talmud was written in Aramaic because in those days the Jews did not understand Hebrew. Today, however, any Jew, even a non-Hebrew-speaking Jew, fulfills his obligation if he says or hears the prayers in Hebrew. To say or hear the prayers in any other language does not fulfill the obligation.

Rabbi Scheuer also maintains that changing the content and text of the prayers represents the worst deviation from the Jewish faith, since the prayers take the place of the sacrificial cult commanded by God. In his opinion, such changes would split Judaism into two separate religions. [pp. 210–11]

Moses Sofer interprets M. *Sotah* 7:1, which permits certain prayers to be said in any language, as referring to prayers that are said at home but not in the synagogue. The fact that the average man does not understand Hebrew is no excuse for using the vernacular in the public service. Sofer believes that everyone should learn Hebrew in order to understand the Hebrew prayers. He reasons that if a person talks to a human king, he has to speak the language of the king. Hebrew is God's language. The world was created by God's Hebrew words. He gave us the Torah in Hebrew. [pp. 213–14]

Moses Sofer states further that in ancient times the Torah was translated into Aramaic during the service, but we no longer do this since people today do not understand Aramaic. However, they did not translate it into the vernacular because rendering a fully adequate translation is impossible. Therefore, this must not be done in the synagogue, although at home the Torah may be translated into any language. Occasional exceptions may be permitted in the synagogue but not on a permanent basis. [p. 222]

Akiba Eger, rabbi of Posen(Poznań), complains that some Jews do not understand Hebrew. This is a disgrace in the eyes of non-Jews, since every other nation speaks its own language and loves it. The Reform Jews teach their children French and Latin, but forsake the holy language. [p. 219]

The rabbis of Padua declare in a letter that the prayers must be said in Hebrew only, even by men who do not understand Hebrew. The rabbis of France objected to the custom of the women praying in French but not in Hebrew. [p. 223]

Rabbi Jacob of Lissa demonstrates the impossibility of translating Hebrew accurately, since the same Hebrew word has several different meanings. Praying in a foreign language may result, therefore, in a misunderstanding of beliefs and commandments. Furthermore, the study of the holy language is a *mitzvah*, as stated by Maimonides. If praying in other languages were permitted, Hebrew would be forgotten altogether. Rabbi Jacob of Lissa maintains, further, that our sages certainly had many other reasons, unknown to us, for retaining Hebrew. [pp. 227–28].

Rabbi Naftali Hirsch Katzenellenbogen, chief rabbi of the Upper District, Rhineland, says that Hebrew is the language transmitted to us from the time of the creation of the world, since God used Hebrew in creating the world. A person praying in Hebrew fulfills his obligation even if he does not understand it. Even difficult *piyutim*, religious poems, should be read in Hebrew although they are not understood. [p. 228]

Moses Sofer, in a responsum, advises to appoint only a pious rabbi who does not read non-Jewish books and who does not speak a foreign language; that is, he must speak Yiddish. He also claims that Maimonides apologized for borrowing from the books of the Greeks, explaining that he did so lest the people of God seek wisdom in the books of non-Jews. [p. 242]

Rabbi Akiba Joseph Schlesinger is quite outspoken against the use of foreign languages in services. He cites an incident in which a pious rabbi preached sermons in German. When this was related to Rabbi Meir Ish Shalom, he replied: "This is the beginning of a disaster. The first German-speaking rabbi is learned. Afterwards, an inferior German-speaking rabbi will be appointed. Finally, they will employ a *goy* as a rabbi." Rabbi Schlesinger then makes a peculiar statement: Most of the rabbis who preached in a foreign language did not live to old age. Some of them were killed, some remained childless, and the children of some became sinners. [pp. 75, 251]

The Orthodox prohibition against replacing Hebrew with the vernacular was not limited to the prayers alone. It embraced other areas as well. (see below p. 147)

In the same work, commenting on Moses Sofer's words, "Be heedful changing your name and language" (i.e., don't change them), Schlesinger says that Sofer does not refer to the family name but to the first name; that is, if one's first name is Aaron, he should not be called Adolf. According to a midrash, our ancestors were redeemed from Egypt for four reasons, one of them being that they did not change their names (*Vayikra Raba* 32:5). In another version the reading is "because they did not change their language." [p. 253]

After quoting more sources to the same effect, Schlesinger points out that the following languages are not among the prohibited languages: Hebrew, Greek, Aramaic, and Arabic. Accordingly, the Torah was given to Israel in these four languages, as interpreted in a midrash (*Sifre, Berachah* on Deut. 33:2; some texts have "Roman" rather than "Greek", see ed. Horowitz-Finkelstein, p. 395). Syriac and Persian are included in Aramaic. Then Schlesinger continues:

"Our ancestors, who were prohibited from speaking Hebrew, changed the language of the nations into Yiddish. Yiddish is, from the viewpoint of Jewish law, just like Hebrew. When M. Sofer ordained that the Jews must not change their language in our time, he referred to Yiddish. Translating the Torah into the languages of the nations entails many sins (see B. *Kiddushin* 49a). The only exceptions are the Aramaic translations by Onkelos and Jonathan ben Uziel (see *Shulchan Aruch, Even Ha'ezer* 38:25). We are allowed to translate the Torah into Yiddish perhaps because it is not a specific language of the nations, but only a corrupt language. However, to translate it into *Hochdeutsch* is prohibited. Our Mishnah (*Sotah* 7:1), permitting the use of foreign language in certain instances, refers to Yiddish (!)." Other conjectures concerning the meaning of M. *Sotah* 7:1 are also given.

Schlesinger also strongly objects to the study of secular wisdom in foreign languages. He also maintains that Reform, pursuing such wisdom, is a real heresy, etc. [pp. 253]

Among the resolutions adopted by the synod of Orthodox rabbis in Nagymihály (now Michalovce, Czechoslovakia) in 1865, the first proclaimed that sermons must not be preached in any foreign language, with the exception of Yiddish. [pp. 264–65]

Rabbi Chayim Bezalel Panet of Tasnád, in a responsum, declares that a man preaching to the people must use the language of his people if he is to be understood, and this language is Yiddish. Subsequently, he attacks Jews who waste their time speaking the language of non-Jews and studying secular subjects. He also attacks the *Prediger*, liberal Jewish preachers, claiming that they are ignorant of Talmud and Codes, and are unworthy as rabbis. They have no fear of God, and therefore they are not effective. [pp. 263–64]

Rabbi Moses Schick, in reply to the questions raised by his disciple, Rabbi Wolf Sofer, concerning preaching in German to people who understand only German, says: "There are many heretics and sinners. All of them started their wickedness by learning foreign languages and the wisdom of the gentiles."

Schick then utters a reasonable view, permitting preaching in German in a place where the people do not want to listen to anything but German. However, he subsequently retracts this opinion because of the opposition of many of his colleagues. Thus, he yielded to pressure against his better judgment. [p. 268]

Rabbi Hillel Lichtenstein complains in a responsum that the Jews of the diaspora, including their leaders, learned to speak the pure foreign language of their country. Therefore, the devil cleaves to them and they interpret the Torah in a blasphemous manner. They are hypocrites and liars, twisting the words of the Torah. The intention of the liberal preachers, he maintains, is to follow non-Jewish ways. They function as rabbis and are considered to be pious men. They also want to be considered Chasidim, and therefore give their people amulets. Rabbi Lichtenstein then flatly declares that no one speaking a foreign language "shall enter our camp, since our camp must remain holy." [p. 291]

Rabbi Jacob Chai Recanati of Pesaro was asked whether the sermons in Verona are preached in Hebrew or Italian. He answered that the sermons are preached in Italian so that everybody can listen, understand, and learn. However, he added, the sayings of our sages and biblical passages are cited in Hebrew, and are explained in good Italian either before or after they are said in Hebrew. [p. 182]

Subsequently, Recanati adds further details pertaining to the prayer services on the Sabbaths and holidays in Verona, such as: The public services on these days are conducted jointly by laymen and a professional reader (cantor). A layman reads the first part of the service followed by a cantor, dressed in cantorial garb, who conducts the main part of the service. The congregation says the *Amidah* ("silent prayer") silently, and the cantor repeats it aloud.

This information is significant inasmuch as it shows that the Jewish worship services in Verona described by Recanati follow in several respects those which are predominant even today in the traditional synagogues. The most fundamental difference between the two is the use of the organ at the services in Verona (*Nogah Hatsedek*, pp. 9 ff). Recanati defends this practice strongly by citing and interpreting many traditional sources, including the Shulchan Aruch. He calls attention to the fact that not a single halachic authority of the past, called *poskim*, even mentions the organ (op. cit. p. 10). The only limitations which he suggests are that a gentile play the organ on the Sabbath and that he be instructed on Friday to do so (ibid, p. 10).

Sefardic and Ashkenazic:
Pronunciation and Versions

Liberal Views

RABBI AARON CHORIN of Arad, replying to a complaint about the use of the Sefardic pronunciation by people (liberal Ashkenazim), says: "Changing the pronunciation from Ashkenazic to Sefardic is certainly permitted, since the sense of hearing testifies that the Ashkenazic pronunciation is unsound, inaccurate." This is confirmed by all the linguists of all times, he asserts.

Chorin subsequently states that Rabbi Nathan Adler of Frankfurt am Main, a rabbi in Moravia, stayed in Vienna for several months and prayed there in a *bet hamidrash* using the Sefardic pronunciation. [p. 196]

Rabbi Mosheh Kunitz of Ofen, in a reply to the Jewish congregation of Berlin, asserts that more than seven-eighths of the prayers said by the Jews ascend to God in the Sefardic pronunciation, and only the small remaining portion ascends in the Ashkenazic pronunciation. His statistics are based on his assumption that there are more than eight times as many Sefardim as Ashkenazim in this world. Consequently he approves of the change from the Ashkenazic to the Sefardic pronunciation. He also cites the case of Rabbi Nathan Adler, who prayed in his synagogue using the Sefardic pronunciation. [p. 198–99]

Eliezer Libermann, replying to Orthodox objections to reforms, defends some of the reforms by citing Sefardic practice.

In defense of omitting the silent *Amidah* he relates his experience in Palestine, where he often observed that great men, when they were pressed for time and had to go to a wedding or banquet or some similar event, said the *Amidah* aloud only. Libermann cites Maimonides among the Sefardic authorities who ordained that the *Amidah* should be said aloud only. Some Ashkenazic authorities also accept this custom. [p. 203]

Libermann also rejects the objection to the use of the Sefardic pronunciation, based on his own "logical" reasoning. All the great linguists, he says, testify that the Sefardic pronunciation is scientifically more accurate. He gives many linguistic details to prove the superiority of the Sefardic pronunciation. [pp. 203–204]

Orthodox Views

The late Chief Rabbi Herzog of Israel points out, in a specific instance pertaining to the location of weddings, that the Sefardim do not have to follow the Ashkenazic practice. [pp. 308, 310]

Rabbi Yechiel Weinberg, in *Seride Esh*, vol. 2, resp. 5 (pp. 7–12), discusses the question of whether children who learned the Sefardic pronunciation in school are permitted to use this pronunciation when reading their Bar Mitzvah portion from the Torah, if the congregation is accustomed to the Ashkenazic pronunciation. After a very lengthy discussion he arrives at an affirmative conclusion. He reasons as follows. Only the Sefardim pronounce the letters correctly, distinguishing between *Alef* and *Ayin*, and between *Tav* and *Samech*. He also cites recent literature to the effect that no objection should be raised against the cantor or Torah reader, regardless of whether he uses the Sefardic pronunciation or the Ashkenazic. An objection in the case of a Bar Mitzvah would be a serious mistake. It would affect the *mitzvah* pertaining to his education, and would endanger the peace of the occasion.

Rabbi Josef Jakobovits of Berlin published a responsum entitled *Halachisches zur Frage der aschkenasischen oder sephardischen Aussprache* (Frankfurt am Main, 1936). After extensive citations of the literature, Rabbi Jakobovits concludes that the change from the Ashkenazic pronunciation of the prayers to the Sefardic is prohibited. He emphasizes that his decision does not refer to the Land of Israel. In the concluding paragraph he refers to Rav Uziel's statement that a question of such far-reaching halachic importance can be decided only by a conference of rabbinical authorities. Finally, he quotes a passage from Ezekiel Landau's *Noda Bi'hudah* (second series, *Yoreh De'ah*, 54): "No custom, no matter how baseless, may be abolished without the consent of the sages."

Chanting the Torah and Prophetic (Haftarah) Portions

A ARON CHORIN, in *Kinat Ha'emet*, cites the objections raised in *Megillah Afah* (Flying scroll) to various reforms. One of the objections is to the fact that the reformers read the Torah without the traditional chant based on the notations given on Sinai. Chorin rejects this objection by claiming that the chanting embodies all kinds of noise and deprives the Torah of its dignity. He then testifies that he himself reads the Torah on Sabbath and festivals without cantillation, which he feels disturbs the devotion and lacks the "taste and smell" (i.e., spirit) of the Torah. He also states that he does not lower his voice, as traditionally customary, when reading the *Tochachah*, the curses in Leviticus 26 and Deuteronomy 28. His reason is that the curses are just as holy as the rest of the Torah, since they, too, were given by God. [p. 196]

Eliezer Libermann, in *Or Nogah*, First Part (pp. 20–21), argues against chanting the Torah readings, asking: "Who heard Moses using or commanding the chant? . . . In every country the Torah is read in a different way. . . . If the original traditional chant is a religious requirement, why is the tune different at various occasions, e.g., on Rosh Hashanah, Yom Kippur, Tishah Be'av?" Therefore he suggests disregarding the chant. [p. 204] In contrast, Moses Sofer, in his second letter in *Eleh Divre*

Haberit (pp. 30–45), argues for the importance of the chant, asserting that it came down to us from Moses. [pp. 221–22]

Rabbi Abraham Sutro, in a responsum, *Shomer Tsiyon Ha-ne'eman* (p. 305), objects to the reading of the Torah without the chant, stating that the reformers, by not chanting, "do not read the Torah but announce it like the wood choppers and the water drawers announce their merchandise in the markets and streets. . . . One who transgresses an explicit prohibition of the Talmud, he transgresses the injunction of the Torah: 'Thou shalt not turn aside from the sentence which they shall declare unto thee' (Deut. 17:11), as is stated in *B. Berachot* 19b . . ." [p. 261]

Instrumental Music
Liberal-Reform Views

THE DISPUTE between the Reform and the Orthodox concerning the use of a musical instrument at services centers around the organ. Other musical instruments are dealt with only peripherally. The basic positions of the two extreme branches of Judaism are obvious. Reform permits instrumental music at religious services while Orthodoxy prohibits it. However, the struggle between the two parties over this issue is more elaborate than the struggle over almost any other issue dividing them.

Let us first present the liberal side of the dispute. Rabbi Shem Tov, son of Rabbi Joseph Chayim ben Samun, in his responsum *Derech Hakodesh* (in *Nogah Hatsedek*), decides that the organ is permitted. Against the opponents, who claim that this instrument, the *ugav* of the Psalms (150:4), is prohibited because the gentiles use it at their services, and also because the use of instrumental music has been prohibited since the destruction of the Temple in Jerusalem, Rabbi Shem Tov argues that the answer is obvious and no elaborate discussion is needed. He maintains that the prohibition of playing musical instruments, as stated in the Talmud (*B. Sotah* 48a; Mishnah *Sotah* 9:11), has reference only to doing so when drinking wine and rejoicing in levity. The biblical source is Isaiah 24:9, "They shall not drink wine with a song." According to Rashi, loc. cit., this means that people must not sing at home and at banquets. This

proves that music is prohibited only if it is accompanied by
levity while rejoicing with wine. However, if it is done for the
opposite purpose—that is, for a *mitzvah*—the words of Psalm
100:2, "Serve the Lord with gladness," apply. This includes
both vocal and instrumental music. Subsequently, Rabbi Shem
Tov Samun cites *Shulchan Aruch, Orach Chayim* 560, Karo
with Isserles' comment saying that in the case of a *mitzvah*, as
at a wedding banquet, everything is permitted. This prompts
Rabbi Shem Tov to conclude that if music is permitted for
human beings whenever a *mitzvah* is involved, how much the
more so is it permitted in honor of God. It is a *mitzvah* to praise
Him with song, drum, harp, and so forth.

In religious life, he continues, the actual practice, even without legal foundation, is of great importance. The actual practice
in all the synagogues is that the cantor sings in honor of God.
The basic form of praising God at services is vocal music. If this
basic form of praising God is permitted, how much the more
so is the secondary form—the use of instrumental music—permissible. [pp. 177–78]

After Rabbi Shem Tov Samun thus "proves" that instrumental music is permissible at services, he discusses the organ,
which he allows for the following reason. The objection of the
Orthodox, which is based on Leviticus 18:3, "Neither shall ye
walk in their statutes," is not a valid objection. This injunction
does not refer to everything done by the gentiles. Rather, it
refers only to those statutes of the gentiles which are perplexing and lack reason. However, both vocal and instrumental
music awaken the heart and make it rejoice; therefore it is
permitted to play and listen to music at services.

After arriving at the above conclusion, Rabbi Shem Tov
offers an elaborate discourse on the laws and customs prohibited in Leviticus 18:3. In doing this he uses traditional
talmudic and rabbinic sources. The purpose of his long dis-

course is to prove that the organ does not fall under the prohibition of "gentile practices." He maintains that gentile practices are prohibited only if they meet the following criteria:

1. They are perplexing and have no apparent reason (see *Bet Yosef, Yoreh Deah* 178). Among these are also practices concerning divination (*Sefer Mitzvot Gadol*, "Laws of Gentile Practices," *B. Shabbat*, end of chap. 6).

2. They breach the ways of modesty and humility. This rule has limitations which are cited by Rabbi Shem Tov.

The conclusion from all the sources cited is that the use of the organ is not concerned with something "unusual" (perplexing, illogical) or with immodesty. To all this Rabbi Shem Tov adds that the prohibition of following gentile statutes applies only to something new which the gentiles invented and made into law. However, singing and playing music in God's praise is of Jewish origin, and the gentiles learned it from the Jews. Therefore, the prohibition of walking "in their statutes" does not apply in this case. On the contrary, the organ is a Jewish statute.

Rabbi Shem Tov Samun also discusses another objection against the use of the organ. The rabbis prohibited the making of an exact replica of the Temple in Jerusalem (*B. Avodah Zarah* 43a–43b). This prohibition includes all the holy objects and utensils of the Temple. Since musical instruments were used in the Temple in Jerusalem, we are now prohibited from using them in our synagogues.

In Rabbi Shem Tov's opinion, however, this objection has no validity. He cites Rashi, who explains that the prohibition applies only if the length, width, height, and other dimensions of the instrument are exactly the same as those of the Temple instruments, but not otherwise. Since we can safely assume that our organ does not resemble the musical instruments of the Temple in every detail, we may use it without any hesitation.

The next argument of Rabbi Shem Tov is based on Maimonides (*Bet Habechirah* 7:5), who states that only lyres, flutes, harps, trumpets, and cymbals were used in the Jerusalem Temple, and does not mention the organ. It would be nonsense to say that the rabbis prohibited all musical instruments, everywhere, under all circumstances. Mishnah *Sotah* states only that the song, including instrumental music, ceased at the banquets. This means that the rabbis did not prohibit instrumental music everywhere and under all circumstances.

After maintaining that he has sufficiently proved his point (i.e., that playing all musical instruments is permitted in the synagogue, since in the case of a *mitzvah* no prohibition had been issued), Rabbi Shem Tov gives an additional reason for permitting the organ in the synagogue: the pleasant music stimulates synagogue attendance, which is desirable, even though the people may not come (primarily) to pray. According to the Talmud (B. *Pesachim* 50b), this is perfectly proper, since the performance of a *mitzvah*, though first done without devotion, will ultimately lead to its performance with true devotion. *Quod erat demonstrandum*: It is permissible and proper to use the organ in the synagogue. [pp. 177–82]

Another liberal decision regarding the use of the organ and other musical instruments in the synagogue was rendered by Rabbi Jacob Chai Recanati of Pesaro, in his responsum, *Ya'ir Nativ* (Verona, 1817). Among several questions addressed to him was one concerning the use of musical instruments, particularly the organ, in the synagogue. The questions include possible objections based on traditional sources, such as Bible, Talmud, Codes. [pp. 183ff]

In his reply Recanati assures the questioners that he found

not even one halachic authority in the entire rabbinic literature who spoke about the organ. He checked a reference to
the organ in the talmudic encyclopedia *Pachad Yitzchak*, but
was unable to locate the passage.

To the question whether the organ should be prohibited because it is an instrument used for idol worship, Recanati replies:
Only an organ that was actually used for idol worship would
be prohibited, but not an organ that was not used for such a
purpose. Recanati compares the organ to wax candles. The
candles would be prohibited if they had been kindled before
an idol. The same holds true for the organ. He bases his decision
on traditional sources. Subsequently he rejects the similarity,
suggested by the questioner, between the *matsevah* (pillar),
which was an object of idol worship, and the organ. The
matsevah is connected with the soil and used exclusively for
idol worship. The organ, on the other hand, is not connected
with the soil and is used for secular purposes as well. It is comparable to a bell, which may also be found in private homes and
is not an object of idol worship, and therefore is not prohibited.
Recanati points out another dissimilarity: the *matsevah* may
be an object of idol worship, while the organ is not.

In further pursuing the issue, Recanati makes a fine distinction between "tune" and "instrument." He maintains that
Rabbi Jacob Weil's words, "No tune played for the idols must
be played to God," are judiciously chosen. Weil intentionally
did not choose the words "musical instrument." This proves
that the use of instruments, among them the organ, is permitted. [p. 185]

Of particular interest may be Recanati's reply to the
possible objection against the use of musical instruments based
on Hosea 9:1, "Rejoice not, O Israel, unto exultation, like the
peoples." Karo, in *Shulchan Aruch, Orach Chayim* 560, explains that the rabbis ordained not to use musical instruments
or other sound-producing instruments in order to cause re-

joicing; and it is prohibited to listen to them because of the destruction of the Temple.

To this objection Recanati replies that Karo's statement in *Orach Chayim* 560:3, speaking of "a universally accepted Jewish custom to say words of praise, songs of thanksgiving and remembrance of God's deeds of loving-kindness over wine," does not refer to vocal music only. It also refers to instrumental music.

Recanati proves his point by citing an actual case, which occurred in Modena, where there were both Italian Ashkenazic rabbis and rabbis from the land of Israel. (Recanati names the Italian rabbis but not the others.) There was also a Jewish orchestra of drums and harps, and nobody tried to prohibit it. Once a problem arose there (see Ishmael Hacohen, *Zera Emet*, *Yoreh De'ah*, chap. 157), concerning whether a bereaved member of the orchestra could play the oboe on the night of Hoshana Rabbah. Rabbi Ishmael Hacohen permitted him to play the instrument, even though the man was a mourner. Had the musical instrument been prohibited, the rabbi would not have permitted him to play it, even if he had not been a mourner. This incident is, for Recanati, a definite proof that playing music in honor of God is permitted. Hosea 9:1 applies to rejoicing with music only where no *mitzvah* is involved, as stated above.

Recanati also cites passages from the Bible and the *Meharsha* in order to prove that the prohibition against using musical instruments refers to the private home, but not to the synagogue. He maintains that musical instruments are permitted in synagogues and instances of a *mitzvah*. Recanati concludes that there is no prohibition against the use of instrumental music at the prayer service, not even as a result of the destruction of the Temple in Jerusalem. [pp. 182 ff]

After this "final" conclusion, Recanati rejects another objection—that the music, by interrupting the prayer, would prevent devotion. In rejecting this objection, Recanati uses both precedents and traditional sources. First, he cites a practice related in the *Sefer Keriat Shema* (Book of reading the Shema) by the rabbis of Corfu. According to this book, in Corfu, on holidays, the *Shema* was chanted with musical accompaniment. After the music had been discontinued for a certain time, two rabbis of Salonika ruled in favor of reviving the old custom. They not only cited proofs, but also obtained the approval of rabbis from Jerusalem (op. cit., p. 11).

Recanati cites a number of halachic authorities, most of them supporting his view. Most interesting is his reference to a passage in the book *Sha'ar Ephraim*, chap. 4, which says that a custom must not be abolished even if it contradicts a law of the Torah; and that we are not responsible for possible harmful consequences. Among the rabbis supporting the use of music at services is Rabbi Judah Aryeh of Modena (Leon da Modena) in his book *Kol Yehudah*. [pp. 187–88]

After all the evidence is adduced, Recanati decides that the use of the organ in the synagogue is permitted, but a gentile should play it on the Sabbath and holidays. A Jew must not play at those times because he might repair the instrument if it were to break down. Recanati supports this decision by citing *Shulchan Aruch, Orach Chayim* 338:1.

Thus, Recanati's liberalism has limits. A further limit to his permissiveness is shown in his objection to a view in *Seder Eliyahu Raba*, which permits one to ask a gentile to repair an instrument on the Sabbath. In Recanati's opinion, the proper thing is to ask the gentile on Friday to play the organ on the Sabbath. [pp. 188–89]

Aaron Chorin, rabbi of Arad, is perhaps the most learned halachist among the early Reform rabbis, as is apparent from his writings, especially his responsum *Kinat Ha'emet* (The zeal of truth).

Chorin recommends that in order to inflame the hearts of the worshippers, the lofty prayers on the Sabbath and holidays should be accompanied by harp and song. For the benefit of a *mitzvah*, musical accompaniment, according to Isserles in *Shulchan Aruch, Orach Chayim* 560:3, is permitted. Only a fool would claim that musical accompaniment of the songs of praise in the synagogue is prohibited because of Leviticus 18:3 "neither shall ye walk in their statutes." Most of the halachic authorities agree that the non-Jewish peoples of Europe are not idol worshippers, since they believe in most of the fundamentals of the Torah. According to the latest halachic authorities, the prohibition of following the gentile laws refers only to those laws that have no reason. Therefore, a matter that has a beneficial effect, such as the musical accompaniment of prayers, does not fall under the prohibition of idol worship. In the instance of a *mitzvah*—and the prayer service on Sabbath and holidays is a *mitzvah*—instrumental music played by gentiles is definitely permitted, as is made clear in *Orach Chayim* 338 and 339. [pp. 193–94]

Rabbi Mosheh Kunitz of Ofen (Buda), in a reply to the Jewish congregation of Berlin (published in Vienna, 1818), defends, in a somewhat novel way, the organ installed in a Budapest synagogue. The organ was installed there in order to attract people and to stir the hearts of women and children so they would love and fear God, as in the case of King Saul: "And it came to pass when the minstrel played, that the hand of the Lord came upon him" (2 Kings 3:15). The fact that a gentile plays the organ is considered by Rabbi Kunitz to be a favorable aspect. He compares it with the widespread custom among the Jews of asking gentiles to kindle and extinguish the candles in the synagogues, disregarding a light *shevut* prohibition. The rabbis abolished many other similarly light (*shevut*) prohibitions. Some rabbinical authorities, relying on the ancient French rabbis, permitted instrumental music for both prayer services and secular rejoicing.

According to Rabbi Kunitz, the most important reason for permitting the organ at services is that it results in the sanctification of God's name. Jews who had been staying away from the synagogues return to them because of the organ. Without the organ, these people would have vanished as Jews. By installing the organ, God's name is publicly sanctified, which is the greatest *mitzvah*. [pp. 199–200]

Rabbi Eliezer Libermann, in *Or Nogah* (Dessau, 1818), enumerates no less than six possible objections against the use of the organ and refutes them by citing traditional sources (ibid., pp. 14–15), as well as his own interpretations. One is particularly interesting: In many churches—for example, in most of the churches in Poland—no musical instruments are used. Had these instruments been required by gentile religious law, they would have to be used in all the churches, just as all the churches use the "holy water" (ibid., p. 15). Since this is not the case, the use of musical instruments in the churches, though customary in many of them, has no religious character. Libermann points out that the psalms were accompanied by instrumental music (ibid., pp. 17–18). Other biblical sources likewise show that instrumental music was used extensively in ancient times. The conclusion is obvious. We have no reason to prohibit the use of the organ or any other musical instrument. [p. 203]

Orthodox Views
on the Use of the Organ
and Other Musical Instruments

THE MOST vigorous attacks against instrumental music, especially at prayer services, are given in *Eleh Divre Haberit* (These are the words of the covenant), published by order of the Hamburg Orthodox Congregation (Altona, 1819).

Rabbi Hirz Scheuer of Mainz permits the use of musical instruments at weddings because of the *mitzvah*, but prohibits it where no *mitzvah* is involved.

The biggest worry of the Orthodox of Rabbi Scheuer's time was that the Sabbath was being ushered in with music in Prague's largest Orthodox synagogue. Rabbi Scheuer rejects the use of this case as a precedent in the following manner. There are nine synagogues in Prague, but the Sabbath has been ushered in with music in only one of them, and in that instance the music is used only up to *Bo'i Beshalom*, which is sung before the Sabbath begins. However, on the Sabbath or holiday proper, no musical instrument is used there. On rare occasions, such as the Sabbath before or after the wedding of rich people, musical instruments had been played in an old synagogue up to *Bo'i Beshalom*. On those occasions men and women sat together mixed, and had to be rebuked for this. This evil custom was abolished over twenty-five years ago, Rabbi Scheuer states.

In conclusion, he emphasizes the stringency of the prohibition. [pp. 211–12]

Rabbi Moses Sofer, the greatest Orthodox authority of the time, briefly discusses the prohibition of instrumental music in his responsum (op. cit., no. 3). He argues: Although we Jews originated the music in the Jerusalem Temple, our sages, who introduced the prayers, did not ordain the use of musical instruments in the synagogue. Thus, the use of instrumental music in the synagogue is prohibited, because, ever since the Temple of Jerusalem was destroyed, there is no rejoicing before Him. We may make music under certain circumstances to make people rejoice—for example, bride and groom, since they are depressed by the *galut*—but never in the synagogue, and especially not on the Sabbath. [p. 213]

Mordechai Benet's reasoning against the use of music (ibid., no. 4, pp. 11 ff.) is quite dialectical. Among his arguments against the use of music at services is his view that music interferes with devotion since it attracts the heart and causes pleasure. [p. 215]

Rabbi Eliezer Fleks, Rabbi Samuel Segal Landau, and Rabbi Leib Melish, all of Prague and members of its "Great Court," point out that the men playing the instruments at *Kabalat Shabbat* in Prague must put away their instruments half an hour before *Barechu*—that is, before the beginning of the evening service proper. On the Sabbath itself, the playing of the organ, even by a gentile, is strictly prohibited. [p. 216]

In a second letter (op. cit.), Rabbi Moses Sofer discusses the prohibition of the organ in greater detail, and advances new conjectures. He maintains, as do some others, that there was no organ in the Jerusalem Temple. In discussing the possible reason why, he suggests that it may have been because of the derogatory meaning of the word *ugav* עוגב, "organ," which literally means "love, lust." He compares this prohibition to the prohibition against bringing water to the Jerusalem Temple Court from a fountain called מי רגלים *Mei Raglaim*, lit. "urine."

Sofer feels that this conjecture is weak, and makes another conjecture which he believes is more plausible. An ancient law of idol worshippers permitted the use of the organ only in the temples of the idol worshippers; therefore, the organ was prohibited in the Jerusalem Temple and in the synagogues. In the exceptional case of the Prague synagogue, the organ playing was stopped before the Sabbath began. Also noteworthy is the fact that this organ was not repaired after it broke down.

Sofer is even more perturbed about the advice given in *Nogah Hatsedek*, p. 7, suggesting that the organ be put into the women's section of the synagogue. Since women cannot play the organ, a gentile man would play it, and this could result in trouble resulting from sexual attraction to the organ player. [p. 221]

Rabbi Abraham Löwenstamm of Emden, in his book *Tseror Hachayim* (Amsterdam, 1820) maintains (p. 6) that the organ is a most beloved and pleasant instrument that lifts the spirit. Nonetheless, it is not found in the theater or in the orchestra, while in the churches it is the only musical instrument used at services, and it is used only exceptionally also at big church concerts, for example, in honoring the king.

Why is it that the organ, a most pleasant instrument, is banned from the house of the king and every orchestra, while in the churches it is the only admissible instrument? Rabbi Löwenstamm suggests that at the foundation of the Christian religion, the organ was chosen and reserved for church use only, and its secular use was banned. Many churches in Poland do not use the organ because it is a very expensive instrument which the poor Polish churches cannot afford. Löwenstamm compares this with the fact that the readers in small synagogues are congregants, while big, wealthy congregations hire expensive cantors. The conclusion of his discourse is that the organ is prohibited in the synagogue on weekdays as well as on the Sabbath and holidays, whether played by a Jew or a gentile. Other musical instruments are likewise prohibited if played by gentiles. However, musical instruments, except the organ, may be played on weekdays. [pp. 235–36]

Very thorough and systematic in discussing the prohibition of the organ is David Hoffmann in his Responsa *Melamed Leho'il*, vol. 1, resp. 16. The responsum is given in connection with a specific question. A rabbi in a congregation had tried to prevent the installation of an organ in his synagogue but was unable to do so. He was then faced with the problem of whether he could remain a rabbi in this congregation if he permitted the use of the organ on weekdays only—for example, for weddings—but not on the Sabbath. He wished to stay in his present congregation, because if he left his place would be taken by a rabbi who would not only permit the organ but would introduce many other reforms as well.

Hoffmann, in his answer, discusses numerous aspects of the problem at great length. His first step is a survey of the various opinions and explanations concerning the matter. [pp. 291–94] After a most elaborate discussion, Hoffmann gives the following opinion. The organ cannot be permitted even on weekdays. However, if a rabbi permits the use of the organ at weddings and in honoring the king, acting under compelling circumstances, and relies on some rabbinical authorities who only prohibit the organ on the Sabbath, Rabbi Hoffmann would not revoke his *semichah* (the rabbinical diploma which he had issued to him) because of this sin. However, the rabbi must publicize the reason for having given the permission lest others consider this as a precedent. Whenever a similar case comes before the rabbis, they must examine it most carefully. [p. 297]

Decorum at Services, Weddings, and Other Occasions

MOST OF the literature dealing with the problem of decorum at services, weddings, funerals, and other occasions of religious significance is written in German. It reflects the attitude of Liberal-Reform Judaism in Germany and represents a desire to adjust the order and dignity of the Jewish service to that of non-Jewish services. The literature on decorum written in German is thoroughly discussed in Jakob J. Petuchowski's *Prayerbook Reform in Europe*, pp. 105–27, under the title, "Order and Decorum," where he translates several significant *Synagogenordnungen*, "Synagogue Orders."

There is no further need for us to discuss details concerning decorum published in German, but we would still like to cite a few additional interesting rules of decorum. In *Zeitgemässe Organisation der gottesdienstlichen Gebräuche in der neuerbauten Synagoge Unruhstadt (Karge)* (1843), p. 3, we read the following:

"It is prohibited under a penalty of 10 Sgr. for several persons to assemble in the vestibule or (front yard) of the synagogue before, after, or during the services" (p. 3).

"#6: Boys under five may be taken to the synagogue only if they have to say the *Kaddish* as mourners. Schoolboys under fourteen must be seated on a special bench for children under the supervision of the teachers. Girls are permitted to enter

33

the synagogue only after fourteen years of age and must sit in a special section for maidens" (p. 6).

"#8: Those who disturb the services for the first time must pay a penalty of 10 Sgr. to be used for charity. If repeated, the penalty is 1 Thaler. Poor people disturbing the services must be immediately expelled from the synagogue by the sexton" (p. 7).

"#25: Nobody is permitted to sing along with the cantor arbitrarily" (p. 11).

"#36: Women and children under thirteen are not allowed to bring willow branches (*hoshanot* on Hoshana Rabbah) to the synagogue. They may perform this ceremony after the services in their home" (p. 14).

"#51: Girls past fourteen, after completing their education, must pronounce their belief in a room of an elementary school in the presence of the rabbi or his assistant" (p. 18).

"#52: Weddings should be performed, as a rule, in the synagogue . . ." (p. 18).

"#55: If somebody wants the wedding to be performed at home, he must pay 3 R thlr. . . . If the couple wants a wedding speech they must make arrangements with the rabbi or his assistant" (p. 18–1).

These rules are signed by three officers of the congregation and the rabbi, Moses Landsberg, and his assistant, M. Bamberg.

Some interesting details from the *Synagogen-Ordnung für die Synagogen des Grossherzogthums Mecklenburg-Schwerin* (Schwerin, 1843) are the following:

"#10: Any conversation with neighbors, noise, all jokes, etc. during the services are strictly prohibited" (p. 22).

"#15: The president has the right to call police to expel a man from the synagogue only in extreme instances, i.e, if the disturbance is so serious that the service might be interrupted" (pp. 24–25).

"#24: The nuisance of mentioning the names of all the deceased since the founding of a congregation, which is still customary in some places, as in Schwerin, should be stopped. The mentioning of the names should be limited to those who died within the last forty years, After every five years, a new limitation should be introduced" (p. 32).

"#1: The custom to call the boy to the Torah on the first Sabbath after he became thirteen years old, i.e., the Bar Mitzvah ceremony, should be retained; however, the boy himself must not read from the Torah" (p. 48).

"#7: Among the prohibited ceremonies at weddings is the breaking of the glass and the escorting of the bride around the groom" (p. 57).

"#10: Women are not permitted to join a funeral procession" (p. 61).

These are merely a few samples of the reforms introduced in Germany in order to improve order and decorum, taken from a vast literature written in German on this topic.

What do the Hebrew sources say about decorum? Eliezer Libermann, in *Or Nogah*, Second Part (see particularly p. 22), advises explicitly that we should learn from the gentiles whatever is good. Decorum at services is one such good thing (custom). He supports his advice by citing traditional authorities, such as Rabbenu Tam's *Sefer Hayashar*, Bachya's *Chovot Halevavot*, and Maimonides' *Mishneh Torah* (*Kiddush Hachodesh* 17:25). [p. 207]

Decorum at services is not an exclusively Reform Jewish requirement. Some Orthodox Hebrew sources make similar requirements, though less frequently and on a smaller scale. Rabbi Eliezer Trietsch of Moravia, in a letter published in *Eleh Divre Haberit*, emphasizes the importance of properly honoring the synagogue. He claims that in many congregations, especially in Germany, carrying on idle conversations in the synagogue is considered permissible. This sometimes leads to shouting and quarreling, a serious sin, which could result in anarchy and confusion. Therefore, men, women, and children must be warned not to carry on idle conversation in the synagogue during the services. [p. 230]

II

Synagogue
Architecture;
Wardrobe of
Functionaries

Most of the Hebrew literature concerning synagogue architecture was written by Orthodox authorities. The Orthodox opposed the changes the Reform made in building their temples which made them resemble churches, or at least differ from the traditional synagogues.

The Bimah

ACCORDING to Orthodox tradition, the *bimah*, usually a (built-in) desk on a raised platform upon which the Torah is placed while reading from it, should be in the middle of the synagogue. However, in Reform temples the *bimah* is usually placed at the end of the temple. This change has also been made in some traditional synagogues.

Let us examine a few incidents which show the seriousness of the problem. Rabbi Moses Schick, in responsum 71, *Orach Chayim*, was asked by a rabbi, who was employed as a teacher, whether he could keep his job after the congregation which employed him introduced reforms, among them the moving of the *bimah* to the eastern side of the synagogue. The rabbi points out that he would attend the services in this synagogue only occasionally, and would like to retain his job since he had to support his family.

In his answer, Rabbi Schick declares that anyone who changes a Jewish custom and imitates the deeds of the gentiles transgresses many prohibitions. On the other hand, he tells the inquiring rabbi, martyrdom does not seem to be required in this case, citing Maimonides in support of this opinion. The prohibitions are transgressed by those who make such reforms, but not by the person who prays in such a synagogue in his innocence because he has no other synagogue to attend, or because of some other weighty reason. Nonetheless, it is a sin to attend such a synagogue, even if one merely stands and sits, but does not pray there.

Schick advises the teacher to tell the officers of the congregation that reforms are prohibited. He should not transgress the law because of sustenance, and must not pray in this synagogue even if he has to go begging. At the same time, he should ask the leaders of the congregation not to take revenge, but to allow him to continue to teach in the *bet hamidrash*. However, should they not yield, he should remember that God does not forsake those who trust him in truth. [pp. 269–71]

Another outstanding Orthodox rabbi, Judah Aszod, in responsum 3, *Orach Chayim*, replies to a rabbi whose congregation had decided, against his will, to change the location of the *bimah*. Rabbi Aszod discusses, among other matters, the question of whether the placing of the *bimah* in the middle of the synagogue is a law or merely a custom. His decision, based on interpreting a passage from Maimonides, is that it is a law to do so. At the end of the responsum he urges the inquiring rabbi to strive with all his might to effect a change of the congregational leaders' opinion in the matter of the *bimah*, and to oppose other changes as well. [p. 280]

Rabbi Jakob Yechiel Weinberg, the last rector (president) of the (Orthodox) Berlin Rabbinical Seminary until 1938, answered a question concerning the *bimah* in 1960 in the following manner (*Seride Esh*, vol. 2, resp. 154, p. 374). After quoting the view of several halachic authorities, some considering the location of the *bimah* in the middle of the synagogue to be a custom, and others claiming it to be law, Rabbi Weinberg gives his own opinion: Though it is prohibited to have the *bimah* anywhere other than in the middle of the synagogue, it is not prohibited to pray or to read the Torah in a synagogue whose *bimah* is not in the middle. Rabbi Weinberg reasons that it was the leaders of the congregation, who changed the traditional place of the *bimah*, who committed the sin, and not the worshippers. It is true that the Hungarian rabbis prohibited anyone from entering a synagogue which did not have the *bimah* in the middle, but this was done at the time of a war against assimilation. Rabbi Weinberg cites a specific case of Orthodox rabbis in Lithuania who did not refrain from attending a certain synagogue where the *bimah* was not in the middle.

Dr. Weinberg considers the prohibition against changing the location of the *bimah* merely a "fence," a precautionary, protective measure, lest people say: "The sages permitted it." He advises the inquirer not to pray in a synagogue where the *bimah* is not in the middle permanently, but in the meantime not to refrain from attending public services in the synagogue because of the change in the traditional location of the *bimah*. [pp. 312–14]

After the destruction of European Jewry, the center of the *bimah* controversy shifted to Israel. Some of the most important responsa on the *bimah*, and on many other issues, have appeared in the yearbook *Noam*, published by the Torah Shelemah Institute in Jerusalem since 1958.

Rabbi Zalman Sorotzkin discusses the location of the *bimah* in *Noam*, vol. 5 (1962), pp. 52 ff. First, he gives Maimonides' rational explanation that the *bimah* should be in the middle of the synagogue so that the reader of the Torah or the preacher can be heard by everybody. He also quotes Karo's lenient interpretation, which says that having the *bimah* in the middle of the synagogue is not a basic requirement but depends on time and place. In Maimonides' day the synagogues were big, and therefore the *bimah* had to be in the middle. However, in later times the synagogues were small, and the reader could be heard no matter where the *bimah* was located. In fact, it is more attractive to have the *bimah* on the side than to have it in the middle. Rabbi Sorotzkin then cites *Chatam Sofer*, who permits one to leave the *bimah* on the side in old, small synagogues, but maintains that no new synagogues should be so built.

In the opinion of Rabbi Sorotzkin, all these leniencies of the law are cancelled by the necessity for the "fence." Because of the "fence," we have to wage open war against the smallest change concerning the synagogue, lest it lead to other changes. In fact, the numerous and more serious changes of the reformers were preceded by moving the *bimah* from the center of the synagogue to the side.

Subsequently, Rabbi Sorotzkin cites measures against reforms decided upon at a conference of Orthodox rabbis in 1866 and signed by Hungarian and a few Galician rabbis. One of the measures concerned the *bimah*, which the reformers had moved from the center of the synagogue in an attempt to imitate the churches of the gentiles. The rabbis of Hungary enumerated eight prohibitions and two positive commandments violated by the reformers. The Hungarian rabbis also ruled that a Jew must not enter a synagogue if the *bimah* is not in the middle, even if he would be the tenth man of the *minyan*. Rather, he should pray alone and omit the *Kaddish*, *Kedushah*, and reading of the Torah, which require a *minyan*. This refers even to Yom Kippur.

Finally, Rabbi Sorotzkin ventures a conjecture. Had the leading Orthodox rabbis foreseen the consequences of the first step of reform—that is, the moving of the *bimah* away from the center of the synagogue—they would have proclaimed a curse and excommunication against this move, for its purpose was to make the synagogues resemble the churches. If this change had been prevented, disastrous consequences could have been avoided. Hundreds of thousands of Jews might have been saved from mixing with gentiles and from assimilation. The decree against moving the *bimah* away from the center, had it been issued when this reform first began, would have been acceptable to all Jews everywhere, with the possible exception of a few who would have deserted the Jewish faith. [pp. 322 ff]

A responsum with respect to the *bimah*, in the same issue of *Noam*, is answered as follows: A pious man may pray in a synagogue if its only fault is that the *bimah* is not in the middle. However, the method of the *yetser hara*, the evil inclination, is to tell the people today, this, tomorrow that, till it tells them to worship idols, and they do it (*B. Shabbat* 105b). The *yetser hara* starts everywhere by persuading men to move the *bimah* from the middle to the side of the synagogue. Afterwards, it persuades them to transgress more important laws, such as the removal of the partition between men and women, and so forth. If the questioner recognizes the principle that Jewish custom is like the Torah, he must move the *bimah* to the middle of the synagogue, because this is a foundation of our faith. [pp. 325–328]

In the same issue of *Noam*, pp. 60 ff., Rabbi Mordechai Hacohen states that the question of the *bimah* was recently (1962) and once again put on the agenda, though it had been discussed for generations. To accept a change in the matter—that is, to move the *bimah* from the center of the synagogue—is to accept a gentile law. This reform shook the House of Israel in Germany and Hungary, since anything new is prohibited by the Torah.

Although the law concerning the *bimah* had been decided by the sages of the past, the author of this responsum holds that a theoretical discussion is still permissible, and acts accordingly. First, Rabbi Mordechai cites halachic authorities who prohibit the placing of the *bimah* anywhere but in the middle of the synagogue. In addition to rabbinic sources, Rabbi Mordechai even cites archaeological evidence. He claims that on the Greek Island of Delos a synagogue from the time of the Second Temple was excavated, and its *bimah* was clearly in the center.

Next he reviews the opinions of the halachists who permit the change, beginning with Joseph Karo, the author of the *Shulchan Aruch*. Karo states that placing the *bimah* in the center is not required, and that in small synagogues it is more attractive to have the *bimah* on the side than in the center. A number of other halachists cited in the responsum agree with Karo.

Interesting is the reference to a number of synagogues which did not have the *bimah* in the middle. Among them are old and new synagogues in Italy and also some in Spain, such as the seven-hundred-year-old synagogues of Córdoba and Toledo. In fact, in the great majority of the Italian synagogues the *bimah* was at the end of the hall, on the west side, opposite the holy ark.

Why did later authorities reject Karo's view even though it was supported by historical evidence? Mordechai Hacohen believes that they did so only to oppose the reformers. The reformers wanted to strangle the old Jewish spirit by citing Karo. Therefore, the outstanding Orthodox rabbis found it necessary to make a "fence" by not permitting the slightest change lest the "sinners" commit other transgressions.

Rabbi Mordechai realizes the weakness of this explanation and tries to resolve the puzzling fact that some pious (i.e., Orthodox) rabbis insist that the *bimah* be in the center of the synagogue, while other rabbis, just as pious, permit the *bimah* to be placed at the end of the structure. In his answer he suggests that in talmudic times the location of the *bimah* in Babylonia differed from that in Palestine. In the latter country, the *bimah* was built on the western side of the synagogue, while in Babylonia and other foreign lands it was placed in the center. Startling is Rabbi Mordechai's final advice, since it is not directly related to the problem under discussion: "In our time . . . we mainly have to protest and to submit to martyrdom in order that a proper partition be erected in the synagogue between men and women, since this is a law of the Torah in everybody's opinion." [p. 328] Thus, in his opinion, the partition between men and women in the synagogue is more important than the location of the *Bimah*.

Other Aspects of Synagogue Architecture; Matters Pertaining to the Wardrobe of the Functionaries at Services

RABBI JUDAH ASZOD, in Responsa, *Orach Chayim*, resp. 39, answers a question addressed to him by several unnamed men. The problem presented is that newcomers to a certain town want to tear down the old synagogue and replace it with a modern structure which would resemble the temples of other religions. They want to conform to the spirit of the time. These men also want to introduce new tunes or modes of singing, and new clothing for the functionaries resembling that used in the temples of other religions. The question raised is whether such a synagogue is permissible.

Rabbi Aszod, in his reply, prohibits the building of new synagogues which resemble churches, the new mode of singing, and the special clothing of the cantors, as he prohibits the changing of all other customs and practices. He maintains that such reforms are contrary to religion, and Orthodox Jews must prevent the building of such synagogues and must refrain from praying in them. Rabbi Aszod then refers to his responsum addressed to the congregations of Weizen and Jormota, where they wanted to build a tower on top of the new synagogue. This, he says, is prohibited by the Torah (Lev. 18:3).

Quite extraordinary is Rabbi Aszod's ruling: "If seven-eighths of (liberal) Jews permit a matter, and one-eighth of Orthodox Jews prohibit it, and they are right, it would be a desecration of God's name to follow the majority rule." [p. 288]

Rabbi Zalman Sorotzkin, in *Noam*, vol. 5, pp. 52 ff., observes that the plague of the "choir *shuls*" (Reform temples) has not spread to Eastern Europe, thanks to the watchful eyes of the great rabbis. When "sinners" in Kovno were building a modern synagogue topped by a cupola and a *Magen David*, Rabbi Isaac Elchanan, the leading rabbi of that city, warned the men responsible for the innovation, saying that should the *Magen David* not be removed from the roof, he would leave the town instantly and never return. The *Magen David* was removed. [p. 323]

III

Holidays, Rituals,
Miscellaneous
Practices

Sabbaths, Holidays

AKIBA EGER, rabbi of Posen, states in a letter: A Jew who neglects just one of a thousand words of the rabbis will cause the downfall of the entire Torah. A person who questions the validity of the Talmud certainly desecrates the Sabbath, since he would not know the detailed requirements. Written and Oral Law are inseparable. It is impossible to accept the one and reject the other. To do this is to be a heretic.

Playing the organ on a Sabbath or a holiday, even if done by a non-Jew, falls under the prohibition: "Neither shalt thou set thee up a pillar" (Deut. 16:22). [pp. 219–20]

Moses Schick, Responsa, *Orach Chayim*, resp. 71, attacks the reformers for stretching the interpretation of Leviticus 18:5, by stating that the commandments are given to live by and not to die by (*B. Yoma* 85b). Consequently the reformers permit everything; they transgress the Sabbath and holiday prohibitions, and as well as many others, claiming that if they did not do so their lives would be in danger.

In the same responsum Rabbi Schick emphasizes the prohibition against extinguishing a fire on a Sabbath, even if the owner of the property were to lose all his possessions and become a public charge. [p. 270]

Rabbi David Hoffmann, in *Melamed Leho'il*, vol. 1, resp. 16, maintains that the reformers began their law-breaking activities with the adoption of the organ. This led to the desecration of the Sabbath and to many other transgressions. [p. 296]

David Hoffman, in *Melamed Leho'il*, vol. 1, pp. 28–29 was asked whether worshippers who transgress the Sabbath may be counted as members of the *minyan*. The men in question had been working and smoking on the Sabbath. In addition, they do not make Kiddush and Havdalah. Hoffmann, in his answer, points out that a man who publicly desecrates the Sabbath cannot be a member of the *minyan*. However, such a man has to be excommunicated before he is denied membership in a *minyan*. Hoffmann quotes authorities who hold that only sinners who transgress the law in order to annoy the pious are to be rejected. Since this is not the case today, the sinners may be considered for the *minyan*.

One of Hoffmann's decisive arguments in favor of including the sinners in the *minyan* is his stress on the importance of the custom. Today the custom in Hungary is to be lenient; how much the more so in Germany. Rabbi Hoffmann then cites a case in which a man who had desecrated the Sabbath was permitted to read the service in an Orthodox synagogue.

Citing responsum 23 in *Binyan Tsiyon*, Hoffmann compares today's Sabbath-transgressors to an infant who was captured by gentiles and grew up among them, without being aware of his Jewishness. Such a Jew is not responsible for transgressing the Jewish laws. This refers particularly to the Jews of America.

Rabbi Hoffmann's final argument in favor of the Sabbath-transgressors is his opinion that today they are no longer called "public desecrators" since the "public," that is, most of the Jews, desecrates the Sabbath, and such a "public" does not count halachically as a "public." [pp. 298–99]

While Abraham Sutro of Münster, in *Shomer Tsiyon Hane'eman* (Altona, 1853), declares that travel by train on the Sabbath is strictly prohibited [p. 262], Rabbi Hoffmann, in *Melamed Leho'il*, vol. 1, resp. 41 (pp. 53–54), permits it in a special instance: Moshe Barbash, a rabbi and native of Russia, who was now residing in Germany, received permission to visit his children in Russia. The trip by train would last about seven days and would possibly necessitate travel on the Sabbath. Rabbi Barbash, a learned man himself, cites sources that would permit him to travel on the Sabbath if a *mitzvah* is involved. This would solve his problem, since supporting, raising, and educating his children, the purpose of his trip, is a *mitzvah*. Moreover, according to Rabbenu Tam every trip other than a pleasure-trip (vacation) is considered a *mitzvah*. In his reply, Rabbi Hoffmann concurs with Rabbi Barbash, and cites further sources in support of the lenient decision, though he does not accept all the proofs cited by Rabbi Barbash. [pp. 299–300]

Rabbi Zalman Sorotzkin, in *Noam*, vol. 5 (1962), pp. 52 ff., attacks the reformers, particularly those of America. Some American rabbis, to imitate the Christians, replaced the Sabbath by Sunday. In some places they cook on Yom Kippur in one room of the temple, and the rabbi announces from the pulpit: "Everybody who is hungry should come and eat on Yom Kippur." They come to the temple in cars and cabs on the Sabbath and Yom Kippur to "pray." [p. 324]

Rabbi Eliezer Libermann, though a reformer, was deeply sorry to hear that "many Jews transgress a number of the prohibitions of the Torah. They desecrate the Sabbath, which is the foundation and root of our entire Torah and religion. The first warning of all the prophets concerned the observance of the Sabbath" (*Or Nogah*, Second Part). [pp. 207–08]

Marriages, Women

MOST OF THE responsa pertaining to marriage, divorce, and related matters contain strong warnings against making any changes, although some exceptions had been approved, or at least tolerated, even by leading Orthodox rabbis. One such exception—the use of instrumental music at weddings, though not in the synagogue—has been discussed above (pp. 29–31). Other exceptions will be discussed later.

Reform Marriages

The most crucial and consequential question is whether Reform marriages are recognized by the Orthodox. In this matter we shall observe a trend toward change within Orthodox Jewry. Let us examine the views of the outstanding Orthodox halachists.

Rabbi Moses Schick, in Responsa, *Orach Chayim*, resp. 305, states that the divorces and marriages of the reformers are invalid. In support of this judgment he refers to Maimonides, *Laws of Testimony*. Since the reformers are like complete gentiles, their daughters and sons are prohibited to the Orthodox for marriage, just as are the daughters of the apostates. The reformers, being heretics, are worse than the Sadducees and Karaites. They are a sect in themselves, and their descendants may be bastards.

Subsequently, Rabbi Schick suggests that his opinion be publicized in order that the ignorant (Orthodox) people should fear for their souls and keep away from the reformers. He also asks Rabbi Abraham Samuel Binyamin, rabbi of Pressburg, to whom the responsum is addressed, to alert the great rabbis, including those of Germany. Rabbi Schick's final advice is that every rabbi who agrees with his responsum on this question should sign it. [pp. 273–75] (more pp. 127–28)

Rabbi Yechiel Weinberg, in *Seride Esh*, vol. 3, resp. 18, addressed to Rabbi Mordechai Borer of Geilingen, discusses the question in the following terms. A Reform rabbi officiated at a wedding. Now the groom wants an Orthodox rabbi to write a *ketubah*. The question is whether a new wedding ceremony is necessary, since the ceremony performed by the Reform rabbi might not have been performed in accordance with the law. However, a further consideration is that perhaps it would be better to be lenient, since performing a second marriage might lead to gossip saying that the first marriage ceremony was invalid, and that the cohabitation prior to the second marriage ceremony constituted lewdness.

In his answer, Rabbi Weinberg maintains that the marriages performed by Reform rabbis are valid. After citing the traditional literature, Rabbi Weinberg points out that the validity of a marriage does not depend on the officiating rabbi, but on the presence of valid witnesses. In the case in question, there were such witnesses present, namely the cantor and the sexton, and therefore the first marriage was valid. Nonetheless, Rabbi Weinberg recommends a second marriage ceremony in the presence of two qualified witnesses. He also suggests telling the husband that the second ceremony is needed for the writing of the *ketubah*, which was not done at the first ceremony. However, the husband should not be told that the first wedding was invalid, lest gossip be spread about the Reform rabbi, and lest the couple worry that they have been engaged in acts of lewdness. [pp. 311–12]

Today, Reform marriages are recognized in the State of Israel only if performed abroad. In Israel only Orthodox marriages are recognized. The reason is well known and needs no further discussion here.

In *Noam*, vol. 7 (1964), p. 399, the question is raised whether a marriage ceremony performed by a Reform rabbi is valid. The answer, given by an Orthodox rabbi, is that such a marriage is invalid unless *kasher* witnesses were present. Otherwise, every intercourse is null and void—that is, an act of lewdness.

Reference is made in the same place to discussions concerning marriages performed by a government official and by gentile courts, and one of the Orthodox rabbis tends to be quite lenient in the latter case. [p. 329]

Marriage to Reform Jews

Rabbi Moses Schick, in Responsa, *Orach Chayim*, resp. 304, says: "It seems that, according to law, we must not intermarry with them (Reform Jews) because of the consideration of bastardy." This means that the nonobservance of some marriage laws by the reformers may result in the bastardy of their children, and a "kosher" Jew, born of Jewish ancestry, is prohibited by law to marry a bastard (Deut. 23: 3; *Shulchan Aruch, Even Ha'ezer* 4). [pp. 273–74; more below pp. 127–28]

Mixed Marriage

Rabbi Moses Schick, in Responsa, *Orach Chayim*, resp. 331, dealing in a derogatory manner with the Brunswick Synod, calls the synod's reference permitting Jews to marry gentile girls a lie. Such marriages are prohibited by the Torah until the gentile converts to Judaism. [p. 279]

Rabbi Judah Aszod, in Responsa, *Orach Chayim*, resp. 6, addressed to the rabbis of Germany and to Rabbi Hirsch Lehren of Amsterdam, chides the rabbis of the Brunswick Synod for their arrogant decision permitting a Jew to marry a non-Jewish woman on condition that their children be raised as Jews. He reasons that according to Jewish law such a marriage has no validity, and therefore the children of such a marriage are non-Jews. He then predicts that the reformers may soon permit incest. [p. 283]

Rabbi Yechiel Weinberg, in *Seride Esh*, vol. 2, resp. 6, p. 12, relates a question asked by Rabbi J. Stranski of Nachod: Can a man married to a gentile woman be counted as a member of the *minyan*? Rabbi Stranski, himself a learned man, discusses the matter briefly without arriving at a conclusion. He cites a source stating that a sinner may be a member of the *minyan* as long as he has not been excommunicated. However, according to another source, this rule has limited validity.

In his answer, Rabbi Weinberg points out that the rule requiring excommunication before disqualifying a man for membership in a *minyan* was valid only as long as excommunication was possible. At present, however, excommunication is prohibited by state law, and therefore the following must be considered: Is this man *liable* for excommunication? If so, he must be considered excommunicated and be rejected for the *minyan*.

Rabbi Weinberg calls this a "fence" for the law, since the "as if" rule is not the full equivalent of a real excommunication. Rabbi Weinberg further cites halachic authorities who rule that calling to the Torah a man who has a gentile wife is likewise prohibited. [p. 316]

Location of the Wedding Ceremony

A prime example of the phenomenon that what was once a serious dividing issue between the Orthodox and the Reform can vanish, or almost vanish, from the scene of struggle is the rift over the location of the wedding ceremony. The issue was: May a wedding ceremony take place in a synagogue or not? And if not, where should it take place?

Rabbi Judah Aszod, in Responsa, *Orach Chayim*, resp. 38, addressed to Rabbi Beck, Holitsch, who asked whether the wedding ceremony may be held in the synagogue, answers as follows. Having the marriage ceremony in the synagogue constitutes a transgression of "Ye must not follow their laws" (Lev. 18:3). This refers to the laws of the gentiles, who perform their wedding ceremonies in the churches. Rabbi Aszod admits it is true that Rabbi Jacob Levi (Molin), the great sage of the Middle Ages (ca. 1360–1427), speaks of marriage ceremonies in the synagogue. However, this is not an acceptable precedent, since the gentiles in those days may not have had their marriage ceremonies in the churches. While based on conjecture, Rabbi Aszod's principal argument is the halachic principle that custom voids law. He further calls attention to many customs which are contrary to law but were upheld by the sages, and maintains that this certainly applies in the present case, where the custom is like a law.

After the conclusion of the discussion, Rabbi Aszod lists eleven reasons why weddings should be performed under the open sky. After enumerating the reasons, he closes by saying that he has more good reasons, but it is time to be brief. [p. 287]

Rabbi Leopold Greenwald, in his *Otsar Nichmod* (*sic*) (New York, 1942), cites a question that was addressed to him by an unnamed person (probably a rabbi). The gist of the question is that Orthodox rabbis in America have been performing wedding ceremonies in the synagogues, and nobody objects. In contrast, the questioner observes, in other countries the wedding ceremonies are held under the sky, as requested by great halachic authorities, whom he cites. This ruling has been observed even in bad weather, in spite of danger to health, and he cites an actual case. A traditional source permitting the marriage ceremony in the synagogue he interprets away by suggesting that this source contained a printer's error. The printer resolved the abbreviation ה״ב = בית הכנסת "synagogue," instead of resolving it correctly בית הנישואין "place of the wedding." The rabbi who raised the question is perplexed as to why the great rabbis of our time disregard the traditional practice and perform marriage ceremonies in the synagogue.

Rabbi Greenwald, in his answer, first remarks that he was quite perplexed when he came from Hungary to America and saw that Orthodox marriages in America were performed in the synagogues, while in former times (in his old country) no pious rabbi ever performed a marriage in the synagogue. Rabbi Greenwald then expresses his disapproval of a New York custom of making a hole in the roof of the synagogue and considering this to provide a wedding under the sky. The requirement of having the wedding ceremony under the sky is a secondary one, that is, of lesser importance. More weighty are the calamities that might result from having the wedding ceremony in the synagogue.

Rabbi Greenwald claims that when he first came to America

he succeeded in having weddings in courtyards and private homes. Later, however, he could not withstand the pressure brought upon him, and began to perform wedding ceremonies in the synagogue. He did this after examining the sources and finding that weddings in the synagogue are, a priori, permitted. However, he was careful that there be no mixed seating. A special reason why weddings in America may be performed in the synagogue is the fact that many uninvited guests would come if they took place in the courtyard of the synagogue, including whites, blacks, and children, who would disturb the joy with their mockery. Rabbi Greenwald strongly objects to weddings in hotels, because nonkosher or questionably kosher food would be served there.

In order to strengthen his permissive stand in the matter, Rabbi Greenwald refutes the ultra-Orthodox by citing authoritative sources and rejecting the conjecture that the above-mentioned permissive source is based upon a printer's error. Among his strongest proofs are precedents that occurred in the Middle Ages and later. He also cites sources that state that we no longer care to observe the custom of having the wedding under the sky, just as we no longer care to have the marriage ceremony only at the time of the increasing moon as a good omen, although the great sages Karo and Isserles advise us to observe this custom.

Early sources do not advise us that the wedding ceremony should take place under the sky. Sources as early as Tosafot (*B. Sukkah* 25b) know of the custom of having the wedding under the sky only in cases where there are so many people that the house could not hold them. This is also the opinion of Jacob ben Asher (*Tur, Even Ha'ezer*, chap. 62).

Since weddings have been arranged in synagogues not only in the Middle Ages but as late as 1883, in Cracow, the real question to be considered is: Why did the great rabbis of

Germany and Hungary change the old practice and move the
wedding from the synagogue to another building, to a courtyard, or preferably to the synagogue courtyard?

Rabbi Greenwald answers this question first by citing an
opinion which says that the change ("reform") was necessary
as a "fence," as stated by Israel David Margoliot Yafeh in
Mecholat Hamachanaim. In former times (*Maharil's* time) the
bride and bridesmaid were the only women to enter the synagogue. They were very young and did not yet menstruate.
Today, however, the bride is usually an adult and may sometimes menstruate. Moreover, nowadays men and women enter
the synagogue with the bride. Therefore, the rabbis introduced
a "fence," a precautionary measure, to prevent possible incest
and to keep menstruating women away from the holy place, and
ordained that weddings should be performed outside the synagogue.

Rabbi Greenwald rejects this explanation. He cites an
opinion of Isserles permitting menstruating women to go to the
synagogue, although he also relates that this is not the custom
"in our land" (Hungary). Another outstanding authority,
Abraham Gumbiner (*Magen Avraham*), permits a menstruating woman to enter the synagogue for a joyous occasion pertaining to her children.

Citing several sources, Greenwald accepts the explanation
that the reason for the prohibition against weddings taking
place in the synagogue is that the Christians require that their
weddings take place in churches. He claims, without docu-
mentation, that at conventions of Catholic priests in 1540, in
Mantua and Byzantium, the law was proclaimed that marriages
must take place in the church. King Charles consented and
confirmed this law. This ruling of the Catholics was not accepted by the Protestants, who hold that a marriage can be
performed, not only by a minister, but also by a judge and in

a place other than the church. Since for Jews the marriage is valid even without the services of the rabbi, some great Jewish sages (Greenwald does not name them) moved the marriage ceremony from the synagogue to other places, in opposition to the Catholic law. (This is not the place to discuss Rabbi Greenwald's inaccuracies in the area of history and Christian theology.)

If a Jew living in a Catholic country insists that the wedding take place in the synagogue, the prohibition of Leviticus 18:3,—that we must not follow the laws of the gentiles—stands. However, in the United States, where most of the people are not Catholics, Leviticus 18:3 does not apply, especially since even among the Catholics, only one in a hundred has his wedding in a church. Greenwald further cites a view of Yosef Colon, related in *Magen Avraham* (*Laws of Purim*, chap. 690): "If matters change from what they used to be in former times, it is permitted to change the custom in accordance with the time." Therefore, it is proper to have weddings in the synagogue, especially since Leviticus 18:3 does not apply in our country, and particularly since our authorities in former times ordained that the bride and groom be blessed in a holy place. However, we must warn the people that men and women should not mix; and that the women should remain in the women's section of the synagogue. [pp. 303–307]

Rabbi Isaac Halevi Herzog, the late Ashkenazic chief rabbi of Israel, was asked by Rabbi Benzion Meir Chai Uziel, the late Sefardic chief rabbi of Israel: "Is it proper to permit the wedding ceremony to take place in the synagogue?" (*Heichal Yitzchak: Responsa by Rabbi I. H. Herzog* [Jerusalem, 1967], vol. 2, resp. 27, p. 103).

In his answer (dated 1942), Rabbi Herzog first remarks that in his native Poland, as in the other countries which were part of Russia prior to the First World War, weddings were performed under the sky, usually in the courtyard of the synagogue. In England, however, where he and his father lived in later years, the weddings were performed in the synagogue. This was also the practice in Belfast, Ireland, where he functioned as a rabbi. Rabbi Herzog had no power to change this, but would not permit the playing of music during the ceremony. Subsequently, Rabbi Herzog expresses his happiness about his immigration to the Holy Land, where this "evil custom" (having weddings in the synagogue) does not exist. He also expresses the necessity of warning the Sefardim, who do not care for having the wedding under the sky, to arrange to have their weddings not in the synagogue, but in another building.

Rabbi Herzog suggests, furthermore, that if the people wish to maintain an aspect of holiness based on the location of the wedding ceremony, it should be held in the courtyard of the synagogue. He also suggests that it is possible to erect a small building in the court of the synagogue, with an opening above the *chupah.* This would be like having the ceremony under the sky. While the Sefardim do not have to erect a similar building (i.e., one with a skylight), they too should erect a special structure in the courtyard of the synagogue. "Under no circumstance must the *chupah* be in the synagogue proper."

More important than the location of the wedding ceremony, according to Rabbi Herzog, are certain customs or behavior traits of some guests at the wedding, often seen when the ceremony takes place in the synagogue. Kissing is one such custom. It is prohibited to kiss small children in the synagogue. At weddings in the synagogue it is impossible to prevent kissing. Relatives and friends kiss each other, both men and women, thus transgressing the prohibition concerning close contact with menstruating women, and with relatives to whom the incest prohibition applies. Rabbi Herzog states that abroad he always issued a warning, in writing and orally, against kissing, but adds that although sometimes people listened to him, often they did not, and he felt very bad about it.

Rabbi Herzog laments the great sin of men and women mixing at wedding ceremonies in our days, since this desecrates the synagogue. In former times this was not the case, since then only the mothers entered the synagogue, or, in their absence, the bridesmaids. Rabbi Herzog makes a strong appeal against introducing innovations (reforms). "The Torah comes from Zion, and the diaspora has to learn from the Land of Israel, and we must not learn from the reforms introduced in Western Europe, which we regrettably could not prevent." [pp. 308–310]

Bat Mitzvah

BAT MITZVAH, a recent institution of Liberal Judaism, also adopted by traditional Judaism without much hesitation, constituted a serious problem to the Orthodox. The most comprehensive recent responsum dealing with this problem from the Orthodox point of view is that of Rabbi Ephraim Grienblatt in *Noam*, vol. 11 (1966), pp. 361 ff.

The question of whether the Bat Mitzvah may be called to the Torah is not even considered, since this is not permissible according to Orthodox law and custom. The central issue is whether a banquet given when a girl attains adulthood (twelve years and one day of age) should be or may be considered a *se'udat mitzvah*, a meal possessing religious character, as is the case with respect to the Bar Mitzvah banquet. The author of our responsum cites many views, pro and con. Let us summarize some of the more significant views.

A banquet given on the occasion of a boy's Bar Mitzvah is a *se'udat mitzvah* only if he gives a religious talk, a lecture, in the course of the banquet. Since a girl cannot be expected to give a religious talk, her banquet is not a *se'udat mitzvah*. It still might be a *se'udat mitzvah*, however, if a man were to give a lecture in her behalf.

According to another view cited in Rabbi Grienblatt's responsum, a girl's banquet, given on the occasion of her reaching the age of majority, has no religious character, because there is no actual visible difference in her religious life before and after attaining adulthood. She does not lay *tefilin* (phylacteries) and does not become a member of the *minyan*, the quorum of ten at religious services, or of the *mezuman*, the quorum of three at the grace after the meal.

Other halachists disagree. One reasons thusly: According to a view cited in the *Shulchan Aruch*, it is a *mitzvah* to make a banquet on behalf of the Bar Mitzvah, just as it is on the day of a wedding. Since the wedding feast is a *se'udat mitzvah* for both groom and bride, the Bat Mitzvah banquet ought to be considered equal to the Bar Mitzvah banquet.

Another halachist suggests a compromise. The girl should not be given a religious banquet, but should rejoice by wearing a new dress, reciting the benediction *shehecheyanu*, and accepting the yoke of the commandments.

Rabbi Grienblatt cites in greatest detail, and with obvious full approval, the opinion of Rabbi Yechiel Weinberg. Rabbi Weinberg is inclined to permit the Bat Mitzvah celebration, provided it is not held in the synagogue, but in a private home or a hall adjacent to the synagogue. He also requires that the rabbi admonish the girl to observe all the commandments. Decisive for the introduction of the ceremony is the motivation: Is it desired for the sake of performing a *mitzvah*, or only to imitate the "heretics" (reformers)? Rabbi Weinberg concludes that the Bat Mitzvah celebration may be continued wherever it has been practiced in the past. Otherwise, it is better not to introduce it. If it is observed, its place is not in the synagogue but in a private home. His final words: If the majority of a congregation desires to introduce the Bat Mitzvah custom, it is not worthwhile for the minority to fight it. It is more important that this custom be made meaningful in order to strengthen the spirit of the Torah and to instill noble qualities in the hearts of Jewish girls.

Miscellany Pertaining to Women

RABBI ABRAHAM SUTRO of Münster (1784–1869), in his *Responsum in Matters of the Synagogue*, published in *Shomer Tsiyon Hane'eman* (1853), had to answer, among other matters, the following question: Are women and men permitted to sing together in the synagogue? In answering this question Rabbi Sutro refers the questioner to his book *Milchamot Hashem*, p. 111, maintaining that to permit this is strictly prohibited, since we accept the principle that "the voice of a woman is *ervah*" (lit. "nakedness") and arouses men sexually (*B. Berachot* 24a). He also cites *B. Sotah* 48a. [p. 260]

Notwithstanding the reasons given in the sources cited, it is an act of arrogance and lewdness for a Jewish woman to enter the men's section of the synagogue since in all the synagogues, as in the Sanctuary of Jerusalem, a special section has been made for the women. The intention of the reformers is to make the chaste Jewish girls into unashamed, lewd women. In Orthodox synagogues, the women are on a higher level (in a balcony or gallery). They are separated from the men's section by a fence and curtain lest the men and women look at each other. In contrast, the reformers reduced the honor of the women to the lowest level, by removing even the curtain.

Concerning the singing of women, the Pope in Rome warned

67

women and virgins not to sing in theaters and circuses, since to do so appears to be an act of lewdness. Now, what the Pope prohibited in a place of entertainment, the reformers permitted in the synagogue, a place of holiness. [p. 261]

David Hoffmann, in *Melamed Leho'il*, vol. 1, resp. 16, predicts that, since the organ was approved and placed in the temples by the reformers, soon they will introduce women's choirs. This would violate the talmudic dictum of *B. Berachot* 24a, cited above. Needless to say, Hoffman's prediction came true. [p. 296]

Rabbi Benzion Fuerer discusses the question of whether it is proper that men in charge of religious education teach girls the Written as well as the Oral Law in great detail (*Noam*, vol. 3 [1960], pp. 131 ff.). Rabbi Fuerer begins his discourse by citing Mishnah *Sotah* 3:4, which contains views both pro and con.

Maimonides' view, giving both an a priori and an ex post facto ruling, is quoted next. "Ex post facto, a woman who studies Torah receives reward, though a lesser reward than men, since she is not commanded to study Torah as are men. However, a priori, or in principle, girls should not be taught Torah because most women lack the proper attitude and the sound mind of men. Their intelligence is inferior; therefore, they misinterpret the Torah. The statement of Rabbi Eliezer, 'Everybody who teaches his daughter Torah is as if he taught her lechery' (above Mishnah), refers to the Oral Law. As to the Written Law, it should not be taught her a priori, but once she was taught it, it is not like lechery."

Subsequently, many other halachic views are cited, two of them being, "The woman is obligated to learn the laws pertaining to women" (Isserles in *Yoreh De'ah* 246,5); and "Women may study a priori the simple meaning of the Written Law, but not in depth" (*Ture Zahav*, ibid.).

Rabbi Fuerer, though Orthodox, takes great pains in interpreting away the negative attitude of former sages and in particular the derogatory view of Rabbi Eliezer in this matter. Rabbi Eliezer's view is explained away by forced interpretation. The essence of this interpretation is that in former times the study of the Torah by women did more harm than good, but in our generation the study of the Torah by women does more good than harm. Rabbi Fuerer qualifies his statement in the following manner. In former times the question was: Should the girls study Torah or nothing at all? Since the girls of today are determined to study, the question is now: Should they study Torah or secular subjects? Since we cannot turn the tide, it is better to let the girls study Torah rather than "lechery," that is, nonsense, secular subjects, and so forth.

A further fact must also be taken into consideration. Whether we like it or not, in our day the female teacher has taken the place of the male teacher. She teaches the Torah to both boys and girls. If we do not teach our daughters Torah and train them as teachers, the liberal teacher will inherit the place of the Orthodox teacher, and will teach the children the falsified Torah.

In order to arrive at his desired conclusion, Rabbi Fuerer renders an unusual interpretation of Isserles' statement that "the woman is obligated to study the laws pertaining to women." The sages only prohibited women from studying the Torah if their study was for the sake of theoretical knowledge. They did not, however, prohibit women from studying for the sake of knowing how to observe the laws. This knowledge they must acquire because the observance of the laws to be performed by the children depends on the knowledge of the teacher. Therefore, as a teacher of boys, a woman must study all the laws, not merely those pertaining to women only, and must study both the Written *and* the Oral Law. [pp. 319–21]

Chatam Sofer, Responsa, vol. 6, resp. 89, discusses the following case. A widow weaned her child three months after birth and wanted to remarry. Rabbi Daniel, who referred the problem to *Chatam Sofer*, instructed her to wait twenty-four months before remarrying, since she should have nursed the child for that length of time in accordance with the Jewish law. However, Rabbi Chorin permitted her to remarry immediately and was willing to perform the ceremony. Chorin granted his permission by reasoning that "our ancestors were fools in this respect, why shall I be a fool, too?"

Chatam Sofer, in his reply, agrees with the questioner in principle. Nonetheless, he speaks of the possibility of extenuating circumstances, which ought to be probed by the great sages. Then he adds that the Orthodox ought to separate themselves from the reformers, and should not intermarry with them. . . . (cf. below p. 127) How important the problem was for *Chatam Sofer* is indicated by his answer to Rabbi Daniel, informing him that he wrote to the great rabbis of Hamburg, Prague, and Brod, asking them for their opinions and would forward their replies to him. [pp. 250–51]

Circumcision

THE QUESTIONS pertaining to circumcision discussed in the responsa literature are focused on the following points: Who is qualified to perform the ritual of circumcision? Is omission of a traditional detail permissible? Should circumcision be denied by an Orthodox *mohel* to the sons of "sinners" (Reform Jews)?

In considering the question of who is qualified to perform the ritual of circumcision, professional competency is a sine qua non and shall not be discussed here. The question raised by the Orthodox is whether a Reform Jew or a woman may be admitted as a *mohel*.

David Hoffmann, in *Melamed Leho'il*, vol 2., resp. 80, (pp. 85, 86) cites Moses Isserles (*Yoreh De'ah* 264:1), who states that a Jew who rejects the entire Torah is like a gentile and cannot perform a ritual circumcision. If such a Jew did circumcise a Jewish boy, the ceremony would have to be repeated, though a complete repetition would be impossible. Only "a little blood of the covenant" must be drawn at the second ceremony.

More lenient is Rabbi Ozer's opinion (ibid.). He holds that according to the *Shulchan Aruch*, a *mumar* (understood by Hoffmann as a heretic or a Reform Jew) who himself is circumcised is admissible as a *mohel*. He is preferable to a woman, even to an Orthodox woman. [p. 301]

Even more lenient seems to be the opinion of Rabbi Akiba Eger of Posen, and of other rabbis cited by Rabbi Hoffmann, who would admit a *mumar* a priori without asking for a second, symbolic, circumcision. Hoffmann then says that this is not really a leniency. Postponing the circumcision until a pious *mohel* could be found would be more of a leniency.

Rabbi Akiba Eger raises the question whether an expert *mohel* who publicly desecrates the Sabbath was admissible. Rabbi Eger answers that if the *mumar* desecrates the Sabbath in the presence of ten *mumarim* (in Jewish religious law ten men constitute a "public"), this is not considered a public transgression. Only pious (i.e., Orthodox) Jews are members of the "public."

In his concluding discourse Rabbi Eger suggests that a *mumar* should not be honored and entrusted with circumcision except when no other *mohel* is available, or in a case of emergency. He defines "emergency" very broadly. If the rejection of a nonobservant *mohel* would lead to arguments, this is a case of emergency.

Most lenient is Rabbi Eger's concluding reasoning: We do not have to investigate whether a mohel desecrates the Sabbath. In fact, it is wise *not* to investigate him, as Scripture says: "But with the discreet is wisdom" (Prov. 11:2).

Rabbi Hoffmann follows Rabbi Eger's lenient tendency. Not everybody who is called a heretic is a complete heretic. A *mumar* who rejects the entire Torah has to be admitted in a case of emergency. [p. 301]

Rabbi Judah Aszod, Responsa, *Orach Chayim*, resp. 6, is directed against the liberal rabbis convened in Brunswick. He attacks these rabbis, among others, for abolishing the *metsitsah*, the sucking of the blood after circumcision. Omitting it endangers the life of the child, as said in the Talmud, and also violates an ancient oral law, called "Law given to Moses on Sinai" (*Halachah LeMoshe Misinai*). The *metsitsah* is also important for another reason: According to Maimonides, it weakens man's excessive sexual desire. [pp. 282–83]

Should circumcision be denied to the sons of Reform Jews by an Orthodox *mohel?*

Rabbi Moses Schick, Responsa, *Orach Chayim*, resp. 304, addressed to Rabbi Chayim Sofer of Munkács, discusses this question.

Rabbi Schick disagrees with the questioner who would deny circumcision to the sons of sinners. Circumcision is a requirement of the Torah, an important law. Occasionally, we may transgress a law of the Torah as a "fence of the law," that is, to protect and strengthen a law. However, denial of circumcision would hardly serve as a "fence." The sinners abhor circumcision. Therefore, if we deny them circumcision, they will be glad to have a good excuse not to circumcise their sons.

We cannot deny them circumcision for another weighty reason: A "fence" can be ordained only by the greatest sages of the generation or their leaders, appointed and recognized by the people. [p. 272]

Gentiles and Jews:
Halachic Aspects

GENTILES PLAYED a role in rabbinic legislation as early as talmudic times. For example, the testimony of a gentile pertaining to the death of a Jewish man could be accepted (*Yevamot* 122a–122b; *Shulchan Aruch, Even Ha'ezer* 17:3). A gentile could be invited by a Jewish court to administer the flogging of a Jew (*M. Gitin* 9:8; *Shulchan Aruch, Even Ha'ezer* 134:9). Even in certain instances of food laws (*kashrut*), the testimony of a gentile was admissible (*Shulchan Aruch, Yoreh De'ah* 98:1, Karo, "unintentional testimony," i.e., he was not aware that his information was considered a testimony).

Above (p. 30) we discussed the gentile's role as organ player in the synagogue, and documented below the custom of hiring a gentile to watch the candles on Yom Kippur night lest fire break out. [p. 221]

Noteworthy is a ruling by three Orthodox rabbis of Padua, Rabbi Menachem Azariah Kastilnovo, Rabbi Jacob, son of Rabbi Asher Luzzatto, and Rabbi Israel Mordechai Kunyon. These rabbis cite a traditional view permitting one to ask gentiles to play musical instruments at Jewish weddings. The authority referred to is Avi Ha'ezri, who permits one to ask a non-Jew to do something pertaining to a *mitzvah*. Another reason given by the above rabbis is that there is no real rejoicing for bride and groom without instrumental music. [223–24]

In regard to halachic aspects pertaining to names and languages of the gentiles see above pp. 10, 11.

Rabbi Schlesinger, citing *Vayikra Raba, Sefer Mitzvot Gadol* and some biblical verses, maintains: "Israel must be separated from the gentiles in clothing, in custom and in speech . . ." He also refers to a responsum of *Chatam Sofer* (*Choshen Mishpat,* resp. 197) addressed to Rabbi Jacob Emden and other rabbis.

Subsequently he quotes the prohibition against the use of foreign languages from P. Talmud *Shabbat* I.4; 3c ff. This was one of the "Eighteen Prohibitions" against the gentiles issued shortly before the war against Rome in 70 c.e. The unique significance of these prohibitions is that they cannot be annulled, even by a court (or legislative body) that is greater in wisdom and larger in membership than the "court" that introduced them. The reason for the exception is that our ancestors risked their lives for these "Eighteen Prohibitions," and therefore not even the Prophet Elijah and his court can abrogate them (see Tosafot, *B. Avodah Zarah* 36a) *Lev Ha'ivri* pp. 21 ff. [p. 254]

As pointed out on p. 10, the languages that were not prohibited are Hebrew, Aramaic, Persian, Greek, Arabic, and Yiddish. In fact, Yiddish has the holiness of Hebrew. [p. 254]

Rabbi Eliezer of Trietsch in Moravia, in a letter (*Eleh Divre Haberit* pp. 87–97), warns against hating one's fellow men, regardless of nationality, because the non-Jews of our day are not like the gentiles of former times. Today they believe in the Creator of heaven and earth and observe the "intellectual" commandments. The gentiles of today belong in the category of "the pious people of the nations of the world" and have a portion in the World to Come.

In continuing his defense of the gentiles, Rabbi Eliezer cites Deuteronomy 28:8, "Thou shalt not despise an Egyptian, because thou wast a stranger in his land." This warning was given us in spite of the fact that the Egyptians mistreated and oppressed us. The implication is clear: We must remember not the evil which they did to us but only the good things. If this is so with respect to the Egyptians, how much more is it incumbent upon us always to mention the good things of the nations in whose midst we live, and who "do us only that which is good." "Never remind a person of the bad things he did to you, only the good things." [pp. 230–31]

While Rabbi Eliezer of Trietsch made a clear-cut distinction between the gentiles of former times and the gentiles of our day, the latter "doing us only that which is good," *Chatam Sofer* differentiates between the respective attitudes of Orthodox and Reform Jews toward the gentiles. In Responsa, vol. 6, resp. 84, replying to Rabbi Baruch ben Meir of Hamburg, *Chatam Sofer* says that the reformers flatter the gentiles by saying, "We are like you." In reality, the reformers throw thorns into the eyes of the gentiles by taking a Christian to play in their temple, just as Samson, the prisoner, played in the temple of the Philistines against his will. We have to fear that the gentiles will say that they are being mocked by the Jews. Moreover, if the reformers would say explicitly that the playing of the organ by a Christian should be disregarded as an integral part of the service because it resembles the playing done by a monkey, the result would be hatred generated between the Jews and the gentiles.

Chatam Sofer also attacks the reformers for their wrong and fearful thoughts with respect to the gentiles in the following terms: For the reformers to say that today we live peacefully among the nations, and therefore should omit the prayers for the reestablishment of David's dynasty and the Temple service, lest we offend the nations, is erroneous. These prayers would not offend our king and our princes. In fact, even they hope to possess Jerusalem, the city where their Messiah is buried. All the nations know that we pray and hope for the coming of our Messiah, and they do not resent it (more pp. 82–83). [pp. 246–47]

Conversion to Judaism

RABBI YECHIEL WEINBERG, in Responsa *Seride Esh,*
vol. 2, resp. 107, p. 256, discusses whether it is permissible to
give a Jewish education to children of a Jewish father and a
non-Jewish mother, who intend to convert to Judaism. He
gives an affirmative answer, then continues by saying that children who are both physically and mentally mature should be
converted before the lessons start. He concludes the responsum with the advice: "Seek an experienced Orthodox rabbi
to carry out the act of conversion." The rest of his discourse
is a repetition of the known procedure of conversion as given
in the *Shulchan Aruch, Yoreh De'ah,* 268:3 ff. [p. 314]

IV

Theology

The principal accusation advanced by the Orthodox against Reform Judaism in the area of theology is that the latter is a heretical movement. The heresy of Liberal-Reform Judaism finds expression in the rejection of the belief in the Messiah, in the disbelief in the restoration of the Temple in Jerusalem with its sacrificial cult, and in the rejection of the Kingdom of David. Followers of Reform Judaism also deny the divine origin of both the Written and Oral Law. They further reject such fundamental beliefs as resurrection of the dead, divine reward and punishment, and the existence of the hereafter. Following are some characteristic opinions of leading Orthodox respondents concerning theological premises.

Written and Oral Law

AKIBA EGER says in a letter (*Eleh Divre Haberit*, pp. 27–28) that our faith in the Written and Oral Law is a fundamental principle of Judaism. Written and Oral Law are inseparable. It is impossible to understand them without accepting the traditional interpretations of our rabbis. A Jew who does not believe this is a heretic. "A Jew who neglects just one of a thousand words of the rabbis of the Talmud will cause the downfall of the entire Torah. . . . He will not lay phylacteries, will desecrate the Sabbath. . . . The same applies to all other commandments . . ." [pp. 219–20]

Mordechai Benet, rabbi of Nikolsburg (op. cit., pp. 11 ff.), declares that both Written and Oral Law originated with God. The Oral Law was rejected only by base branches of the Jewish people: the Sadducees in the time of the Second Temple; the Karaites in the days of Judah Gaon (the Middle Ages). Their remnants are completely separated from the Jewish community, because without the Oral Law, which includes the traditional interpretations of the rabbis, they cannot understand even a single *mitzvah*. [pp. 214–15]

Moses Sofer says (op. cit., p. 9): "The Jews who deny the validity of the Oral Law, established by our sages, are heretics." [p. 212]

The Messiah

IN TRADITIONAL Jewish thought, the coming of the Messiah is closely connected with the belief in the return of the Jewish people to the Land of Israel, the rebuilding of the Temple in Jerusalem, and the restoration of the sacrificial cult. Therefore, these beliefs will not be treated separately in our discussion.

Moses Sofer (*Eleh Divre Haberit*, p. 9) attacks the reformers for omitting the prayers for the coming of the Messiah, the return of the Jewish people to the Land of Israel, and the restoration of Temple and sacrificial cult in Jerusalem. The reformers omit these prayers not merely because of their disbelief in these fundamentals of our religion, but also because they fear that the gentiles may consider such beliefs to be proof of the Jews' disloyalty to their host countries.

Rabbi Sofer's reply does not concentrate on the theological differences between Reform and Orthodox Judaism, but rather on proving that the beliefs in question do not constitute, or even indicate, disloyalty to our gentile hosts. He reasons as follows: First, we have historical proof that our desire to return to the Land of Israel was not considered disloyalty to our host countries in the past. When Nehemiah, in spite of his high-ranking position in the Persian Empire, expressed his desire to return to the Land of Israel, the Persian king expressed no misgivings and graciously honored Nehemiah's request. Rabbi Sofer's next step is to praise the rulers and host nations in whose midst we have lived like prisoners since the destruction of the Temple. We have to pray for their welfare. We believe that they will be rewarded by God for their kindness to us. Nonetheless, we are not being ungrateful if we hope and pray to return to our land. On the contrary, the other nations will praise God if He responds to our prayers. If we are well off, they will benefit, too. Finally, Rabbi Sofer cites Maimonides (*Mamrim*, chap. 3) in chiding the reformers for their disbelief in the words of the prophets who predicted the restoration of the Third Temple and the coming of the Messiah, and also for their disbelief in the utterances of our sages. [p. 213]

Rabbi Moses Sofer, in a reply to Rabbi Baruch of Hamburg (Responsa, vol. 6, resp. 84), who asked for his opinion, among other matters, about the reform of omitting the references in the prayers to the coming of the Messiah, the restoration of Jerusalem, and so forth, says the following. The *Amidah*, containing the prayer for the restoration of David's dynasty, was said three times daily by Daniel, and by the priests performing the sacrificial service, even though the latter were under Hasmonean rule and that of Herod. Even more weighty than historical precedents are the numerous laws in the Mishnah and both *Talmudim*.

Rabbi Sofer now draws a conclusion. Since the Hasmonean rulers did not feel offended by the reciting of prayers for the rule of David's dynasty, therefore neither will the gentile kings feel offended (see above p. 7). [p. 213]

Rabbi Eliezer of Trietsch (op. cit., pp. 90–92) maintains that even during the time of the Second Temple, when the Jewish people dwelt in their land and had a king and high priest, they still prayed for the coming of the Messiah. Subsequently, he points out that the belief in the Messiah is one of the thirteen basic beliefs, according to our great philosophers and rabbis, such as Maimonides and Joseph Albo, and is fully explained by Don Isaac Abrabanel. The reformers deny the belief in the coming of the Messiah, and, therefore, in their prayers they omit references to the ingathering of the exiles, the redemption, and so forth. [pp. 229–30]

Rabbi Abraham Löwenstamm of Emden, in his book *Sefer Tseror Hachayim* (Amsterdam, 1820), repeats and reemphasizes the importance of the belief in the coming of the Messiah. He also maintains, as does Rabbi Moses Sofer, that this belief does not in any way contradict our love for the rulers of our host nations. This belief is the obligation of every Jew. [p. 240]

In the last chapter of his book, entitled "The End of Days" (pp. 170–81), Rabbi Löwenstamm discusses in great detail the question of the Messiah, the return of our "captives" to the Land of Israel, and the restoration of the Temple and its cult. In this chapter, Rabbi Löwenstamm declares that a Jew who does not believe in the coming of the Messiah, in Israel's return to their land, and in the restoration of Jerusalem, the Temple, and its cult, is *not a Jew*. Such a person is not even to be called a human being. Our beliefs do not contradict our love for our king and the country of our present habitation. Therefore, we are not permitted to omit even one single letter from our prayers pertaining to the Messiah, the Holy City, and so forth. Rabbi Löwenstamm then presents a long, elaborate discussion, giving both the Christian view of their Messiah (Jesus), and at much greater length the traditional Jewish position, supported by biblical and later sources. Among his more significant views and arguments are the following (p. 75b): "As long as there are . . . nonpious Jews on earth, and gentiles who do not believe in the Jewish faith at all, redemption [i.e., the Messiah] has not come." Furthermore, he maintains, Jews are not permitted to rebel against their rulers. On the contrary, they must pray for peace for them and their country.

Most unique and interesting is Rabbi Löwenstamm's assertion that even when the days of the Messiah come, we will not be permitted to help ourselves. Even then we will have to remain quiet and abide by the orders of the ruler. Every nation and ruler, out of their good will and great love for us, will have to take us to the Land of Israel, and place the crown of royalty upon the head of our Messiah. "We long that they send us with the desire of their soul to Jerusalem . . . and appoint David, our Messiah, king. However, if they do not want to do this out of their full desire, then, even if we see that we have the power to go to Jerusalem by force, we are not permitted to do anything on our own lest we break the oath imposed upon us by the God of our fathers . . ." [p. 241] Needless to say, the Jews in our time who fought for the independence of the State of Israel acted in disagreement with Rabbi Löwenstamm's admonition.

Rabbi Moses Schick (Responsa, *Orach Chayim*, resp. 304), in his reply to Rabbi Chayim Sofer of Munkács, first repeats the latter's complaints and suggestions that there are wicked people who desecrate God, publicly rebel, and reject the belief in the Messiah, the Kingdom of the House of David, and the restoration of the Sanctuary. As a punishment, Rabbi Chayim Sofer suggests that they be excommunicated and their sons not be circumcised. Rabbi Schick disagrees with Rabbi Chayim Sofer regarding the suggested punishment. He reasons that excommunication is prohibited by law. He also opposes Rabbi Sofer's suggestion that their sons not be circumcised (see above p. 73). He also opposes another suggested punishment that we should not consult Reform Jewish physicians who attend liberal synagogues. Entering a building, for example, a liberal synagogue, in which there are no idols or objects related to idol worship, is not prohibited. Nonetheless, it is still a *mitzvah* to keep four cubits away from these heretics. [p. 273]

Heresy: Various Aspects

ORTHODOX RABBIS of Prague, members of the "Great Court," wrote a short letter (*Eleh Divre Haberit*, p. 17) in which they first complain about the present generation in which sinners and heretics have gained power. They then complain about the new customs invented by the reformers, who also despise the Torah and the customs of our ancestors. They add that those who violate traditions lack faith, and that their intention is to acquire a higher reputation among the gentiles. However, these reformers are neither Jews nor Christians. The book *Nogah Ha-Tsedek* (The light of righteousness), written by Reform rabbis, these Orthodox rabbis consider to be evil darkness. All it contains are cunning lies, intended to lead the pious Jews astray. The prayers of the reformers turn into sins, since they transgress the words of the sages. [pp. 215–16]

Rabbi Eliezer Trietsch, in a letter to the Hamburg Orthodox court (op. cit., pp. 22–24), says that the fact that, in a specific instance, an Italian rabbi and Aaron Chorin of Hungary had been asked to give their views on certain matters of the Jewish religion, but the rabbis of Germany, Moravia, Bohemia, and Poland, and the great rabbis of Hungary, had not been asked, proves that the questioners were not interested in learning the truth but only in falsification of law and tradition. [pp. 217–

18] Rabbi Eliezer maintains that Rabbi Chorin is not merely a heretic, but also totally ignorant so far as Talmud and other rabbinic sources are concerned. He enumerates the changes Rabbi Chorin made and shows that they are contrary to law and tradition. Jews who follow his instructions are denying the fundamentals of Judaism. [p. 217]

Rabbi Abraham Löwenstamm, in *Sefer Tseror Hachayim* (p. 20b), points out that standing without a hat is contrary only to piety, but walking four cubits (about two yards) without it is prohibited by law. He then says that since the Jews have accepted the custom of piety as a law, to violate the custom is arrogance and heresy (see below pp. 105 ff). [p. 237]

Rabbi Löwenstamm also discusses, among other issues, another problem of traditional theology about which he was asked: "Is it permissible to pronounce the Tetragrammaton letter by letter? (p. 68)." Citing traditional sources, he strictly prohibits doing so. According to Tosafot and Obadiah of Bertinoro, the punishment for pronouncing the Tetragrammaton is limitless. A proof for the prohibition of the pronunciation of the Tetragrammaton is the fact that it has no vocalization of its own in the Bible. If we were permitted to pronounce it, it would have to have a vocalization of its own so we would know how to pronounce it. A person who pronounces the Tetragrammaton commits a grave sin and, according to most sages, will not live in the World to Come. [pp. 239–40]

Rabbi Moses Sofer (Responsa, vol. 6, resp. 89) declares that the reformers are sectarians and heretics like the Sadducees, Boethusians, Karaites, and "Saul" (Paul). "They have their own sinful religious practices and are heretics, while we, the Orthodox Jews, observe the true Jewish religion. This distinction, however, is only theoretical or theological. In reality, we are not permitted to declare them a separate sect, since we do not have the permission of the secular authorities to do so" (see above p. 70). [pp. 250–51]

In reply to a letter from Germany entitled *Shelome Emune Yisrael* (The perfectly faithful of Israel), signed by 116 Orthodox rabbis, seven rabbis of Jerusalem concur with their German colleagues. The essence of these letters is a strong complaint against the decisions of the Brunswick convention of the liberal rabbis. These liberal rabbis are heretics about whom the Orthodox pray every day, "The heretics shall have no hope." They are like the men of Sodom, like the Karaites, etc. (*Shomer Tsiyon Hane'eman* [Altona 1847], p. 20a–20b) [p. 258]

Rabbi Chayim Bezalel Panet, in his responsum against the "wicked" (reformers), a reply to Rabbi Hillel of Kolomea (Responsa *Derech Yivchar*, resp. 1), attacks the Reform rabbis. Rabbi Panet maintains that they and their followers are a sect that desecrates the Sabbath, eats pork, etc. These preachers, he says, have no fear of God. He concludes his responsum by saying: "It is better to attend the church of the non-Jews and listen to the sermons of their ministers than to enter a choir-synagogue [=liberal synagogue] and listen to the sermons of those preachers. . . . in their words there is hidden heresy . . ." [pp. 262–63]

Most outspoken in condemning the liberal Jews is Rabbi Moses Schick. In one of his responsa (*Orach Chayim*, resp. 37), he says that Maimonides is right when he maintains that nothing stands in the way of repentance. Even the wicked and heretics are accepted, if they repent (*Laws of Repentance*, end of chap. 3). Rabbi Schick concurs with Maimonides, but interprets the words "All are accepted if they repent" as referring to God, who knows the thoughts of man. However, we human beings have limited vision and cannot know if a repentance is genuine or not. Therefore, we have to accept another ruling by Maimonides: "We do not accept certain sinners, even if they repent" (*Avodah Zarah* 2:5).

Pious Jews are unable to read the minds of the liberal Jews. Rabbi Schick's conviction is that the repentance of liberal Jews is not sincere. "They are just waiting for the right opportunity to come. . . . Therefore, every Orthodox Jew has to watch out not to fall into the net of the *Neologes* [liberals]. . . . God-fearing people must keep afar from them. . . . Beware of making peace with them . . ." [pp. 266–67]

In another responsum (*Orach Chayim*, resp. 70), Rabbi Schick elaborates on his view that secular knowledge leads to heresy. As soon as the Jews speak the language of the gentiles and acquire secular knowledge, they neglect the Torah or forget it altogether. They also abandon the *mitzvot* and piety. Many of them become heretics. They all begin their sinful lives by studying foreign languages and secular wisdom. It is the obligation of the Orthodox to reject and destroy everything that interferes with the study and observance of the Torah. Among Rabbi Schick's specific dislikes is philosophy, and he quotes Rabbi Asher (Responsa, 55): "Thank God that He saved us from it [i.e., philosophy]." Schick objects to citing men like Maimonides, who acquired secular knowledge and remained pious. They are a minority and do not disprove Schick's opinion, which concerns the majority. [p. 268]

Schick continues his struggle against the "heretics" in a later responsum (op. cit., resp. 305). Before attacking the "heretics" directly, Rabbi Schick chides the Orthodox rabbis for their silence, in contrast to Ezra and his followers, who expelled the Samaritans from the Jewish community. Rabbi Schick suggests publicizing the truth, that is, the punishment, concerning the "heretics," those evil rabbis who banded together and printed sinful legislation (protocols). He also states that he regrets that these men cannot be excommunicated, due to a prohibition by the government. Rabbi Schick states further

that "the evil, heretical rabbis denied the divine origin of the
Torah, as many of their heretical books testify. For this reason,
they are not Jews, but are worse than non-Jews. They are not
trustworthy in regard to Jewish law and custom, even less
trustworthy as teachers and rabbis. . . .

He elaborates: "The rabbis prohibited the daughters of the
Sadducees and Karaites for marriage even after they accepted
the Jewish faith. The Reform Jews should be treated even
worse. They are heretics.

Rabbi Schick adds: "Since they are like gentiles, we are
prohibited from praying in their houses of worship. Wicked
people, that is, the reformers, are not members of the *minyan*
and cannot officiate as reader, even if ten kosher [Orthodox]
Jews are at the services. They are not our co-religionists and
cannot represent us. All this should be publicized. The publication will alert the great rabbis, who, in turn, will decide what
to do to give strength to the Jews who want to strengthen
the Torah and will, at the same time, thwart the counsel of
the wicked." [pp. 273–75]

Rabbi Isaac Beer Bamberger, a renowned Orthodox rabbi
of Würzburg, once rendered the lenient decision that it is
permitted to be within the same community with the Reform
congregation of Frankfurt on the Main if this congregation
swears before the Orthodox community that they do not want
a complete separation from the Orthodox in regard to every
precept of the Torah.

Rabbi Schick of Brezova strongly objects to Rabbi Beer's
leniency (Responsa, *Orach Chayim*, resp. 306). He compares
the reformers to Korah (Num. 16). "The incident of Korah
serves as precedent for our sages, that we have to separate from

the wicked. They are like non-Jews. We have to separate from them more than from the gentiles. According to our sages we may accept certain sacrifices from the gentiles, but not from the apostates, not from those who publicly desecrate the Sabbath and from heretics, i.e., not from the reformers, since they belong to this category of transgressors.

"Moreover, they cannot join us even after death. It is prohibited to have a common cemetery with them, since the law rules that a wicked person must not be buried next to a righteous [=Orthodox] person. This law cannot be observed in a common cemetery without much quarrel.

"There is also a further reason for the separation. Experience has taught us that while the first generation of Orthodox Jews associating with the reformers will not become sinners, the second generation will."

Rabbi Schick refuses to accept a bid of the liberals suggesting that each of the two Jewish branches should elect its own rabbi, but should still remain within one community. Rabbi Schick is supported in his opinion by Rabbi Moses Sofer.

At the end of the responsum, Rabbi Schick begs Rabbi Beer to change his mind, "lest God's name be desecrated by you." [p. 276]

Rabbi Tsvi Hirsch Lehren and Rabbi Eliyahu Abraham Prinz printed an attack against the reformers, whom they call "Karaites." Rabbi Moses Schick approved of their action (Responsa, *Yoreh De'ah*, resp. 331). In doing so, he called the reformers, who had assembled in Brunswick and published their decisions in the *Protokolle der ersten Rabbinerversammlung*, sectarians and Karaites. According to Rabbi Schick, he who rejects the Oral Law is a heretic. It is prohibited to eat food they declare to be kosher. It is a *mitzvah* to burn their books, since they are the books of sorcerers and heretics. Every matter which they decided or are going to decide is null and void, just as is their permission to marry gentile girls. [pp. 278–79]

The heads of the congregation in Weissenberg complained that the sinners trample on the laws and customs contained in the *Shulchan Aruch*. Their letter of complaint was sent to Rabbi Judah Aszod, an outstanding Orthodox rabbi. In his reply (Responsa, *Orach Chayim*, res. 36), Rabbi Aszod concurs with the heads of the congregation. In doing so, he points out that, except for synagogue customs, no custom can be changed, even after the reason for it has become invalid. A custom overrides a law (*Shulchan Aruch, Choshen Mishpat* 232:19). "Since the customs of the synagogues are still valid, we are not allowed to change them. No one must violate the customs of the *Shulchan Aruch*, which were accepted by men and confirmed by God. Where there are knowledgeable sinners, there is more lawlessness. A thousand ignorant sinners do not count as one pious man." (see p. 112)

Rabbi Judah Aszod believed that publication of this responsum might help to turn the tide. If not, he maintained, God would punish the sinners. [p. 285]

The leaders of the congregation in Gyula (Hungary) complained in a letter to Rabbi Judah Aszod (Responsa, *Orach Chayim*, resp. 37) that the new rabbi had omitted certain prayers and changed the liturgy of Rosh Hashanah. In his reply, Rabbi Aszod supports the leaders of the congregation and declares that even Yom Kippur will not atone for the sins of the rabbi. He has no portion in the World to Come. Rabbi Aszod read the new rabbi's Rosh Hashanah sermon and declared that in it the new rabbi desecrated God's name. (cf. below p. 100)

According to the *Shulchan Aruch* (*Yoreh De'ah* 246:8), it

is prohibited to study Torah with a rabbi who sins, even if he is a great scholar, and even more so is it forbidden to rely on his decisions.

At the end of the responsum, Rabbi Aszod suggests sending copies of his letter to certain outstanding rabbis, asking for their support. [pp. 285–86]

Rabbi David Hoffmann, though himself an illustrious Orthodox rabbi and scholar, in his *Melamed Leho'il*, vol. 2, resp. 80, does not impart to the term "heretic" as broad a meaning as do many of his colleagues. Rather, he concurs with Rabbi Akiba Eger's more lenient definition or interpretation of the term *mumar*, "heretic," when discussing the admissibility of a nonobservant *mohel* (see above p. 71). He holds that we cannot summarily declare that everybody who is called a heretic is a complete heretic, like a *mumar* who rejects the entire Torah. We must judge them favorably, at least in a case of emergency. [p. 302]

Rabbi Zalman Sorotzkin, in *Noam*, vol. 5, pp. 52 ff., condemns the Reform rabbis of the United States because they do not believe in the divine origin of the Torah, meaning that they are heretics. Therefore, they permit what is prohibited in the Torah (see above pp. 42–43). The number of apostates is frightening.

The evil inclination (*yetser hara*), which speaks through the mouth of the reformers, has a cunning method. Today he tells people to transgress minor prohibitions, and tomorrow to transgress major prohibitions, until finally he says to them, "Worship idols," and they do it (*B. Shabbat* 105b; see above p. 43). [pp. 224–25]

Rabbi Mordekhai Hakohen (*Noam*, vol. 5, pp. 60 ff.) declares that anything new is prohibited by the Torah—that is, it is to be considered heresy. The implication is that the reformers are heretics. "The Reform movement in Germany and Hungary shook up the House of Israel." [pp. 325 ff] (see also pp. 143–45)

V

Gentile Authorities

THE GENTILE authorities often interfered with Jewish religious life. Occasionally the interference originated with the gentile authorities, as, for example, when Napoleon requested that certain questions be answered by the "Sanhedrin" which had been constituted by his order. This famous instance of interference is extensively described in various publications and will not be discussed here. Our intention is to concentrate rather on interference by the gentile authorities initiated by the feuding Jewish groups, Reform and Orthodox, as they respectively struggled for and against the introduction of reforms.

In most instances, the Orthodox sought the help of the secular authorities in order to prohibit the innovations introduced by the leaders of the reformers. The Reform leaders often reacted to the complaints of the Orthodox leaders by making counter-complaints before the gentile authorities. Let us first concentrate on the complaints initiated by the Orthodox before the gentile authorities, this being the more significant and spectacular category of complaints.

Rabbi Baruch (son of Meir), head of the Hamburg Orthodox *bet din*, in a letter written in 1819 to Rabbi Moses Sofer, lists a number of complaints against the reformers and their recently introduced reforms. He also informs Rabbi Sofer about sending word to the congregational leaders, who were appointed since the Napoleonic wars by the government, asking them to prohibit the use of the new reformed prayerbook, and so forth. He then continues: "We found it necessary to present our words to the gentile authorities." Subsequently the Reform Jews acted as "informers," telling the gentile authorities that the decision of the Orthodox was unlawful. By going to the gentile authorities, Rabbi Baruch maintains, the reformers desecrated God's name.

At the end of his letter, Rabbi Baruch praises the gentile authorities as men of reason and knowledge for instructing the *bet din* to bring evidence from noted sages to substantiate their complaint. Therefore, he asks Rabbi Sofer to reply immediately. [pp. 242–44]

To the points cited from Rabbi Baruch's letter, Rabbi Sofer (Responsa, vol. 6, resp. 84) replies: God showed us favor before the gentile authorities in that they instructed the leaders of the Hamburg Jewish community to solicit the opinion of the sages, among them his own. In his detailed reply, discussed above in another context (pp. 82–83), Rabbi Sofer argues that the Jews' prayers for the restoration of David's dynasty, for the Temple in Jerusalem with its sacrificial cult, and for Palestine as the land of the Jews, in no way offend the present host nations. The reformers, by deleting these prayers, have committed a sin.

Subsequently, Rabbi Sofer attacks the reformers, charging that some of their reforms reflect dishonesty and mockery of the gentiles. The reformers try to flatter the gentiles by saying, "We are like you, etc." [pp. 246–47]

In brief, this discourse by Rabbi Baruch and Rabbi Sofer reveals that the Orthodox first complained to the gentile authorities about the reformers because of their newly introduced reforms. Afterwards, the reformers approached the same gentile authorities defending their reforms. Finally, the authorities asked the Orthodox to substantiate their claims by submitting the opinions of leading rabbinical authorities. This implies either that the Orthodox were given an opportunity to defend themselves, or that they were given the privilege of making the final decision. Subsequent history indicates that although the gentile authorities were inclined to maintain the status quo here, as in most other instances, they were basically uninterested in the implications of these complaints.

Rabbi Akiba Joseph Schlesinger, in *Lev Ha'ivri* (pp. 21 ff.), reproaches the reformers for their innovations and other doings, including their activity as informers to the gentile authorities and, specifically, to gentile courts. However, he does not give details about the accusations of the reformers. [p. 256]

Rabbi Moses Schick, in Responsa, *Orach Chayim*, resp. 37, expresses his satisfaction with the success of the "*Chevrah* of Guardians of the Faith." Due to its endeavor, God gave victory to the Orthodox. As a result, the emperor, judges, and *Landtag* (legislature) endorsed and confirmed the Orthodox organizational statute and their laws. This short reference implies that the Orthodox approached the gentile authorities with complaints against the reformers and their reforms, and were upheld by them. The particulars of the complaints are not transmitted. [pp. 285–86]

Rabbi Judah Aszod, in Responsa, *Orach Chayim*, resp. 6, states that the liberal rabbis who convened in Brunswick ought to be excommunicated, but that state law prohibits excommunication. He expresses his trust that God will exert beneficial influence on the governmental authorities in the matter.

The latter statement allows the inference that the Orthodox submitted complaints against the Brunswick decisions and the rabbis assembled there. Subsequent events do not prove that they were successful. [pp. 282–83]

Rabbi Judah Aszod, in Responsa, *Orach Chayim*, resp. 36, complains that the "sect of innovators," that is, the liberal Jews, effected the closing of the Orthodox synagogue and school of Weissenberg by the non-Jewish authorities. Rabbi Aszod suggests that the Orthodox should pray at home without a *minyan* rather than attend the liberal synagogue. In this instance, the Liberal-Reform complaints to the gentile authorities were successful, an exception to the usual outcome of complaints and counter-complaints. Details are missing. [pp. 284–85]

Rabbi Judah Aszod, ibid., resp. 37, received a communication from the leaders of the congregation in Gyula. According to the communication, leaders of that congregation complained that the new rabbi omitted certain prayers and changed others. Therefore, they would not permit him to preach anymore. Subsequently, the rabbi himself complained to the gentile authorities that the congregation would no longer permit him to preach. (cf. above p. 92)

In his reply, Rabbi Aszod states that since this rabbi was appointed by the gentile authorities against the will of the congregation and its leaders, various measures should be considered that would lead to his dismissal. Among his suggestions are revocation of this rabbi's *semichah* by Rabbi Deutsch, who supposedly issued it. In his reply Rabbi Deutsch stated that he never gave the man *semichah*. Next, Rabbi Aszod suggests to solicit three more letters from three famous rabbis and to present these letters to the emperor and the governmental officials. Rabbi Aszod is confident that these letters will sufficiently influence the gentile authorities to dismiss the controversial rabbi. [pp. 285–86]

Rabbi Jonathan Alexandersohn, who was dismissed from his position as a rabbi of Hejöcsaba (Hungary) due to his liberal tendencies, complained about Rabbi Moses Sofer before the gentile authorities of Miskolc in 1834 because Rabbi Sofer was sending money to the poor of Palestine. In his opinion, this was against the law. His complaint had little or no effect (see L. Greenwald, *Toldot Mishpachat Rosenthal*, p. 50, and *Letoldot Hareformatsion Hadatit*, p. 26, n. 57).

Rabbi Israel Jacobsohn, appointed by the governmental authorities as the rabbi of Kassel and its district, endeavored to introduce his reforms throughout Westphalia. Subsequently, the Orthodox complained to the ruler. With Napoleon's defeat, the government of Westphalia toppled too, and Jacobsohn's influence and power was ended (cf. Greenwald, *Letoldot Hareformatsion*, p. 42).

Afterwards Jacobsohn went to Berlin, where he built a temple and introduced his reforms. The authorities, obviously acting on the complaint of the Orthodox, closed this temple and prohibited all prayer reforms, since such reforms were considered to be the basis for the founding of a new sect, and the founding of a new sect was prohibited by law (ibid., pp. 42–43).

After the famous Hamburg temple, with its Reform service, opened its doors, Orthodox rabbis submitted a complaint to the government. The decision of the Hamburg Senate was that the Orthodox bet din had the right to put the matter before the great Jewish leaders. If these leaders opposed the reforms, then the temple would be prohibited. However, due to special circumstances, the temple was not closed (ibid., pp. 43–44).

A noteworthy instance of governmental interference in Jewish affairs occurred in 1847. In that year a Reform convention was called for Mannheim, but it was delayed by the gentile authorities as the result of complaints voiced by the Orthodox (ibid., p. 59, n. 17, citing Geiger).

The interference of the governmental authorities in Jewish affairs was not always occasioned by the request of feuding Jewish groups. Occasionally the initiative came from the governments themselves. Such an instance, for example, was the initiative taken by Emperor Joseph II (1780–90). He planned to emancipate the Jews of his lands and give them equal rights. By doing so, he believed, the Jews would be assimilated into the gentile environment. In order to facilitate their assimilation, he issued a law in 1783 requiring the Jews to give up Yiddish and Hebrew and to use only the language of their host-country. He also ordained that Jews must cut their beards and must be drafted into the army. However, zealous Jews petitioned him to revoke some of his ordinances, particularly concerning cutting the beard, and he granted their requests (see ibid., p. 64).

In the first half of the nineteenth century, only one Hungarian congregation, that of Pest, accepted all of Holdheim's reforms. However, this synagogue did not last long. It was closed by the government in 1849, and most of its members converted to Christianity. The reason given by the government for closing this synagogue was a most bizarre one: The synagogue had initiated the Hungarian revolt against Austria! (ibid., p. 65, n. 4).

The governments of Hungary, in most instances, opposed Jewish reforms, as they opposed all sectarian movements. In some places, however, the gentile authorities allowed the introduction of reforms in the hope that they would eventually lead to the conversion of the Jews to Christianity (ibid., p. 80, n. 40, calls attention to the Responsa *Bet Hillel* in this matter).

In 1850 the reformers of Pest approached the governmental authorities of Vienna with a request for a permit to build a Reform temple, but they were rebuffed. The response of the

Vienna authorities was: "If you want to improve on the religion of the Jews, then accept the Catholic faith, which represents an improvement over the Jewish religion and all other religions . . ." (ibid., p. 81).

At the Orthodox convention in Michalovce in 1865, a number of prohibitions were issued against reforms and subsequently published [pp. 264–63]. However, the prohibition against studying secular subjects was not put in writing because it was contrary to the law of the country (ibid., p. 86).

In 1867 the Orthodox Jews of Hungary went to Emperor Franz Joseph with a petition requesting a permit for the establishment of an institute called "Guardians of the Faith." This institute would guard and regulate Jewish religious life; that is, guard against the assimilationists. It would particularly be concerned with preventing the founding of a seminary, as planned by the liberal Jews. However, the liberal Jews were not idle. They published statements in papers and books reiterating the necessity for adjustments, including the adoption of Hungarian names, clothing, and language. The liberal Jews were supported by Baron József Eötvös, a friend of the modern Jews.

At a meeting in his office attended by thirty Jewish representatives, among them a few Orthodox, Baron Eötvös, after listening to the internal differences of the Jews, declared that he recognized only one Jewish religion.

On July 30, 1868, the Hungarian government ordained that the Jews elect a representative body to settle their differences. Of the 220 delegates elected, only 88 voted against the establishment of a seminary. A noteworthy detail is the fact that Hildesheimer, the spokesman before the minister of education, Baron Eötvös, whom he asked for protection against the assimilationists, did not know what he wanted. He fought all his life for the establishment of the seminary, and at the end he voted against it (ibid., p. 93).

We have cited only a few instances of governmental interference with Jewish religious life. The governments rarely interfered on their own initiative. In most cases they intervened at the request of one or another of the parties to a dispute. The usual pattern was for the Orthodox, or the liberals, or both, to submit complaints to the secular authorities, asking for their help against the opposite Jewish group. As was said above, in most cases the Orthodox leaders complained to the government against the liberals who introduced reforms. More often than not, the complaints of the Orthodox were considered by the authorities, who disliked reforms and often prohibited them because they opposed sectarian movements on principle.

Books on the history of the Jewish religion give many more instances of governmental interference with Jewish religious affairs. We did not repeat them here since our task is to concentrate on the struggle over reforms as found in Hebrew sources. Many additional cases of governmental interference in Jewish life are found in English books. One of the most recent significant books, that includes such instances is the German volume of H. M. Graupe (see Bibliography).

VI

Custom: Its Role in the Struggle over Reform

THE DEGREE of importance ascribed to the realm of custom has a major role in the struggle over reform. In general, the Orthodox insisted on the fundamental importance of "custom," while the reformers felt at liberty to retain, modify, or drop customs quite freely, as they also did with the laws. Let us cite a few significant instances.

Rabbi Eliezer Libermann, in *Or Nogah*, lists among the eight accusations made by the Orthodox against the reformers that they transgress the prohibition of changing the customs of our ancestors, a prohibition based on Proverbs 1:8, 6:20, "And forsake not the teaching of thy mother." [p. 201]

Libermann attempts to refute this Orthodox accusation by citing and interpreting certain talmudic passages (ibid., p. 22). According to the Talmud, he asserts, we are permitted to change religious practices, including customs. The most weighty passage cited by Libermann is *B. Chullin* 6b, which relates that Judah the Prince permitted the eating of the vegetables of Bet She'an without tithing them, a practice formerly prohibited. When objections were raised, Judah refuted them by citing 2 Kings 18:4, relating that King Hezekiah destroyed the brazen serpent that Moses had made because people considered it an object of idol worship. Other pious kings, Asa and Jehoshaphat, who had destroyed all other objects of idol worship, did not destroy the brazen serpent, in order to give to later pious men an opportunity to distinguish themselves. For Libermann, this is the basic source for the justification of making changes in the realm of law and custom, and for permitting matters hitherto prohibited. [pp. 204–205]

In the Second Part of *Or Nogah*, Libermann attacks the two extreme groups of the Jewish people. One extreme likes the burden of customs no matter what their origin and significance, even if they were introduced by an ignorant person or by a woman. Proponents of the other extreme are even worse, and lack faith altogether. They deprecate everything that is part of an old heritage, no matter how meaningful it may be. Men of the first extreme group cannot distinguish between truth and untruth, between good and bad. [pp. 206–207] The men of the second extreme group, he admonishes by saying that they must not transgress any of the Oral Laws imposed upon us by the holy sages of the Talmud, "since both were given us by one Shepherd." [p. 207]

The importance of custom from the Orthodox point of view is emphasized by every rabbi who attacks the reforms and reformers in *Eleh Divre Haberit*.

Rabbi Meshulam Zalman Hakohen of Fürth is the first such rabbi who objects to the violation of laws and customs by the reformers. He is among the few Orthodox rabbis who do not indulge in personal attacks; instead he prays to God that He will pour His spirit upon the reformers so that they can serve Him as in former times. [p. 210]

Rabbi Hirz Scheuer of Mainz, ibid., declares that we are permitted to change or abandon a custom only if there is clear proof that it had been introduced originally due to an error. [p. 211]

Rabbi Moses Schick, Responsa, *Orach Chayim*, resp. 71,

claims that a Jew who changes a Jewish custom, and instead follows the deeds of the gentiles, transgresses many prohibitions. [p. 269]

The rabbis of Padua, in a letter included in *Eleh Divre Haberit*, No. 14, cite the view of rabbis in France who object to the custom of women praying in a language other than Hebrew. [pp. 223–24]

Rabbi Judah Aszod, Responsa, *Orach Chayim*, resp. 3, discusses the question of whether placing the *bimah* in the middle of the synagogue is a law or merely a custom (see above p. 40). Significant is the decision implied in the question: The law is superior to the custom, in spite of the often-expressed opinion that the custom is just as important as the law and occasionally even supercedes the law. Thus, for example, Rabbi Sorotzkin declares that the Jewish custom in accordance with *B. Menachot* 20b, *tosafat* (lit. "custom of our fathers") is like the Torah. Rabbi Judah Aszod (op. cit., resp. 38) accepts the rule that the custom voids the law. This is true, he maintains, not merely for the case before him—the location of the wedding ceremony—but in many instances in which the custom is contrary to law [pp. 286–87].

Under compelling circumstances the Orthodox themselves changed some customs and conformed to Reform customs, without referring to them as such, and giving other reasons instead. Thus, for example, they moved the place of the wedding from outside the synagogue into the synagogue. In justifying this change, they referred on the one hand to compelling circumstances, and on the other hand to old sources (see above pp. 62–64). Such an old source is, for example, Joseph Colon, who states: "If matters change . . . it is permitted to change the custom in accordance with the time" (ibid.).

Occasionally, an Orthodox authority will admit that a

custom is an evil one, but will go along with it because he has no power to stop it. Such a custom is, for example, having the wedding ceremony in the synagogue; the late Chief Rabbi Herzog of Israel admits that he had to permit this evil custom while he was a rabbi in England (see above p. 63).

Perhaps the most significant instance in which the Orthodox and the Conservatives adopted a Reform custom is that of the Bat Mitzvah. This was done under the pressure of the spirit of the time, which required equality for women. Although the Liberal-Reform origin of the Bat Mitzvah ceremony has not been denied by traditional Judaism, they did make certain changes, lest it be equated with the Bar Mitzvah ceremony or the Bat Mitzvah ceremony as practiced in Liberal-Reform temples (see above pp. 65–66).

The term "custom" does not always refer to a ceremony, a prayer, etc., which is not in the category of laws. "Custom" may also refer to the mode of implementing a law. A significant example is the question of whether a man who publicly desecrates the Sabbath could be counted as a member of the *minyan*. David Hoffmann, though himself Orthodox, after analyzing the conflicting opinions, concludes that today's custom in this matter is to be lenient. He even knows of a custom permitting a man who has desecrated the Sabbath to read the service in an Orthodox synagogue (*Melamed Leho'il*, vol. 1., pp. 28ff.; see above p. 52). However, not every Orthodox rabbi who admits transgressors of the law to the *minyan* does so by relying on the strength of the custom based on precedent. Some support a custom by utilizing theology, and may also cite a biblical passage in order to uphold the custom under discussion. Thus, some rabbis hold that a non-observant Jew attending an Orthodox service is, at least temporarily, a *baal teshuvah*, a penitent, who is halachically a pious Jew and, therefore, a member of the *minyan*.

An exegetical reasoning for admitting a nonobservant Jew to the *minyan*, which I heard from the late Rabbi Jakobovitz of Berlin, is the following. According to Genesis 21, on Sarah's request Abraham dismissed Hagar and Ishmael. When the water which Abraham gave them was finished, Hagar placed the child under a bush and sat down at a distance lest she see the child die (ibid., vv. 15, 16). "But God heard the boy wailing, and the angel of God said to Hagar . . . Do not be afraid, for God has heard the boy's cry where he was. . . . Then God opened Hagar's eyes and she saw a well . . . and gave the boy a drink" (vv. 17, 19).

This incident constitutes a serious problem. God in His infinite wisdom knew that Ishmael's descendants would be wicked people. Why, then, did He save Ishmael's life? The answer lies in the words, "God has heard the boy's cry where he was." At the time when Ishmael was crying under the bush, he was a suffering human being, not a sinner. Therefore God saved him, disregarding his and his descendants' future transgressions. The same holds true for transgressors attending a traditional service. While they are in the synagogue, praying with the rest of the congregation, they are not sinners and, therefore, count as members of the *minyan*. (cf. B. Rosh Hashanah 16b)

As in the above instance, Rabbi Hoffmann senses the weakness of basing a controversial custom on a precedent alone. This is particularly so if the originator, or the circumstances of the precedent, are not known, as is true in the case of the *minyan*. For this reason, he also suggests halachic reasons for the custom of admitting nonobservant Jews to the *minyan* [pp. 297–98].

Rabbi Hoffmann's opinion is in conformity with the view expressed in a short letter of the Orthodox "Great Court of Prague" (see *Eleh Divre Haberit*, p. 17). In this letter, the Orthodox complain about the newly invented customs of the reformers, who despise the customs of our ancestors. May we, at this point, emphasize the fact that even within traditional Judaism distinctions are made between one custom and another. Some traditional customs are rejected by traditional rabbinical authorities on the ground that they are based on an error, others because they are considered *minhag shetut*, a foolish custom.

According to historians of the law, customs are often used as the source of a law. In fact, as long as a custom is observed scrupulously, no supporting law is necessary. However, when a custom weakens, it can and often is strengthened by making it a law. According to Rabbi A. Löwenstamm (*Sefer Tseror Hachayim*, p. 20b), once the Jews accept a custom of piety as a law, its violation is heresy [p. 238].

One of the strongest advocates of the paramount importance of the custom is Rabbi Judah Aszod (Responsa, *Orach Chayim*, resp. 36). Nonetheless, he permits a change in a custom of a synagogue, provided that the reason for such a custom has become invalid. After this seemingly lenient position, he adds the warning that since the reasons for customs of the synagogues are still valid, we are not allowed to change them. Obviously, all he intended to accomplish by his seemingly lenient opinion was to justify the widely varying customs among Orthodox synagogues throughout the world. (see above p. 92).

In conclusion, we may say that the Orthodox *in principle* strongly adhere to the old customs. We emphasize the words "in principle," because if we compare the customs listed in the *Shulchan Aruch* with those observed today by the truly Orthodox, we shall find that many of the original customs have been tacitly dropped. On the other hand, some recent Reform customs, such as the Bat Mitzvah ceremony, have been adopted by traditional Judaism, although with some modifications. The liberal thelogy of the Reform makes dropping old customs and adopting new ones no problem, and they have made ample use of this freedom, particularly in dropping old customs.

VII

Internal Changes and Reforms

BOTH REFORM and Orthodox Judaism underwent numerous internal changes in order to adjust to new situations, to the spirit of the time, or to other circumstances.

The fundamental difference between the Orthodox and Reform in making the changes is that the former undertook them in spite of their basic doctrinal opposition to changing existing laws and customs under most circumstances, while the latter had no impediments. On the contrary, the reformers openly advocated the necessity for changes, discussed them in synods and other meetings, and introduced them in their communities as soon as the synods approved of them. The deliberations of the Liberal-Reform synods are properly and fully analyzed and discussed in several authoritative books and numerous articles, written primarily in German and English (see Bibliography). There is no need here to repeat, reanalyze, or reevaluate the internal struggle within the Liberal-Reform movement, particularly since our task is to concentrate on the struggle over Reform as reflected in Hebrew sources. Still, we shall need to discuss a few instances of internal developments within Reform Judaism, since they are found in the Hebrew literature and therefore fall within the scope of our study.

Our primary attention in this chapter is focused on the internal struggle, or internal changes, within traditional Judaism as related to the reforms introduced by Liberal-Reform Judaism.

Many of the internal changes within Orthodox Judaism pertain to reforms or adjustments that were originally adopted by Reform Judaism, but were immediately and vehemently opposed by early Orthodox leaders.

Between the mode of the original rejection and the later adoption of a change by the Orthodox, there is a fundamental difference. The rejection was accompanied by the utmost publicity, using the strongest language possible, emphasizing both the ignorance and the wickedness of the innovators. On the other hand, when the same "reform" was later adopted by the Orthodox, reference to the former opposition was limited or not mentioned at all. Occasionally, the necessity of countering with the means (or "weapon") of the opposition is the justification for the adoption of a certain reform by the Orthodox.

Speaking of internal changes and differences, we find a significant disagreement among the Orthodox rabbis with respect to the use of the organ (see pp. 28 ff). Let us point here to but two details: (1) The rabbis of Padua, though basically concurring with the Hamburg *bet din*, state that "playing the organ on a Sabbath, even by a non-Jew, is prohibited in places where this was a previously prohibited practice . . ." The obvious implication is that the organ may be played on the Sabbath where doing so happened to be the practice in the past. (2) The use of the organ in a Prague synagogue caused quite a turmoil among the Orthodox rabbis. It took a large part of *Eleh Divre Haberit* and many more responsa (see D. Hoffman, *Melamed Leho'il*, vol. 1, pp. 11 ff.) to ban the organ from the synagogue. Those who opposed the use of the organ in the synagogue were greatly troubled and annoyed by the precedent in Prague, where an organ was used in an Orthodox synagogue, though not actually on the Sabbath. This precedent seemed at first to indicate, or set in motion, a new trend, the adoption of a reform, but was later reversed due to vehement opposition. As a result, after the organ in Prague broke down, it was not repaired.

The problem of the organ is one of the few exceptions to the general tendency in modern Orthodox Judaism toward a cautious adoption of the various reforms which were at first strongly opposed. A few examples of the more typical pattern follow:

Translating and Printing
the Talmud; Printing Sermons

RABBI JUDAH ASZOD (Responsa, *Orach Chayim*, resp. 4) attacks the Jews who print translations of the Talmud in the languages of non-Jews. He gives two reasons for the prohibition: (1) According to the Talmud (*B. Sanhedrin* 59a), non-Jews must not study the Torah (including the Talmud). For them to do so would have harmful consequences. (They would use it against the Jews, as has been done by many anti-Semitic "scholars.") (2) As stated in Leviticus 19:14, "Thou shalt not give a stumbling block before the blind."

Rabbi Aszod then points out that the calamity of translating the Talmud began with the "new teachers" (Reform rabbis) printing their sermons, which included sayings of the sages. The next step would be the printing of extensive sayings, followed by printing the entire Talmud. [pp. 281–82]

The strong opposition to the translation of the Talmud by the earlier Orthodox leaders has simply been disregarded by the Orthodox of the present day, who have translated the Talmud. However, we must recognize that circumstances have changed. In Rabbi Aszod's time (nineteenth century), the Jews who wanted to study the Talmud did not need a printed translation. They received all necessary instruction in the *yeshivot*. However, in our day the *yeshivot* have declined both in numbers and in the stature of their teachers. As a result, the translation of the Talmud is needed by modern Jews, both Reform and Orthodox, almost as much as it is needed by the gentiles. Preventing the gentiles from studying the Talmud, and then using their knowledge against the Jews, is no consideration today, since all the possibly offensive passages from the Talmud and other Jewish literature have already been extracted and amply utilized in anti-Semitic publications.

Secular Learning, Modern Scholarship, Seminaries, Modern Jewish Schools ("Day Schools")

W E DISCUSSED above (p. 10), in certain specific contexts, the strong objections of Orthodox leaders against pursuing secular studies. Historical evidence showing that great men of the past, such as Maimonides, acquired considerable knowledge in various fields of secular learning, was interpreted by the Orthodox authorities of the past century in such a manner as to preclude its use as a precedent. It is an interesting phenomenon that the objections vanished within a single century. Today, pursuit of secular studies among the Orthodox is as common, or almost as common, as among the liberal Jews. Only the ultra-Orthodox plead today against secular knowledge.

In contrast, the liberal leaders of the last century emphasized the importance of acquiring secular learning, even inserting theological arguments into their reasoning. Thus, for example, Rabbi Eliezer Libermann maintained that it would be a sin to reject or deprecate secular wisdom and science. In his opinion, we have to use secular knowledge in support of our faith. "Just as faith alone without knowledge is not possible . . . thus, on the other hand, knowledge and research are impossible without the assistance of faith" (*Or Nogah*, Second Part, pp. 4–6). [p. 206] Subsequent religious leaders, both Orthodox and liberal, do not insist on the necessity of faith for secular studies. This is just another example of the phenomenon that some religious beliefs and practices are being quietly abandoned even by the Orthodox when they become outdated.

The Orthodox leaders of the last century did not oppose merely the pursuit of secular learning; they also objected to the modern scholarly study of Judaism.

Rabbi Akiba Joseph Schlesinger, in *Lev Ha'ivri*, pp. 21 ff., complains about the Jews who acquire secular knowledge, and is even more outspoken in his attacks against the Reform Jews who want to establish a seminary, "God forbid." He calls this undertaking real heresy and apostasy, and maintains that they intend to establish a seminary in order to separate Israel from God by force. "How many rabbis did they ordain, who cause people to sin . . . Vienna, Breslau . . . Everybody who supports this foreign [i.e., non-Jewish, anti-Jewish] matter, his soul is not the soul of Israel. . . . They are the *erev rav*, the mixed multitude [i.e., the mob that left Egypt with the Jews and caused all the misfortune that befell the Jews during their forty-years journey through the desert]." (cf. p. 143) [pp. 256–57]

Rabbi Chayim Bezalel Panet, in Responsa *Derech Yivchar*, (resp. 80), objects to the establishment of a seminary (in Budapest), as do other Orthodox leaders. The objective of the seminary would be, he believes, to destroy the foundation of our religion. "They want to establish a seminary so that the Torah be forgotten by Israel, thinking as the generation of the flood . . ." [p. 144]

In spite of all the strong objections to the establishment of a seminary, the Orthodox later followed suit and established their own seminaries.

Because of the paramount significance of this phenomenon, let us elaborate on it a little further.

Modern Jewish schools and seminaries were long an anathema in the eyes of the early Orthodox. We do not find stronger opposition within the ranks of the Orthodox than in this area.

The best example is the unparalleled discord that occurred among the Orthodox when Rabbi Azriel (Israel) Hildesheimer introduced secular studies in his *yeshivah* in Hungary (Eisenstadt, Kismarton), and especially when he wanted to establish a secular (day-)school for children in Jerusalem. The outrage was so boundless among the Orthodox extremists that one of them, Rabbi Chayim Sofer, even suggested to Rabbi Meir Auerbach of Jerusalem that he call a great assembly in order to excommunicate Rabbi Hildesheimer (see Hillel Lichtenstein, Responsa, *Bet Hillel*, resp. 13, more p. 148). [pp. 289–90]

In spite of the vehement opposition of the Hungarian rabbis to the establishment of modern Jewish schools, even to the point of compelling Rabbi Hildesheimer to leave Hungary, he continued his efforts in behalf of modern Orthodox Judaism, and succeeded in establishing in Berlin the Jewish theological seminary named for him. This changing attitude has been accepted gradually, without any reference to the vehement opposition of the early Orthodox rabbinical leaders.

The Use of the Vernacular

THE STRONG opposition of the Orthodox leaders to the use of the vernacular both for prayer and sermon is well known and expressed in various responsa cited in the second part of this book (see also pp. 5 ff.). We will mention just one such reference. *Chatam Sofer*, Responsa, *Choshen Mishpat*, resp. 137, advises: "Appoint a pious rabbi who does not read secular books and does not speak a foreign language [except Yiddish] . . . since this is like bringing [putting] an *asherah* into the Temple of God." [p. 10]

Subsequently, this attitude on the part of the Orthodox underwent a thorough change. Adjustment was made to the Reform position, although not acknowledged as such, and not without a struggle. A few significant instances follow.

Rabbi Samson Raphael Hirsch was one of the first outstanding Orthodox rabbis to modernize the old Orthodox ways in more than one respect. When he was rabbi in Nikolsburg, he took walks through the streets of the town accompanied by his wife, which his predecessor, Rabbi Mordechai Benet, had not done. Most of his Orthodox contemporaries opposed, and even ridiculed, him for his modern ways. They called him a "reformer," which in a sense he was, because he modernized Orthodox Judaism more than any other Orthodox rabbi (cf. Greenwald, *Letoldot Hareformatsion*, pp. 55–56).

In fact, Hirsch spoke only German, not Yiddish, and wrote only in German. Among his other "reforms" were placing the *chupah* in the synagogue, and making a wedding speech before the bride and groom. However, he still would not permit women, other than the bride and her mother, to enter the main (men's) section of the synagogue, even for the wedding ceremony. It once happened that the women entered the men's section of the synagogue during a wedding ceremony, but they were not permitted to remain there. Rabbi Hirsch ordered them to leave (ibid., p. 56).

Today, in many synagogues men and women are not separated at non-Reform weddings. This represents a significant internal change which occurred without much debate; a Reform practice adopted but not recognized as such.

Without conventions or great debates, the Orthodox rabbis of Germany adjusted to the needs of their times and preached their sermons, as did Rabbi Hirsch, in good German. The Orthodox rabbis did not pay attention to the emphatic prohibition by Rabbi Moses Sofer against the use of foreign languages by the rabbis (see *Chatam Sofer, Choshen Mishpat* 177). Neither did they care for the example of Rabbi Ezekiel Baneth (1773–1864), who entered into a *semichah* the stipulation that the ordination would be invalid if the recipient of the *semichah* were to preach in a foreign language—that is, not in Yiddish (see *Lev Ha'ivri* p. 19). This change, that is, the acceptance of sermons in German, was a necessity, since German was the only language understood by German Jews. It was the most effective means to stem the tide toward reform and towards conversion to Christianity. This was well understood by the Orthodox congregations when they elected eloquent German-speaking rabbis, such as Rabbi Isaac Berneys, chosen as rabbi of a Hamburg Orthodox congregation as early as 1821.

"Intermarriage"

ORTHODOX RABBIS of the last century strongly opposed
marriages between Orthodox and Liberal-Reform Jews. They
warned of the calamitous consequences which could result
from such a marriage. Let us give but a very few examples.

Rabbi Moses Schick repeatedly warns his people of the
dangers of marrying Reform Jews. His primary concern is the
serious consequence, bastardy, that might accompany such an
"intermarriage." "Their divorces and marriages are, of course,
invalid. . . . Since they are like complete gentiles, their daughters
and sons are prohibited for us . . . we are not permitted to intermarry with them, even if they return and accept the true [i.e.,
Orthodox Jewish] faith" (Responsa, *Orach Chayim*, resp. 305;
see also resp. 304). [pp. 273–74]

Rabbi Schick was not the first or only opponent of "intermarriage" with reformers. Among other Orthodox rabbis who
issued similar warning, though not as detailed as those of Rabbi
Schick, is Rabbi Moses Sofer. (see above p. 87) Orthodox should
not intermarry with them (Responsa, Pt. 6,) Rabbi Sofer
admits that his strict position and desire for a complete separation of the Orthodox Jews from the Reform Jews cannot be
carried out. Therefore he admits that whatever he said about
this matter is valid only from the viewpoint of theoretical law
[p. 251]. Theoretical laws have already Talmudic precedents

(see M. Guttmann, *Zur Einleitung in die Halacha*, vol. I, Budapest, 1909, vol. II, Budapest, 1913).

The strict separation between the Orthodox and Liberal-Reform Jews in matters of marriage has continually been giving way to a conciliatory practice. The warning of bastardy is seldom heard today. An internal change took place among the Orthodox rabbis, who consider marriage to a Reform Jew preferable to marriage to a non-Jew. This change has been taking place without rabbinical synods or spectacular conferences. It is another nonadmitted reform, adjustment to the realities of Jewish life.

This phenomenon is not without precedent. A similar one occurred already in Talmudic times. *Tosefta Yevamot* 1:10; (*B. Yevamot* 14b) points out that in spite of the major differences in marriage and divorce laws between the Schools of Hillel and Shammai the Jews, irrespective of their adherence to the one School or the other, "intermarried," as stated: "Although the School of Shammai differed from the School of Hillel in regard to co-wives, in regard to sisters, in regard to a woman whose marriage is in doubt, in regard to an old divorce document, in regard to a case in which a man divorces his wife and she then lodges with him in a lodging place, the School of Shammai did not refrain from marrying women of the School of Hillel, and the School of Hillel did not (refrain from marrying women) from the School of Shammai, but instead they practiced truth and peace among themselves in order to fulfill that which is written, 'Love ye truth and peace.' (Zech. 8:19)."

Stringency Serving the Purpose of Leniency

Annulment of Marriage

Occasionally, Orthodox authorities of our day recognize the validity of religious ceremonies performed by Reform rabbis. This applies particularly to Reform wedding ceremonies, the reason being the assumption that *kasher* witnesses (i.e., Orthodox witnesses) would have been among the guests at the ceremony (see Yechiel Weinberg, *Seride Esh*, vol. 3, pp. 41–42). Therefore, Reform weddings performed abroad are recognized in Israel, even by the Orthodox.

Moreover, even if they know with certainty that the wedding ceremony was invalid, they still may recognize the validity of the marriage. Such an instance would be when the couple acknowledges the faulty ceremony or absence of *kasher* witnesses, and considers the first cohabitation as the true marriage "ceremony." Jews observing the couple living together (in a Jewish neighborhood) suffice as witnesses.

Rabbi Moses Feinstein, in *Igrot Moshe, Even Ha'ezer*, resp. 77, maintains that the above leniency does not apply to American Jews, since the great majority of them do not know the Jewish law. He utilizes this argument in a specific instance in which the apparent leniency would have resulted in a calamity and in reality would have yielded a more stringent decision. The case, in brief, is as follows.

A woman was married in a Reform temple. There were no *kasher* witnesses present. The couple lived together, in a gentile neighborhood, for only a few weeks, then separated. Civil courts annulled the marriage, which, according to a physician's testimony, was never consummated. The woman, therefore, was still a virgin. The husband refused to give her a *get*, a Jewish divorce, which refusal would have made it impossible for the woman to remarry. Rabbi Feinstein avoided this calamity and solved the problem by citing sources that permitted him to invalidate the woman's marriage, thus making it possible for her to remarry.

In this case, the woman and an Orthodox rabbi first attempted to secure a Jewish divorce. This implies that they initially recognized the validity of the Reform marriage ceremony. However, since the man refused to give his wife a Jewish divorce, the recognition of the validity of the Reform ceremony was revoked. It is obvious that the stringent ruling invalidating the marriage was made in order to arrive at a humane and realistic solution to the problem. [pp. 340–42]

Invalidation of a Conversion to Judaism and of a Subsequent Marriage

The most famous and controversial invalidation of a conversion to Judaism and the marriage that followed this conversion occurred recently in Israel. The incident was not as simple as the one cited above, in which a Reform marriage was annulled by an Orthodox rabbi. In the case before us, which led to heated arguments among various Orthodox rabbis and scholars, no Reform rabbi was involved. The case, in brief, was as follows.

Hanoch Langer and his sister, Miriam, both Jewish army veterans of the Six-Day War, wanted to get married to their respective fiancées. Their intended spouses were *kasher* Jews, regarding their descent. That is, they were not *mamzerim*, "bastards." However, Hanoch and Miriam were denied the permit to marry their chosen spouses by rabbinical courts in Tel-Aviv and Petach Tikvah, while the Highest Rabbinical Court in Jerusalem refused to reverse the decision of the lower courts. All the courts agreed that Hanoch and Miriam were *mamzerim*, and, according to Jewish law, a *mamzer* is not allowed to marry a *kasher* Jew (see *Shulchan Aruch, Even Ha'ezer*, chap. 4).

This ruling of the rabbinical courts caused tremendous turmoil in Israel. The predicament of the two young people was pitiful and degrading. Their future happiness was at stake. Jewish law and equity seemed to be irreconcilable in the case of the *mamzer*, though the *mamzer* was innocent of any sin or crime.

The problem of the *mamzer* was a pressing one even in talmudic times. The Talmud finds certain methods of terminating *mamzerut*, which, according to the law of the Torah, is a permanent status. Deuteromy 23:3 rules: "A *mamzer* is not permitted to enter the congregation of the Lord; not even the tenth generation may enter the congregation of the Lord." The phrase "tenth generation" is generally understood to be synonymous with permanent status, that is, forever.

One of the talmudic methods of purifying the offspring of the *mamzer* cannot be applied today. According to this method a *mamzer* could marry a female slave (of gentile stock). The child of this marriage would be a slave, and after this slave was freed he became an unblemished Jew (Mishnah *Kiddushin* 3:13). This method, though accepted and listed in the Codes as valid law, cannot be utilized today, since slavery no longer exists.

Another talmudic method of purifying the offspring of a male *mamzer* would work on a larger scale in Reform Judaism, which approves of mixed marriages. According to the Talmud, if a *mamzer* (a *mamzer*, in halachic terminology, is always a Jew) has a child by a non-Jewish mother, the child is a non-Jew. After this child is converted to Judaism, it is a *kasher* Jew. Thus, we have here a paradoxical situation. The traditional law denies the validity of mixed marriages. However, if a *mamzer* transgresses this law, it will benefit his children. They are not *mamzerim* but gentiles, who will become, upon conversion, *kasher* Jews. (*B. Kiddushin* 67 ff., Mishnah and Gemara; *Yad, Issure Bi'ah* 15:3; *Shulchan Aruch, Even Ha'ezer* 8:5). It is surprising that the endless debates about mixed marriages do not consider this point. The reason may be that Reform Judaism disregards the laws about *mamzerim*, as it disregards many other laws that do not seem to be equitable; for example, the exemption or exclusion of women from certain religious observances.

The most effective method of terminating the stigma of the *mamzer* is for him to move to a place where he is unknown and able, therefore, to conceal his blemished ancestry (see B. *Kiddushin* 71a). In this case, not even the Prophet Elijah, among whose tasks is the clarification of obscured and unresolved matters, would ever reveal the identity of the *mamzer* (Mishnah *Eduyot* 8:7).

This method works in most countries, but not in Israel, where the rabbinate keeps a record of *mamzerim* in its files. Lately, it almost literally opened a Pandora's box and led to the most passionate debate in many years among rabbis in Israel and abroad.

The facts, in brief pertaining to the above incident, are the following:

Hava Ginzberg, a fourteen-year-old Jewish Girl of Lukow, Poland, eloped with Bulak Borokovsky, a Catholic man. She converted to the Catholic faith and married Mr. Borokovsky in a church. Not much later, Mr. Borokovsky was circumcised and was called Abraham Borokovsky, a clear indication that he converted to Judaism, and he married Hava in a Jewish wedding ceremony. The implication is clear: Hava returned to Judaism.

A few years later (in 1933), Hava, her husband, and her child emigrated to Palestine. In 1944 Hava separated from her husband and lived with Mr. Otto Joshua Langer, without first securing a *get*, a Jewish divorce. In the same year she married Mr. Langer, with an Orthodox rabbi officiating.

Only several years after two children, Hanoch and Miriam, were born to the Langers, were Mr. Borokovsky and his first wife, Hava, divorced before the rabbinical court of Tel-Aviv.

Since Hava remarried without first securing a Jewish divorce, the Rabbinical District Court of Tel Aviv decided that Hanoch and Miriam Langer were *mamzerim* and communicated this information to the Ministry of Religions and every office for the registration of marriages.

When Hanoch and Miriam and their intended spouses applied for marriage permits, these were denied them because the records showed that Hanoch and Miriam were *mamzerim*.

They were, of course, upset. They vehemently fought the decision, appealing to the public and hiring a lawyer. Still, rabbinical courts in Tel-Aviv, Petach Tikvah, and Jerusalem all refused to issue them marriage permits. Finally, Chief Rabbi Shlomo Goren, with a court of nine rabbis, decided the issue in favor of Hanoch and Miriam, declaring that they were not *mamzerim*. Rabbi Goren based his decision on hearings of witnesses, including Mr. Borokovsky and Hava Langer. The testimony of the witnesses convinced Rabbi Goren that Mr. Borokovsky's conversion to Judaism was invalid and possibly fictitious, and therefore his marriage to Hava had no validity. This having been the case, Hava was not Jewishly married to her first "husband" when she married Mr. Langer, and, therefore, the Langer children were not *mamzerim*. Promptly after Rabbi Goren's decision, Hanoch and Miriam Langer married their respective fiancées.

The argument that followed Rabbi Goren's decision became even more passionate than the discussions that preceded it. "Strict constructionists," ultra-Orthodox rabbis, insisted that the conversion of Mr. Borokovsky was valid, and that the decision of Rabbi Goren was motivated by other than halachic considerations. This, they claimed, is a blunt violation of Jewish law. Practically every Orthodox rabbi in Israel has taken a stand, either pro or con, regarding Rabbi Goren's decision, as have many Orthodox rabbis in other countries, including America. Among the noted American rabbis and scholars who have taken a strong stand in the matter is, for example, Rabbi Emanuel Rackman, a moderate Orthodox rabbinical authority, whose opinion was published in the weekly *American Examiner–Jewish Week*, December 21, 1972 through January 1973. He emphatically approves of Rabbi Goren's decision and supports his stand with suitable interpretations of talmudic and later sources. More significant, however, is his accusation of "a moral cancer in the Orthodox community" (*Jewish Week*, Jan. 18–24, 1973, p. 9). Rabbi Rackman charges that "religious Right, and secular Left both labor to frustrate Goren" (ibid.). Opponents of Rabbi Goren threatened supervisors of *kashrut* in New York with reprisals if the latter were to support their union leader, who sided with Rabbi Goren (ibid.).

Among the noteworthy American opponents of Rabbi Goren's decision, and of Rabbi Goren, are Rabbi Nisson Wolpin, New York City, editor of the *Jewish Observer*, organ of the Agudath Israel; and Rabbi J. Immanuel Schochet, professor of philosophy, Humber College, Rexdale, Ontario, Canada.

Rabbi Wolpin attacks Rabbi Rackman, among others, because Rabbi Rackman "violates Orthodox dogma by dismissing current leading Torah authorities" who objected "to Rabbi Goren's disregard for halachic dicta . . . to his obvious bowing to secularist-political pressures, rather than acting on the merits of the case" (*Jewish Week*, Jan. 11–17, 1973, p. 11).

Rabbi Schochet attacks Rabbi Rackman for several of his statements and most vehemently criticizes him for calling Goren's opponents "a people who lost their perspective and are guilty of unprecedented malevolence and a shameless act un-equalled in Jewish history . . ." Rabbi Schochet calls this ut-terance a "shameless arrogance that finds its equal in the hateful outbursts of anti-religious and anti-Semitic sources only." He also cites an article by the Israeli journalist Shmuel Snitzer in *Ma'ariv* of Dec. 1, 1972. Mr. Snitzer's main accusation is that Rabbi Goren did not want to divulge the truth, but instead wanted to arrive at a popular decision. For this reason he se-lected judges of the same mind, whose names remained anony-mous. It is also possible, Mr. Snitzer suggests, that Rabbi Goren did not even convene his court, but talked to its members individually. Such a secret court is a kangaroo court, Mr. Snitzer maintains (*Jewish Week*, Jan. 11–17, 1973).

The great importance of the matter is evident in the fact that the then President Shazar sought to enlist support for Rabbi Goren in America. In fact, during his five-day visit to the United States in 1972, Shazar "spent much of his time seek-ing support for . . . Chief Rabbi Goren, who has come under bitter attack in right wing Orthodox circles for his contro-versial ruling in the celebrated Langer 'mamzer' (bastard) case." Shazar met with the highly respected Orthodox rabbis, the Lubavitcher Rebbe and Rabbi Joseph Soloveitchik (see article by Gary Rosenblatt in *Jewish Week*, Jan. 11–17, 1973, p. 5).

To sum it up, the active involvement in the matter by Presi-dent Shazar clearly illustrates the paramount importance of realistic humane considerations, no matter what formidable halachic obstacles must be overcome. In this respect, Rabbi Goren is supported by halachic authorities of the past. These men and their schools sought a livable interpretation of the Halachah, not merely by a liberal interpretation of old laws, but also by the introduction of new measures and practices, whenever needed. Noteworthy is the fact that Rabbi Shlomo Goren denies the accusation of his critics that he considered other than strictly legal aspects ("other" implying humane, opportunist, or Liberal-Reform aspects) in rendering his decision (see a brief summary of his responsum presented in an interview and published in America in *Hadoar*, Dec. 8, 1972, pp. 74–75).

Rabbi Goren's decision may be a violation of the letter of the law, as maintained by his adversaries. However, the alternative would not merely have violated equity and caused considerable unhappiness to four innocent, upright human beings, but would also have resulted in a serious crisis in Judaism (see editorial "Dangerous Crisis in Judaism" in *Jewish Week*, Jan. 18–24, 1973, p. 8). (see A. Guttman "Equity in the Halakhah" in *Justice, Justice Shalt Thou Pursue* N.Y. 1975 pp. 86–92)

This instance, more than any other, demonstrates that the struggle over reform, so prominent in the last century, has not ended. It indicates that after Reform Judaism abandoned the acceptance of the authority of the Halachah, the struggle over reform continued within the individual branches of Judaism, but over different issues.

VIII

Tone of the Controversies

THE STRUGGLE over reform has not always been conducted politely. This is particularly true of the struggle expressed in the polemical responsa and other polemical writings. We shall limit our presentation to characteristic or illustrative instances published in Hebrew, since our task is to demonstrate the struggle over reform as reflected in Hebrew sources.

The derogatory, insulting statements found in the responsa and related literature were not only uttered by Orthodox leaders against the Reform leaders and Reform community or vice versa. We find that such utterances have even been made by Orthodox rabbis against other Orthodox rabbis who had attempted to introduce some necessary reforms or modernization.

We can readily observe an interesting development in this area. When Reform Judaism first broke away from tradition, the vitriolic attacks were directed almost exclusively against Reform and its leaders. However, in later times such attacks tapered off and objections were more frequently expressed internally, that is, within the respective branches of Judaism. This transition resulted from the realization by the main branches of Judaism that each is here to stay and that derogation and insult would be of no further use. In the past, derogations directed against the opposite branch of Judaism have been an integral part of the disputations, which later died down since there were no prospects for victory.

We use the words "tapered off" advisedly, because we still find occasional outbursts reminiscent of earlier times. Thus, in *Noam*, the Israeli Orthodox yearbook of current responsa, we find the following definition of a Reform rabbi: "A reform rabbi [spelled derogatorily ראבּיי] is one of those who do not believe at all in the Torah, unbelievers and heretics" (*Noam*, vol. 7 [1964], p. 399). [p. 329]

During the early period of the struggle over reform, most of the derogatory statements were made by the Orthodox against the Reform. Occasionally, however, we also find such utterances by leaders of the Reform against the Orthodox. One example follows.

Rabbi Eliezer Libermann, in criticizing the Orthodox in his *Or Nogah* (Second Part) states, among other critical remarks: "Their [i.e., of the Orthodox] eyes are blinded and, therefore, they cannot see the truth." [p. 206]

Let us now examine some characteristic derogatory statements made by leading Orthodox rabbis against the reformers.

Rabbi Mordechai Benet of Nikolsburg issues a warning against Rabbi Aaron Chorin of Arad, saying: "Heaven forbid to accept any instruction from him because he is an ignoramus in Talmud and Codes. Instead, all his endeavor is in the realm of logic [speculation, philosophy, theology]" (*Eleh Divre Haberit*, p. 16). [p. 215]

Orthodox rabbis of Prague, members of the "Great Court," state in a letter that the intention of the reformers is to acquire a higher reputation among the gentiles so that the latter will say that the reformers, by making changes and narrowing the gap between Judaism and Christianity, are wiser than the other Jews. However, in reality the reformers are neither Jews nor Christians (*Eleh Divre Haberit*, p. 17). [p. 216]

The same letter says that the despicable book *Nogah Ha-tsedek* (lit., "The light of righteousness") ought to be called

"Evil darkness." It contains cunning lies only, calculated to blind the eyes of the Jews, etc. [p. 216]

Rabbi Mordechai Benet, op. cit., p. 21, devotes a whole paragraph to derogatory remarks about *Or Nogah*. He says there, among other things: "This book *Avon* (i.e, *Sin*; the derogatory abbreviation און = אור נוגה means "sin") is nothing but a two-edged blasphemy (pun on: two-edged sword) . . . words of perversity. It turns light into darkness and darkness into light. . . . They are words of nought, etc." [pp. 216–17]

Rabbi Eliezer of Trietsch, op. cit., pp. 22–24, states that the reformers deny the roots of our faith, the words of the holy prophets and the sages, and insult the angels of God. He also attacks the forgeries contained in *Or Nogah*, abbreviating the title as *avon*, "sin." Furthermore, he cites against the reformers the biblical verses Proverbs 14:11; 37:17, which condemn the wicked. [pp. 217–18]

At the end of his letter, Rabbi Eliezer prays that God may uproot the uprooters of the roots of our religion, that is, the reformers.

Noteworthy are the original remarks of Rabbi Abraham Eliezer Halevi (rabbi of Trieste) against the reformers (op. cit., p. 26): "The Hamburg reforms are the greatest evil since the exile from Palestine. God will not forgive these wicked people (reformers). The rabbis and sages who have access to the royal court should see to it that the reformers be persecuted until destroyed, that is, until they repent." [pp. 218–19]

Rabbi Moses Sofer, op. cit. pp. 41–42, in calling attention to the difference between the Orthodox and the Reform in regard to honoring the gentile king, maintains that the Orthodox rabbis should alert the people in all their sermons that honoring the king and the authorities of the land is a commandment of the Torah.

The reformers, on the other hand, do not believe in religion and fear the king merely because of his power lest he kill them.

They fear and honor him in his presence only, but at home they despise him. But for the pious people, the opposite is true. [p. 222]

Sofer, ibid., p. 44, claims that the persecutions and pogroms in various lands were caused by the reformers, who committed the sins of leaving God, and ingratiating themselves with the nations rather than keeping separate from them. [p. 222]

Perhaps the most derogatory criticism of the reformers is found in a letter by Rabbi Samuel of Amsterdam and Amersfoort. The letter reads like a sermon of tirades, utilizing quotations from the Bible and later literature against the reformers. For example, the writer of the letter calls the reformers "little foxes who destroy the vineyard of the Lord of Hosts" (Song of Songs 2:15, *Eleh Divre Haberit*, p. 64). Rabbi Samuel says that "contagious leprosy" (Lev. 13:51, 52) flourishes among the reformers (*Eleh Divre Haberit*, p. 64). [pp. 224–25]

Rabbi Jacob of Lissa (ibid., pp. 76–82) asserts that Rabbi Eliezer Libermann wrote his *Or Nogah* strictly as a business enterprise—his sole intention was to fill his purse with money. Just as most of the nights he spent in Posen were devoted to gambling, printing his book was done only for money. Occasionally he utters sensible words, but they are probably plagiarism (lit. "stolen"). [p. 226]

Rabbi Hirsch of the Katzenellenbogen family, rabbi of Wintzenheim, begins his letter with a tirade against the reformers (ibid., pp. 83–87). He says, "We have been plundered, shamed; robbers came upon us, kidnappers, who took the children from the arms of Jacob" (ibid., p. 83). "There are many false prophets in our midst . . . who seduce you with their smooth talk. . . . They spread the spirit of defilement over the entire earth, over all the great congregations, near or far. They want to be called Jews, but are worse than the Karaites and the sects of the Sadducees and Boethusians" (ibid., p. 84). "These arrogant simpletons . . . turn light into darkness and darkness into light, because they walk in darkness and have no light" (ibid., p. 85). [pp. 228–29]

Rabbi Moses Sofer (Responsa *Chatam Sofer*, vol. 6, resp. 84) calls the reformers "little foxes, scum of diaspora (lit. 'darkies') who rose to cause destruction." [pp. 244–47] Rabbi Sofer concludes another responsum (ibid., resp. 86) with a tirade against Rabbi Eliezer Libermann, the author of *Or Nogah*. [p. 250]

Rabbi Akiva Joseph Schlesinger, in his *Lev Ha'ivri* (pp. 21 ff), says with respect to the Jews who speak a foreign language (i.e., not Hebrew or Yiddish), or who make any change in the "ways of Israel": "while the judgment of the wicked is twelve months [in Gehinom; see *B. Rosh Hashanah* 17a] the punishment of the heretics, sectarians, and informers . . . and those who deviate from the ways of Israel [i.e., Reformers] . . . is that they descend to Gehinom and will be punished there for many generations . . ." [p. 256] "The reform is real heresy and apostasy which may come to realization by establishing a seminary, God forbid." [ibid.] "Amalek did not cause as much harm to the Jews as did the evil family of the reformers. They lead the children away to sectarianism and heresy. May God . . . avenge the blood of His servants . . . and the sin committed against the Jewish children whom they eternally killed in school. . . . Land, o land, do not cover their blood!" [ibid.] "They are *erev rav*, the 'mixed multitude' (see Exod. 12:38) "who caused endless trouble to the Jews after the Exodus from Egypt during the forty years of wandering through the wilderness." [p. 257]

Rabbi Chayim Bezalel Panet, replying to Rabbi Hillel of Kolomea (Responsa *Derech Yivchar*, resp. 1), says about the reformers: They are ignoramuses in Talmud and Codes. They are unworthy rabbis. One of the Reform educators ate for many years in a house of gentiles. "In their words there is hidden heresy that many people do not notice." [pp. 263–64]

In a responsum addressed to Rabbi Jeremiah of Ujhely (ibid., resp. 80), Rabbi Panet complains about the liberal rabbis who are ignoramuses and smooth talkers, and do not know Talmud and Codes. "The great men of our time would hit them over the head and ridicule them. . . . Even in other fields of wisdom they are nothing in contrast to the Orthodox sages." [p. 264]

Rabbi Moses Schick, in a responsum addressed to Rabbi Chayim Sofer (Responsa, *Orach Chayim*, resp. 304), writes: "It is a *mitzvah* to keep four cubits away from the heretics (reformers)." [p. 273]

In a responsum addressed to Rabbi A. S. Binyamin (ibid., resp. 305), Rabbi Schick states that "the heretics, evil rabbis, i.e., reformers, banded together, attacked the Torah . . . wrote heretical books. They are no Jews, but are worse than non-Jews. . . . They are not trustworthy. What they slaughter is nonkosher. They are unfit to be witnesses and judges. Their divorces and marriages are invalid. They are like gentiles in every respect, and therefore we are not permitted to marry their sons and daughters. Moreover, they may be bastards, still another reason not to marry them. Since they are like gentiles, we are not allowed to worship in their houses of worship. They are wicked people . . . (cf. above p. 90) This should be publicized. It will do much benefit." [pp. 273–74]

Rabbi Schick, in a responsum addressed to Rabbi Ts. Hirsch Lehren and Rabbi Eliahu Abraham Prinz (ibid., *Yoreh De'ah*, resp. 331), praises these rabbis for attacking the Karaites (that is, reformers) in print and adds: "I am also ready to smash and break the molars of the sinners to the limit of my strength. . . . The Satan joined the liberal rabbis who convened in Brunswick. They blasphemed God. Made arrogant statements. They were not rabbis but Karaites. At night they went to bed with nothing, and in the morning they opened their eyes and were rabbis." [p. 279]

Rabbi Judah Aszod, in a responsum addressed to the rabbis of Germany and to Rabbi Hirsch Lehren of Amsterdam (Responsa, Orach Chayim, resp. 6), attacks the liberal rabbis who convened in Brunswick. He compares these rabbis to Zimri, who committed a lewd act with a Midianite woman (Num. 25:6 ff.). They are treacherous people, a mob. They are arrogant. Their decisions are like broken shards. [pp. 282–83]

Rabbi Aszod (ibid. resp. 36) attacks the liberals because they are sinners who trample on the *Shulchan Aruch*. He recommends that every pious man must keep away from them. If there are knowledgeable men among them, then there is even more lawlessness there. They are a sect of innovators. God will punish them. [pp. 284–85]

Rabbi Hillel Lichtenstein, in a responsum addressed to an unnamed rabbi (Responsa *Bet Hillel*, resp. 39) says: "The devil of every nation cleaves to the Jews who speak the pure language of their respective countries. . . . They interpret the Torah in a blasphemous manner, twist its words any way they want."

It is prohibited to keep peace with the modern preachers. They are worse than their sinful ancestors, because the latter were known as sinners. However, the modern preachers dress themselves in the garb of the rabbinate in order to be considered pious men. Moreover, they also want to be considered Chasidim, mystics who bless Israel and give them amulets. [p. 291]

Even Rabbi David Hoffmann, a modern Orthodox leader, occasionally uses derogatory terms when he attacks the reformers. Thus, for example, he calls reforms "great calamities" (*Melamed*

Leho'il, vol. 1, resp. 16). [p. 292] In the same responsum he refers to the liberal rabbis as "destroyers" who committed all sorts of abominations. [p. 296]

Rabbi Zalman Sorotzkin (*Noam*, vol. 5, pp. 52 ff.) states that the progressive Jews resemble gentiles; their temples resemble the temples of other nations. In the United States every Reform "rabbi" builds a prohibited altar for himself. He permits what is explicitly prohibited in the Torah. [p. 323]

Internal Derogation

IN THE course of the struggle over reform, the insulting, derogatory tone found in many controversies was not limited to disputes between the Orthodox and Reform. We find similarly rude outbursts in many controversies within the main branches of Judaism. We will not discuss here the controversies within Reform Judaism, since they are readily available in English or German publications. We shall present here merely a few instances of derogatory utterances made by Orthodox leaders and rabbis against their Orthodox colleagues, found in Hebrew sources and, therefore, little known. Several examples follow.

Rabbi Akiva Joseph Schlesinger relates in *Lev Ha'ivri* (p. 18a) that some men of the Orthodox congregation of Rabbi David Deutsch in Neustadt hired a teacher to teach their children the "foreign" language of the land. Though the teacher was obviously Orthodox, Rabbi Deutsch opposed him because of his modern education. He believed that the knowledge of the "foreign" (i.e., non-Yiddish) language might lead to further modernization and heresy. Therefore, during a Sabbath afternoon service, he publicly insulted the teacher. He said, "This arrogant fellow came to uproot the Torah. May he be uprooted! . . . the child who is under his tutelage will become a sinner." The next day, the teacher was dismissed. [pp. 252–53]

One of the most significant disparagements of a noted Orthodox rabbi and leader was uttered by Rabbi Hillel Lichtenstein (Responsa *Bet Hillel*, resp. 13), addressed to Rabbi Meir Auerbach of Jerusalem.

In this responsum, Rabbi Azriel (Israel) Hildesheimer, for whom the Berlin Orthodox rabbinical seminary was named, is called a "man of deceit, a liar, solely interested in monetary gain, wearing a garb of righteousness like a pig that stretches forth its hoofs so that many are caught in his net." Rabbi Lichtenstein claims that he publicizes this as a warning against this "abominable troubler," who intends to destroy the Jews, uproot the Torah and the fear of God, and increase heresy in Israel. "The city [in Hungary, where he formerly officiated as rabbi] and its surroundings, which before were like the Garden of Eden, have been left after him as a wilderness, destroyed by foreigners."

Rabbi Lichtenstein then adds a quotation from *Machaneh Chayim* by Chayim Sofer: "The wicked Hildesheimer is the horse and the wagon of the evil inclination, *yetser hara*, . . . the demon of Esau rides on him. All the sinners who rose over a period of many years did not accomplish as much as he did in destroying religion and faith. All of Hungary would have turned to heresy by him . . ."

Rabbi Lichtenstein continues by claiming that establishing Jewish secular (i.e., day) schools instead of *cheder* schools and *yeshivot* is "like willfully taking Jewish children to the priest . . . so that he sway them to deny God . . . and sprinkle upon them that water. . . . He who does this is a worse enemy than Pharaoh and the wicked Haman. . . . And such wicked people are worse than the enticing priests, called missionaries, since the latter rarely succeed. . . . Everyone who has brains in his skull clearly sees the heresy . . . of that abominable wicked man [i.e., Hildesheimer]. . . . He destroys them so that they would not have eternal life." [pp. 289–90]

The most recent and significant controversy within the Orthodox community that included insults and deprecatory remarks is the famous case of the Langer brother and sister (see above p. 130–36). These derogations are too lengthy to quote here, but references to them may be found in the Israeli newspapers (see, e.g., *Ma'ariv*, Nov. 22, 1972, p. 3).

IX

Summary and
Conclusions

MANY BOOKS and articles have been written in recent years about the struggle over reform during the last century and a half. Most of them were written in German and English, and utilized primarily German and English sources. Hebrew sources were used only to a limited extent. Our task in this book has been, on the one hand, to make the most important Hebrew sources reflecting the struggle over reform available to interested historians, and, on the other hand, to demonstrate their significance for a better understanding of this struggle.

Most of the Hebrew sources reflecting the struggle over reform, or reforms, belong to the responsa literature. This means that they were responses to queries asked either by rabbis or by laymen about real, practical problems pertaining to Jewish religious life and thinking. Most of the responsa were written by Orthodox rabbis and scholars, expressing their objections to reforms. Since both the writers and the recipients of the responsa belonged to the same branch of Judaism, no formal dialogue between Reform and Orthodox Judaism is represented.

If we have a struggle, we expect one side to win, although a stalemate is also a possibility. Consequently, we desire an answer to the question, Who won the struggle? The answer has been clear from the beginning. In this struggle there was no winner.

It resembles, in some respects, the religious disputations between the Jews and Christians of the Middle Ages, where there were no winners or losers. The feuding parties knew from the outset that, no matter how strong the arguments of the opposition, neither would give in. This being the case, we have to wonder what purpose, if any, the fierce struggle served.

Reform and Orthodox, in continuing their controversy, had somewhat different goals. The Reform introduced and fought for reforms in order to adjust Judaism to the prevailing material and spiritual values of the Christian culture. The Orthodox fought the reforms, on the one hand, because they feared assimilation, which they thought would lead to the destruction of Judaism, and, on the other hand, because after centuries of ghetto life they were unaccustomed to making major adjustments. Theological and halachic reasons, though prominent in their arguments, were, in reality, of secondary importance, serving mainly as tools to achieve their primary goals.

All the responsa and other Hebrew literature discussing reforms, pro or con, concentrate on laws, customs, and other aspects of observances. Theology is incidental and is usually referred to in support of a custom or law. The Orthodox rabbis of the first half of the nineteenth century use theology considerably more than their liberal colleagues. The former employ theology as a polemical weapon, while the latter more often use theology defensively.

Neither the Reform nor the Orthodox position remained unchanged from the beginning of the nineteenth century until the present. Methodologically, the Reform leaders, mostly rabbis, at first endeavored to justify the reforms by citing traditional sources, such as the Talmud, Maimonides, the *Shulchan Aruch*, and so forth. Later they abandoned this method when they openly and officially rejected the authority of the traditional sources, including the traditional interpretation of the Bible. This break with the old method greatly facilitated the introduction of reforms, since a thorough knowledge of old rabbinic sources was no longer necessary to legitimize the changes. At the same time, it clearly separated the main branches of Judaism.

This distinction had several advantages. The main advantage was reduction of friction; standing on different platforms, the Orthodox and Reform had less room for further polemical arguments. For Reform Judaism and its leaders, the intensive study of the Talmud and related literatures decreased greatly in importance. Instead, they could devote more time to secular learning, allowing a quicker and fuller integration into the culture of the host country. Also, the Reform leaders no longer had to compete with their Orthodox adversaries in the field of traditional learning; their devotion to secular learning early placed them at a disadvantage in this area. For the Orthodox, the main advantage of the separation was that it enabled them to devote more time and energy to internal problems that were daily becoming more urgent after they left the protective walls of the ghetto. They were able to solve these problems, one by one, either by using talmudic methodology or by adopting or tolerating certain customs and practices, some of which had been introduced by the reformers. These internal reforms of the Orthodox, though not as spectacular as those of the Reform, are substantial.

Of particular significance is the fact that no matter what the rabbis decided, the common people, both Orthodox and Reform, continued to maintain social contact with their "denominational adversaries." Orthodox and Reform Jews, in spite of warnings and spiritual threats by their rabbis, continued to socialize and to intermarry. The authority and power of the medieval rabbis diminished considerably once the European governments introduced a law prohibiting excommunication, which had been the most potent weapon of the rabbis in the Middle Ages and also in antiquity.

The struggle over reform on a large scale began with the modernization of the worship service. The changes most vehemently opposed by the Orthodox concerned the text of the prayers; the introduction of German prayers; the elimination of the chanting of the biblical portions; the introduction of musical instruments; the loosening of the requirement of a quorum (*minyan*) at services; and changing the traditional physical facilities of the public service, such as architecture, *bimah*, wardrobe, and so forth.

The oldest and most serious problem for the Orthodox of the last century was that of the organ. David Hoffmann's contention that the reformers started their law-breaking activities with the adoption of the organ (see above p. 296) was not the only reason that the strongest Orthodox attacks ever launched were against this reform. More weighty was the fact that simultaneously with the organ, other reforms were also introduced, in Hamburg and elsewhere. These other reforms, pertaining mainly to prayers, were even more anti-traditional and, therefore, more objectionable than the organ itself. Nevertheless, the organ drew more fire. It was conspicuous, expensive, and liable to create a division between wealthy and poor congregations. For a while it even seemed that large Orthodox synagogues might adopt the organ. A big Orthodox synagogue in Prague actually had an organ, although it was used only until the beginning of the Sabbath and not on the Sabbath itself. The Orthodox justified the presence of this organ in an Orthodox synagogue by saying that it had already been installed there at the time of the Second Temple in Jerusalem—that is, long before the Christians adopted it in their churches. Consequently its presence was not a reform. Nonetheless, due to the vehement Orthodox opposition to the organ, the organ of the Prague synagogue was not repaired once it broke down.

The issue of the organ is unique in another respect also. We find in other instances that the Orthodox eventually adopt reforms against which they initially fought; for example, the sermon in the vernacular, secular education, day schools, education of girls, and so forth. However, in the case of the organ, the trend is reversed, as a result of an exceptionally strong counter-reform activity.

Not all Orthodox leaders believe that the organ was the source of all the calamity caused by the reformers. Some believe that the moving of the *bimah* from the middle of the synagogue to the side was more radical. One Orthodox leader even asserts that if the rabbis had prevented the moving of the *bimah* to the side of the synagogue—at the beginning an attainable goal—there would have been no Reform movement. The *bimah*, in contrast to the organ, is not a serious issue today. Many traditional, even Orthodox, synagogues do not have the *bimah* in the middle of the building. Nonetheless, the controversy about the *bimah* has not yet ended.

The removal of the partition between men and women in the synagogue is harshly criticized by the Orthodox. In criticizing this reform the Orthodox have to answer the question why many Eastern European synagogues do not have the partition so important to the Orthodox of Central and Western Europe. The answer is that the Eastern European Jews do not need the partition since they constantly look into the prayerbook while the Jews in other lands do not do this, and therefore need a protective partition (curtain).

Less conspicuous than the introduction of instrumental music into the Liberal-Reform worship service, but more substantial, were the reforms pertaining to the service: abandoning the second day of the holidays, admitting women as members of the choir, introduction of the *Bat Mitzvah* ceremony, and so forth. The Orthodox strongly opposed every one of these reforms, although they later adopted some of them, without openly admitting it.

Concerning the reformers' changing the text of prayers, the Orthodox opposition has been uncompromising from the earliest times to date. The leading Orthodox rabbis of the past century assert that any change of a prayer text is heresy.

More complicated, due to a mishnaic ruling, is the defense of the requirement that prayers must be said in Hebrew only. Mishnah *Sotah* 7:1 permits the saying of certain prayers, among them the *Shema*, the *Amidah*, and the grace after meals in any language. The words "in any language" are interpreted by Orthodox authorities as having limited validity. According to some rabbis, the phrase refers to women who do not know Hebrew; others maintain that the words refer to prayers said at home; one rabbi believes that the Mishnah refers merely to Greek, Aramaic, Persian, and Arabic. According to another rabbi, the Mishnah refers to Yiddish.

Reform rabbis take Mishnah *Sotah* 7:1 literally, but do not reject Hebrew as a permissible language for prayer. They emphasize the importance of understanding the prayer, while the Orthodox claim that a person praying in Hebrew does not have to understand it. The rationale of the Orthodox is as follows. Full understanding of certain prayers, for example, the *piyutim*, is often too difficult even for learned men. The important thing is that the person praying be aware of what he is doing.

Since the reformers stress the importance of understanding the prayers, but do not reject Hebrew on principle, they suggest retaining the Hebrew for some prayers which should be studied in religious schools. Interesting is a Reform view that the language of the prayer service should not, in all lands, be that of the vernacular. Hebrew should be retained in Eastern Europe, because the Jews there understand Hebrew, while in other parts of the world, where Hebrew is not understood, the vernacular should be the main language of the prayers.

The reason given by the Orthodox leaders for the paramount importance of the Hebrew is that God used the Hebrew language while creating the world. He talked to Moses and the other prophets in Hebrew. It is interesting to note that the Reform leader Aaron Chorin concurs with the Orthodox in maintaining that God spoke Hebrew.

The language of the sermon constitutes another problem. Even though some Orthodox rabbis were able to preach in Hebrew, the majority of the people did not know enough Hebrew to understand a sermon preached in Hebrew. For this reason, the opinion was given by an Orthodox rabbinical authority that Yiddish, being a corrupt language, and not spoken by any foreign nation, is not considered to be a foreign language, and therefore is permissible for preaching and teaching. Other Orthodox rabbis declare that Yiddish has the holiness of Hebrew and should be used for preaching and teaching, but not for the prayers. In their opinion, the language of the prayers must remain Hebrew.

The pronunciation of Hebrew became a controversial issue with the ascent of the Reform movement. Many early Reform rabbis adopted the Sefardic pronunciation. One reason was that scholars of Semitic languages have proved that the Sefardic was the original pronunciation of the Hebrew. Furthermore, Sefardic has a better sound. In addition, most prayers ascend to heaven in the Sefardic pronunciation, because the Sefardim constitute the vast majority of the Jewish population on earth.

The Orthodox of the non-Sefardic community, that is, most of Europe (and later America), opposed the change on halachic grounds, just as they opposed changing the text of the prayers. For a long time they opposed the use of the Sefardic pronunciation even by the Ashkenazic community in Palestine. The recent decision of the Israeli Chief Rabbinate permitting the Sefardic pronunciation for Ashkenazic services in Israel has been disregarded or opposed by many Orthodox rabbis and congregations. It is noteworthy that, in spite of the effort of Reform rabbis in behalf of the Sefardic pronunciation, the Reform worshippers have refused to heed the advice of their rabbis. They have been using the Ashkenazic pronunciation everywhere, except in Israel. The resistance of the worshippers to the change in pronunciation is one, if not the main, reason for the Reform rabbis' return to the Ashkenazic pronunciation. Today, Reform Judaism does not have a language problem with which to contend.

For the Orthodox, the language issue became crucial after the emancipation, when Orthodox Jews, like their Reform brethren, became an integral part of their host nation. The younger generation of the Orthodox participated in the cultural life of the host-nation, and attended secular (Christian) schools and universities. As a result, they neglected and often forgot the Yiddish tongue of their parents. Subsequently, an internal struggle among the Orthodox ensued, in which the progressive wing prevailed. The radical Orthodox leaders tried in vain to prevent the youth from abandoning their ghettolike patterns of life. Their vehement opposition to secular culture; to establishing a modern, though Orthodox, seminary; to Jewish day schools; and to teaching and preaching sermons in the vernacular was in vain. The following of these radical Orthodox leaders dwindled to a small splinter group. The Orthodox rabbis in many congregations in the last century were already preaching in the vernacular and were just as eloquent as their Liberal-Reform colleagues. The word "vernacular" had, at first, a somewhat narrow meaning. It meant only German. This was true even in America, and, strange as it may seem, even among the Reform Jews. According to Einhorn, the German language had a holy character because the books of Mendelssohn, of the *Wissenschaft des Judentums*, and of the Reform were written in German (see H. M. Graupe, *Die Entstehung des modernen Judentums*, p. 224).

Another significant reform concerned the requirement for the *minyan*, quorum of ten men, for public worship service (and for some other occasions). The Reform abandoned this requirement, although at first, they did so with some hesitancy. Aaron Chorin reasons that the *minyan* should be retained only at services conducted with reverence and decorum; otherwise God would get angry. Therefore, only Reform services require a *minyan*, and the Orthodox services do not, since the latter are disorderly.

Neither the Reform nor the Orthodox accepted Chorin's opinion. The Reform abandoned the requirement of the *minyan* completely. Some Conservative congregations modified the requirement by permitting women to be counted as members of the *minyan*. The Orthodox permit a small boy (under thirteen) to be counted as the tenth man of the *minyan* if he holds a Torah scroll (or a Hebrew Bible) in his hand during the entire services.

For the Orthodox the question of who should or should not be counted as a member of the *minyan* is a serious problem and a controversial issue. Should a transgressor of the law be admitted to a *minyan?* May a Reform Jew be admitted? A Jew married to a gentile woman? We have seen the Orthodox views on both sides. Today most Orthodox congregations are lenient in this matter; otherwise they would lose many of their members; and would often lack the tenth man needed for the *minyan.*

Decorum at prayer services and weddings was another area of friction between Liberal-Reform and Orthodox Jewry, particularly in Germany. Liberal congregations in Germany often included rules of decorum in their statutes. Decorum has been the rule at services in the churches, and the reformers held that Jewish services ought to be as dignified as Christian services.

The rules of decorum were often quite strict. Occasionally, they prescribed penalties for the transgressor. The penalty could be a fine, or expulsion if the transgressor was too poor to pay the fine; the police could be called to expel a troublemaker, and so on. Among the prohibited ceremonies or practices, and listed as such in Reform congregational statutes, were the breaking of the glass at weddings, and the participation of women in funeral processions.

The Orthodox did not reject decorum on principle, but would not stress it too much. They demanded that the synagogue be honored properly by stopping idle conversation, which could lead to the serious sin of yelling and quarelling. Some Orthodox leaders urged their congregants to emulate the Sefardic way of decorum by refraining from spitting and talking during the services.

The struggle between Reform and Orthodox was not as consequential in the area of the life-cycle as it was in the area of the prayer service. This was in part due to the fact that marriage, the most important single event in a person's life-cycle, is, in contrast to the prayer service, an infrequent happening. Even a Jew who attends services only on Yom Kippur is involved in a religious expression of his faith through a prayer service much more often than he is involved in a marriage ceremony, which is generally experienced only once in a lifetime. Another reason for the lesser importance of marriage in the struggle over reform was the progressive secularization of gentiles and Jews alike. The power of religion over man, so prominent in former times, diminished progressively after the Middle Ages, as did the authority of the religious leaders. In addition, human emotion often played a decisive role, particularly after young men and women began to rebel against marriages arranged by their parents and to make their own choices instead. In making these choices, love was generally more important than affiliation with the Reform or Orthodox community.

Early Orthodox leaders, among them Moses Schick, declared Reform marriages and divorces to be invalid. An Orthodox Jew, according to some authorities, was not permitted to marry the child of a marriage performed by a Reform rabbi, even if the individual became Orthodox, because that individual might be a bastard. Later Orthodox authorities, like Rabbi Yechiel Weinberg, are often more lenient. A priori, they require an Orthodox ceremony. Ex post facto, they recognize the Reform ceremony. The rationale is that the validity of a marriage does not depend on the officiating rabbi but on the presence of valid (i.e., Orthodox) witnesses. We may always assume, they say, that some Orthodox persons were among the guests and can be considered as witnesses to the ceremony, thus validating the marriage. This is also the position of many Israeli Orthodox rabbis with respect to Reform marriages contracted abroad.

The Orthodox and Reform also disagree in regard to marriages and divorces executed by secular officials. The Orthodox do not recognize divorces by civil courts while the Reform do. In regard to marriages performed by the civil authorities, the Orthodox are divided among themselves. While all object to such a marriage a priori, the opinions differ with regard to the ex post facto cases. This matter is of importance for the Orthodox primarily because it raises the question of whether a Jewish divorce would be needed if there were no Jewish marriage. The rabbis who require a Jewish divorce (*get*) rely, at least in part, on the talmudic dictum that a man would not engage in a lewd intercourse (*B. Yevamot* 107a). Moreover, once the couple goes to the civil authorities, the intention of marriage is obvious, and this suffices, according to some rabbis, to recognize the civil marriage ex post facto and thus to make a Jewish divorce mandatory.

More questionable and controversial is the validity of a common-law marriage. According to some Orthodox rabbis, such a marriage, though reprehensible, does have validity ex post facto, if the couple live in a Jewish neighborhood and Jews see them entering their home, that is, living as husband and wife, and therefore they require a Jewish divorce to terminate such a marriage.

Reform conversions, if not done in accordance with traditional law, are, as a rule, not recognized by the Orthodox, not even ex post facto. Therefore, a gentile converted by a Reform rabbi or *bet din* has to submit to an Orthodox conversion to be accepted by the Orthodox. The full circumcision does not have to be repeated since this is impossible. However, a little drop of the "blood of the covenant" still has to be drawn to halachically validate the circumcision.

Ben-Gurion raised the issue: Who is a Jew? The most controversial issue in defining a Jew, in the opinion of the rabbis who answered this question, is the validity of a conversion not performed in accordance with traditional law, or the lack of a formal conversion. The Orthodox, for example, do not recognize as a Jew the child of a gentile mother by a Jewish father, even if the child was raised as a Jew, was given Jewish religious education, and had a Jewish confirmation in lieu of a formal conversion. For most Reform rabbis, these acts suffice and are accepted as a valid form of conversion.

The process of women's liberation in the realm of Jewish life and thought has been slow, even in Reform Judaism. For example, the noted Reform rabbi Eliezer Libermann places women and ignorant people in one category, certainly not in conformity with the modern belief in the equality of men and women. When Reform leaders discuss the question of the *minyan*, the admissibility of women is seldom mentioned in their Hebrew responsa. Not even Holdheim, who wants to retain the *minyan* for Reform services, suggests that women be members of the *minyan*.

The Orthodox could not change talmudic-rabbinic law excluding women not only from the *minyan* but also from the observance of other commandments, such as phylacteries, fringes (*tsitsit*, *talit*), obligatory attendance at prayer services (positive commandments to be observed at a specific time), and so forth. However, in the struggle over reform, they had to make exceptions. Such an exception is the training of women to be teachers of Judaism in the religious schools, even though, according to an accepted talmudic opinion, women should not be taught Torah. The rationale is that in the schools of our day the children are taught religion by women teachers. Consequently, if the Orthodox do not train Orthodox women as teachers, Reform teachers will teach and misinform the children. Thus the Orthodox justify the change.

Laws and customs pertaining to women were not included in the prohibition against teaching them Torah. These they had to study, in order to know how to observe them. The prohibition referred to laws to be observed by men. However, in our time, when women teachers also teach the boys, the latter prohibition was interpreted away (i.e., removed) by Orthodox authorities, lest the Reform teachers teach the boys the wrong (i.e., Reform) views and observances.

The pressure of the *Zeitgeist*, coupled with the growing awareness of equity, prompted traditional Judaism to follow in the footsteps of Reform Judaism with regard to some new observances. Among these were the adoption of the Bat Mitzvah ceremony, though with modifications, and the introduction of the Confirmation ceremony for both boys and girls (the latter by Conservative Judaism).

One of the most serious problems of Orthodox Judaism today concerns the *mamzer*, the "bastard." The humiliating predicament of the *mamzer*, himself or herself innocent of any wrongdoing, cannot be reconciled with today's sense of equity. The problem is not serious for Reform Judaism, which, in principle, renounced the binding force of biblical and rabbinical law. Nonetheless, it is still a problem for the Reform Jew who wishes to marry an Orthodox person.

In the diaspora, the strict position of the Orthodox leaders of the last century gave way (with some exceptions) to a more lenient, understanding practice. The suspicion of bastardy is not raised when an Orthodox Jew marries a Reform partner. The halachic backing for this humane practice is the talmudic dictum: "All the families are presumed to be *kasher*," that is, of unblemished descent (*B. Kiddushin* 76b). The scope of this dictum was later limited (see ibid.).

Particularly crucial is the problem of bastardy in Israel, where Reform Jews have to comply with the traditional marriage laws. While the religious leadership, beginning with the early talmudic period, has been well aware of the undeserved suffering of the *mamzer*, and has tried to terminate the humiliating status, at least for the children of the *mamzer*, the Ministry of Religion of Israel keeps in its files lists of persons not eligible for (a "kosher") marriage due to a blemish in their descent, bastardy being the worst of the blemishes (see Rabbi Mosheh Zemer, "Mamzerut," in *Shalhevet*, 7–8, September 1971). Such records are not being kept in other countries.

We discussed the vehement internal struggle among the Orthodox concerning the *mamzer* problem in the specific case of the Langer brother and sister. The favorable decision of Chief Rabbi Goren was greeted with a sigh of relief by the majority of traditional Jews, but was attacked as illegal and opportunist by a number of rigid Orthodox authorities.

Does Rabbi Goren's decision constitute a turning point in the attitude of Israeli Orthodox religious authorities in solving the perennial problem of bastardy, and, indirectly, is it a step toward permitting and recognizing marriages performed by Liberal-Reform rabbis? The answer to this question is almost certainly no. In his responsum, Rabbi Goren arrives at his decision solely on the basis of halachic considerations. Only his opponents accuse him of basing his lenient halachic decision on humane considerations and, therefore, rendering it illegal. Rabbi Goren does not admit that humane considerations affected his legalistic reasoning and decision.

In this respect, Rabbi Goren follows in the footsteps of noted halachic authorities of the past. They rendered liberal decisions which would have encountered strong Orthodox opposition if given by Reform rabbis. This opposition was avoided because they offered elaborate halachic justifications of the respective decisions without discussing the humanitarian aspects. Therefore, such decisions could not be used as precedents to consider the humanitarian element in halachic issues as a matter of principle and to modify the law accordingly.

Let us give but one other example.

Rabbi Moses Sofer was asked to decide the following case (*Responsa Chatam Sofer, Even Ha'ezer*, resp. 78): While Yudl Kohen was out of town, his home was burglarized. When the burglars left, Yudl Kohen's wife alarmed the neighbors, informing them about the crime just committed. She said that she was grieved more by the fact that the burglars had raped her than by the loss of property. After she repeated her complaint to the courts, learned Jewish men informed her that she had to be divorced by her husband, a *kohen* (priest), since traditional Jewish law requires that a *kohen* divorce his wife if she has extramarital intercourse, even if raped.

Soon afterwards she changed her story, saying that she had not been raped and had made this claim only to inflame the authorities so that they would exert more effort to catch the burglars and would punish them more severely. All the burglars did was to lie on her quietly without raping her, lest she alarm the neighbors.

Upon his return, Mr. Kohen at first accepted the original statement of his wife (i.e., that she was raped), but the next day he changed his mind and accepted her second statement.

Rabbi Sofer, after a very long halachic discourse, decided that her second statement was the true one—she had not been raped, and, therefore, was not to be divorced by her husband. Among his reasons was a reference to the necessity for considering the custom of burglars: they try to avoid noise, and therefore they do not rape women but only lie on them quietly, to keep them from raising their voices.

What happened there is quite obvious. After the woman heard of the law prescribing a mandatory divorce in her case, she changed her story. Her husband went along with her and accepted the second version. Rabbi Sofer decided that the second version was the true one. Furthermore, the burglars, who were caught in the meantime, concurred with the woman and Rabbi Sofer, saying that they had only lain quietly on Mrs. Kohen to keep her from screaming.

Rabbi Sofer's decision obviously circumvented the application of a strict law. In order to strengthen the decision, even the words of the criminals (who may have been instructed) were considered.

It seems quite evident that Rabbi Sofer's decision was

prompted by humanitarian considerations, but he does not admit it. Had he done so, he would have been castigated by his colleagues, for whom only exclusively halachic considerations were important. Due to his superior stature, Rabbi Sofer's decision was questioned by no Orthodox rabbi, though no rabbi could have overlooked the forced reasoning that led to the humane decision. On the other hand, this responsum, because of its intricate halachic structure, could not serve as a precedent in liberalizing the law, which makes divorce mandatory if the wife of a *kohen* is raped.

Reform Judaism, since it has rejected the special status of the *kohen*, is not affected by this strict law. Even from the Orthodox viewpoint, it does not affect the validity of marriages if disregarded. If a *kohen* did not divorce his raped wife, she continued to be his legal wife. According to traditional law, the husband in such a case should be coerced (employing a legal fiction since a forced divorce is invalid in most instances), even by flogging, to divorce his wife, but this is not done, even in Israel, where matters of divorce lie in the hands of the Orthodox rabbis. The *Zeitgeist does* not permit this today, not even in Israel.

An area of friction and fundamental disagreement between Orthodox and Reform is that of the significance of customs. According to Orthodox tradition, customs are often as binding as laws and must not be abolished even if they contradict a law of the Torah. A custom may be changed, even in the view of some Orthodox authorities, if circumstances change and the reason for the custom becomes invalid. However, these authorities are not inclined to admit that the reasons for a custom have become invalid. More often than invalidated, customs may be silently disregarded when considered outdated. Thus, for example, the traditional custom of having weddings only at the time of the increasing moon has not been followed for a long time. The Orthodox leaders in most places no longer insist that their followers distinguish themselves from the gentiles by their clothing, a requirement of the *Shulchan Aruch*, based on talmudic sources.

On the other hand, Reform Jews adhere, sometimes even in a particularistic way, to certain customs, ceremonies, and practices which they consider meaningful. Thus, for example, there is a *minhag America* which is, to a considerable extent, different from European and Israeli liberal or Reform *minhagim*. This is in perfect accordance with traditional thought that local customs should be retained. Traditionally, law unifies world Jewry while custom diversifies it.

The most fundamental difference between Reform and Orthodox Judaism lies in the area of theology. Early Orthodox leaders declared the Liberal-Reform movement to be a heretical one. They equated it with the Sadducean and Karaite movements, accordingly proclaiming time and again that Reform Judaism was a separate sect. A few of the Orthodox authorities were so serious about this view that they prohibited "intermarriage" with Reform Jews. Moreover, they proclaimed that it was better to attend Christian church services than to worship in a Reform temple. "Heretics are worse than non-Jews," was the reason given.

In spite of the fundamental theological cleavage between Orthodox and Reform, there was no sectarian break between the two main branches of Judaism. The break was avoided because observances, *mitzvot*, have always constituted the essence of Jewish religious life. Theology and philosophy are, from the viewpoint of the average Jew, peripheral. The heated arguments of rabbis and scholars in the fields of theology and philosophy have been of little interest to the Jewish people as a whole. They considered such arguments to be the scholarly enterprise of the rabbis and scholars and of little consequence for Jewish life.

The theologians and philosophers of both Reform and Orthodox changed their directions and turned inward after they saw the futility of their belligerent arguments and scholarly quarrels with the "enemy." Thus, for example, the Orthodox of our century no longer say: "Thank God that He saved us from philosophy!" as they did occasionally in the past. Both branches recognize the value of philosophy and theology, but neither is exploiting them in attempts to convince or condemn the "adversary," the other branches of Judaism. All are now in the process of clarifying theological concepts for a better understanding of their respective beliefs and practices. It is fortunate, indeed, that the Jewish laity has been little interested in theology and philosophy as far as religious life is concerned. The rabbis of our day are well aware of this and therefore seldom concentrate on theology when preaching or teaching.

It was to be expected from the outset that the struggle over Reform would be conducted by the leaders of Reform and Orthodox Judaism on a subjective level. Nonetheless, they occasionally transgressed the limits of fair discussions in two ways. The less weighty and reprehensible of these was the derogatory and insulting tone of some of the leading participants, coupled with occasional outright false accusations and calumnies. More serious were the accusations by rabbis and congregational leaders lodged against the opposite branch of Judaism before the gentile authorities. Such accusations often resulted in interference by these authorities in Jewish life, for example through the closing of synagogues and temples. Only after the struggle over Reform lost momentum was this reprehensible approach discontinued.

Once both Reform and Orthodox leaders of Judaism realized that efforts toward victory were futile, unsupported even by their own followers, the emphasis of the struggle over reforms shifted. It is now primarily an internal problem within the individual branches of Reform, Orthodox, Conservative, and, to a lesser extent, Reconstructionist Judaism.

A more significant shift in Jewish life in the present century has been toward an emphasis on the common foundations, values, and aspirations of the Jewish people, regardless of their religious affiliation. This shift began in the last century with the resurgence of Zionism, and gained great momentum in our century due to two towering events in Jewish history: the Nazi holocaust, and the establishment of the Jewish state of Israel. These events made all Jews, regardless of their religious affiliation, realize that they were one people, members of *Kelal Yisrael*. While this awareness all but terminated the feud among the various branches of Judaism, it also created some new problems. One of the problems that begged an answer because of its crucial importance for the Jewish state was the definition of a Jew. Before the establishment of Israel, this was a religious issue and was solved separately by the individual branches of Judaism in accordance with their beliefs. However, for political reasons, the State of Israel needed a definition that was in harmony with both Orthodox and Reform Halachah or religious thought, or at least one that would not offend either. Ben-Gurion's question, "Who is a Jew?" addressed to Jewish leaders of all the branches (October 27, 1958) in hopes that the answers would permit him to solve the problem of Jewish identity without offending anyone, would have been unrealistic in past centuries. It is possible now because of the diminished authority of all religion in today's secular world. For this reason, in spite of the fact that hundreds of Hebrew responsa are being written every year by Orthodox rabbis, they seldom include attacks on Reform Judaism. However, even the followers of these rabbis pay little or no attention to the warnings of their leaders, who are all but totally ignored by the Reform. We have included in this study a few such responsa to show that efforts, however faint, are still being made to continue the struggle over Reform. These efforts may best be characterized as "a voice calling in the wilderness." On the other hand, the ancient ideal of *Kelal Yisrael* experiences today a revival supplanting the divisive forces of the past two centuries.

Part Two

SOURCES

This section includes both extensive original translations by the author from the Hebrew Responsa Literature as well as paraphrases and summaries by him. For clarity, the translated passages are printed without quotation marks, and the paraphrases are enclosed in brackets. The author's explanatory notes are in parentheses.

SELECTIONS FROM נוגה הצדק
Nogah Hatsedek
[The Light of Righteousness]

Responsum *Derech Hakodesh* [The Way of the Holy]
by Rabbi Shem Tov, son of Rabbi Joseph Chayim ben Samun

I was asked by my Jewish brethren in a distant land to give my humble opinion in the following matter:

Is it permissible to play the musical instrument called *organo* (in Italian), and in the German *Orgel*, in the synagogue? Some say that this is the *ugav* mentioned in the Psalms (150:4). Some people object to its use because it is the custom of the gentiles to play it in their houses of worship. Furthermore, it is an accepted rule that "song" (music) is (since the destruction of the Temple) prohibited. What is the law to be followed in this instance?

My reply: I do not know why this question is raised. It is clear that the matter is permissible and in no need of (elaborate) discussion.

The sages only prohibited the playing of, and listening to, musical instruments when drinking wine when associated with rejoicing and levity, as we find in *B. Sotah* 48a, Mishnah (9:11): "When the Sanhedrin ceased, singing ceased at the banquets (or wedding feasts; taverns), as it is written: 'They shall not drink wine with a song' (Isa. 24:9)." According to the Talmud, ibid., Rav Huna abolished the song. This means, according to

Rashi, people must not sing at home or at banquets. This shows that the prohibition of singing applies only if it is done in levity while rejoicing with wine. However, when it is not done in levity, as in our case, where it is done for the opposite purpose, i.e., for a *mitzvah*, to make the hearts of men, women and children who come (to the synagogue) to listen, rejoice when performing a *mitzvah*, this being the root of worshipping God as it is written: "serve the Lord with gladness" (Ps. 100:2), it is clear that it is proper and fitting to have music, vocal as well as instrumental. . . . Joseph Karo said in *Orach Chayim* 560: "It has been a custom of all Jews to say words of praise or (to sing) a song of thanksgiving and the remembrance of God's loving-kindness over wine," to which Isserles adds: "Likewise, for the needs of a *mitzvah* everything is permitted, as, for example, at a wedding banquet." If they expressly permitted it for human beings whenever a *mitzvah* is involved, how much the more so is it permitted for God's honor. . . .

[Rabbi Shem Tov now reasons that the passage cited from M. *Sotah* 9:11 implies that song (for Rabbi Shem Tov: song= music) is only prohibited at banquets (or in taverns), but everywhere else it is permitted.] The *Sotah* passage cannot be taken as pars pro toto (generalized) and used to refute our case, since we are talking about a *mitzvah*. In this instance everyone agrees that it is permissible, as stated in Tosafot, ibid., . . . If this is permitted to honor man, it is certainly permitted in honor of God. Moreover, it is a *mitzvah* and an obligation to praise Him by rejoicing with song, drum, harp. . . .

We have established that the actual practice (as opposed to Halachah) is paramount in importance. It is an established practice everywhere that the cantor sings in honor of God on the Sabbath and holidays . . . in the presence of the congregation and great rabbis. . . . This being so, how much the more so should the use of musical instruments be permitted. Since you permit music to be sung (in the synagogue), and it is basically vocal, how much the more so should instrumental music be permissible.

Since it has been proven that vocal as well as all kinds of instrumental music is permissible in honor of God, we come now to our problem: Is the organ, which is specifically used in the churches, permissible to us, since, at first glance, its use by us would appear as a transgression of the injunction: "Neither shall ye walk in their statutes" (Lev. 18:3).

It is obviously clear that this is not a valid objection. Are we forbidden to do anything that gentiles do? The Torah only prohibited those deeds or statutes (observed) by gentiles which were perplexing and lacked any reason. However, the playing of this instrument, for which there is good reason, (since) vocal and instrumental music awakens the heart and makes it rejoice . . . makes it obvious that there is no (aspect) of prohibition in playing or listening to the organ. . . .

Only a perplexing matter is prohibited, as Joseph Kolon said, cited by *Bet Yosef* in *Yoreh De'ah* 178: There are two categories prohibited as gentile laws: The one, where no reason is apparent . . . i.e., when a Jew follows a practice of gentiles which has no obvious reason, it certainly appears as if he followed them *and* gave his consent.

Sefer Mitzvot Gadol, in *Laws of Gentile Practices*, confirms the above by stating in section *Mitzvot Chukot Hagoyim* (Commandments concerning the laws of the gentiles): "In tractate *Shabbat* all the tradition of the rabbis concerning (religious) laws of the gentiles and 'Ways of the Emorites' (of idol worship) are listed. I examined there in *Shabbat*, end of chap. 6, and did not find even one that did not concern divination or something perplexing that has no known reason. In fact, none of them (listed in tractate *Shabbat*) has a discernible reason. This is what *Semag* wrote: . . . 'their statutes' are the perplexities, 'the ways of the Emorites' are the divinations. Even though the Talmud says concerning both 'Ways of the Emorites,' it is explained in *Semag* that there are two ways of the Emorites: (1) divination; (2) laws of the gentiles.

The second matter prohibited because of "Law of the Gentiles" is, in my humble opinion, the one of breeching the way of modesty and humility. This gentile custom is prohibited, if the law is in accordance with the *tana* of the *baraita* in the *Sifre*: "Do not say since they wear purple (garment), I shall wear purple, etc. . . . The way of the Jews is to be modest. . . . Yet, even this is only prohibited when he does it to resemble them, and not for another reason. This is inferred from Rashi's statement: "Even if the custom of the Jews is to wear a certain kind of clothing and the gentiles wear a different one, if the Jewish garment does not indicate Judaism or modesty more than the gentile garment, it is not prohibited to wear the clothing customarily worn by Gentiles. . . ."

You were shown the opinion of a great man who explained the term *chok*, "statute" (of gentiles). Our case is not analogous because it (the use of the organ) is not concerned with something "unusual" (perplexing, illogical) or with immodesty. These two fall under the category of "Statutes of the Gentiles" and are prohibited in the Torah, according to rabbinical interpretation.

Furthermore, it is obvious that the concept of "adherence" to the prohibition "in their statutes . . ." does not apply here. This concept only applies to something new which they invented and made a law. However, the source and root of this matter, i.e., to sing and play music in His praise and glorification, is of Jewish origin, as explained in the Mishnah and by Maimonides. The Levites made music in our Sanctuary daily with all kinds of instruments. Following this example, the gentiles likewise do that which they learned from us. This being so, the prohibition

". . . in their statutes . . ." does not apply here. On the contrary, the organ is *our* statute.

I heard people saying that another prohibition may apply here. The rabbis prohibited (us) from making an exact replica of the Temple of Jerusalem. See *B. Avodah Zarah* 43. Since the Levites used musical instruments in the Sanctuary, we are not permitted to do the same thing in the synagogue. This argument does not hold either. The prohibition applies, as Rashi explains, only if the measurements are exactly the same as those of the Temple, length, width, height, etc. If, however, a small change is made, it is permitted. . . . Who can say that our instrument (organ) resembles, in every detail, the one which was in the Sanctuary?

It is apparent in Maimonides, *Bet Habechirah* 7:5, that only lyres, flutes, harps, trumpets, and cymbals were used in the Sanctuary, no other instruments. If someone would say that no musical instrument should be used, after the destruction of the Temple, because the Levites used them, (I would answer) this is nonsense. Had it been so, the rabbis should have, for this reason, prohibited all musical instruments, everywhere, every time. Why does the Mishnah in *Sotah* say that after the Sanhedrin ceased, the song ceased at the banquets? The rabbis should have prohibited it everywhere, under all circumstances.

The rule, resulting from all that is written and explained above, is that in honor of God and his Torah, singing and playing all musical instruments are permitted in the synagogue, since in regard to (the observance of) a *mitzvah*, no prohibition had been issued by the rabbis.

There is a further reason for the matter (the use of the organ). By having it (i.e., music) men and women come to the synagogue to pray and to listen to the pleasant music; and our sages said: "A man should always busy himself with Torah and commandments, even though he does not do it for the sake of *mitzvah,* for out of doing it first not for the sake of *mitzvah,* he will (come to) do it later for the sake of the *mitzvah!"* (*Pesachim* 50b).

My humble opinion is that it is permissible and proper to praise God with the organ. This view has the approval of the outstanding rabbi of this place . . . and of his court.

This is my opinion, written and signed when the weekly portion, including Genesis 35:11 (i.e., *vayishlach*), is read in the year 5577 (1816).

Leghorn

Shem Tov, son of Rabbi Joseph Chayim ben Samun

Attestation of the rabbi, *dayan,* and scribe of the Congregation Leghorn:

"It is true that I copied everything written above to be sent to the congregation that asked the question. . . ."

Samuel, son of Rabbi Moshe Hakohen

Responsum *Ya'ir Nativ*
[He maketh a path to shine (Job 41:24)]
by Jacob Chai Recanati

[Recanati was asked by his brethren Adat Yeshurun (the Congregation of Yeshurun) of Ramah to answer the following questions:]

1. How many synagogues are in Verona?

Answer: Verona, which has a thousand Jews, has two synagogues. One is the large building in which they pray according to the Ashkenazic custom; in the other (smaller) one they pray according to the Sefardic custom.

2. Are the words of admonition, called "sermons" by the people, said in Hebrew or Italian?

Answer: They are said in Italian in order that the women, children, and other people, who do not understand Hebrew, may listen and learn. However, the sayings of our sages, and biblical passages which are cited as proof texts, are said in Hebrew and explained and clarified in good Italian, either before or after they are said in Hebrew.

3. Is the prayer service said aloud or silently?

Answer: Until *Barechu* there is a man who reads the prayer before the ark word for word. When he reaches *Barechu* the cantor goes before the ark, dressed in a garb prescribed for him by the congregation, which is different from that of the rest of the people. He reads the service up to *Ga'al Yisrael* and (continues) praying silently with the congregation. Afterwards, he prays (repeats the *Amidah*) aloud.

4. Is the playing of the *ugav*, organ (*organo, Orgel*), in the synagogue prohibited or permitted in order to make the songs and praises offered to the living God sound more pleasant?

Answer: In my opinion this question involves three laws and decisions. I shall explain them one by one.

The first one: Is there apprehension in using the organ because of idol worship since gentiles play it today before the idols? Just like the *matsevah*, "pillar," about which Rashi wrote in section *shoftim* (in Deuteronomy): "Even though it was beloved in the past, now it is hated since they made it a law (requirement) for idol worship."

The second one: Is the organ included in the prohibition of rejoicing in our time because of the destruction of the Temple, as stated in *B. Sotah* (48a): "The question has been raised: What is the source of the prohibition concerning music? Mar Ukba replied: 'Rejoice not, O Israel, unto exultation, like the peoples' (Hos. 9:1)." Karo decided accordingly in his *Shulchan Aruch, Orach Chayim* 560, saying: "The rabbis ordained not to use musical instruments nor any kind of sound-making instrument with which one rejoices; and it is prohibited to listen to them because of the destruction of the Temple."

The third one: Do we have to fear (by playing the organ)
that the words of the prayers would be interrupted and the devotion be prevented?

In regard to these three objections I shall bring clear proof
that there is, in my humble opinion, no need for concern. The
aspects of permission will be more evident when I shall clarify
them one by one . . . :

I am telling the truth that, in examining the literature of the
poskim (halachic authorities), I did not find even one who
speaks about the organ. I found that in *Pachad Yitschak* (a
talmudic encyclopedia by Isaac Lampronti, 1679–1756), in the
article *Organo*, the statement of the author: "Re whether the
use of the organ is permitted or prohibited, see the opinion of
the rabbi, author of *Shte Yadot*, p. 100." I searched in the book
Shte Yadot by Rabbi Menachem of Lonzano, but found nothing
in it. Perhaps the reference is to another book which has the
same name but is not available to me.

My reply to the first objection: The prohibition with reference to idol worship is only applicable when the organ was
used for purposes of idol worship. Had the prohibition been
unlimited (i.e., if we could not use any organ) the use of wax
candles in the synagogues ought to be similarly prohibited,
since they honor the idols with them too. Yet such a prohibition does not exist, because the respective prohibition refers
only to lights (lamps) and candles of wax of idols proper. This
means: They had been kindled before an idol. . . . These are prohibited even if they serve as a pledge or were sold to Jews . . .
as decided by *Bach* (*Bayit Chadash* by Joel Sirkes), *Yoreh
De'ah* 139:13. . . . But this (the use of a candle or an organ that
had not been used for idols) is of no concern and the organ is,
therefore, permitted.

However, the *matsevah* is different because it is fixed and
connected (with the ground) and is used exclusively for idol

worship . . . which is not the case with the organ, since it is not fixed and connected with the soil and is used for secular purposes in other places (not only in churches) and for other than religious purposes, too. It resembles a bell, which is also used in private homes, and is not called a "law" (i.e., object) of idol worship even though it is used in houses of idol worship. . . . Therefore, nobody prohibits the bell. Furthermore, sometimes they worship the stone of the *matsevah* itself.

Furthermore, our master decided (ibid., 143:15): "It is prohibited to listen to musical instruments of idols, etc." Had the organ been prohibited, the text should have read: "It is prohibited to listen to musical instruments of the kind that is used for playing before idols."

In regard to the prohibition by Jacob Weil, cited in *Ba'er Hetev*, note indicator 11: The wording "No tune played for the idols must be played to God," refers to the tune only. However, he does not use the words "musical instrument." This clearly proves that the instrument, organ, is permitted. . . .

My reply to the second objection: Karo states in *Orach Chayim*, 560:3, end, "It has been a universally accepted Jewish custom to say words of praise, songs of thanksgiving and remembrance of God's deeds of loving-kindness over wine." Should you say that this has reference to vocal music (i.e., that only vocal music is permitted), but we have not yet heard that instrumental music is permitted, I shall refute you by giving actual cases. In Modena . . . were Italian and Ashkenazic rabbis, Rabbi Padova, Rabbi Lipshitz, Rabbi Ephraim Cohen, the two latter ones Ashkenazim, and other great rabbis from the Land of Israel. There is a society (orchestra) of drums and harps, and nobody tries to prohibit it. The last witness is the outstanding rabbi Ishmael Hacohen of blessed memory. In his book *Zera Emet, Yoreh De'ah*, chap. 157, a question is printed: During the intermediate days of Sukkot, a death occurred in the family of a member of the orchestra that was scheduled to play on the night of Hoshana Rabbah. I was asked whether he (the bereaved) may play the oboe, his usual instrument. . . . After an elaborate discussion he permitted it. Had the musical instrument been prohibited, the rabbis would not have permitted him to play the instrument even if this man had not been a mourner. This proves that playing music is definitely permitted in honor of God. The prohibition of Hosea 9:1 has reference to rejoicing (with music) only where no *mitzvah* is involved, as decided by Karo, ibid., and as I stated above.

I saw in *Meharsha* (Rabbi Samuel Edels's *Novellae* on the Talmud) . . . that Hosea 9:1 is to be interpreted in accordance with Psalms 69:13: "They that sit in the gate talk of me; and I am the song of the drunkards." 69:14: "But as for me, let my prayer be unto Thee, etc." Here we have some indication permitting prayer with music. The psalmist says: The songs of the drunkards are prohibited, but I play the instrument while praying even in the diaspora. . . . Thus it is clear that playing during the prayer service is different (i.e., permitted), and Hosea 9:1 does not apply here. This is also the apparent implication of Rashi's words in *Sotah* (ibid.): "A prohibition was issued in their (i.e., the former) generation not to use (instrumental) music in their homes." This excludes synagogues and instances of a *mitzvah*. . . . Thus we find that there is no prohibition against the use of instrumental music at the prayer service even due to the destruction of the Temple, and it is permitted.

Now I come to the third objection: Do we have to be concerned about the interruption of the words of prayer by the music, which would prevent devotion? I happen to have a little, but very good, book entitled *Sefer Keriat Shema* (Book of reading the Shema), printed in Salonika in 1755. In it are cited the words of the rabbis of Corfu stating that the *Shema* was chanted there on holidays, accompanied by music. Afterwards, for some reason, they stopped the music. . . . However, Rabbi Eliezer of Mordo and Rabbi Judah Halevi of Salonika ruled in favor of the old custom not to eliminate the (incorporation of) music (when the *Shema* was chanted on holidays). They cited proofs in favor of the matter and also received the consent of rabbis from Jerusalem. See op. cit., p. 11. Also, Rabbi Benveniste Gatinio of Salonika supported him, and raised the issue whether in a matter of custom, according to Rabbi Joseph and other authorities, an aspect of prohibition might be present, since a custom must not be considered if it leads to some calamity.

However, there is no consensus in the matter, since *Bach* (*Bayit Chadash* by Joel Sirkes) elaborates on the issue and upholds the custom. Also, Rabbenu Asher reversed his view, which he had formerly held in his responsa, when he wrote his *Decisions*. Also . . . *Sefer Hachasidim*, chap. 114; and in the book *Tosefet Bikure Ketsir Chitim* thirteen rabbis signed their names; and in the book *Sha'ar Ephraim*, chap. 4, it is stated that a custom must not be abolished even if it contradicts a law of the Torah, and we are not responsible for (possible) harmful consequences. Therefore, the law is that the custom of Corfu be upheld even if it has evil consequences. The consent to this was given by Rabbi Judah Chazak along with other rabbis. In the year 1784, when the matter became known to the rabbis of Venice that the music had been abolished by the rabbis of that place many years before, they ordained not to use music any more. Rabbi Gatinio . . . and with him eight rabbis of Salonika replied to the opinion of the rabbis of Venice and solicited testimony from wise, pious men who visited Corfu saying that the music there does not result in blurring of the words of prayer. The resulting decision was that the *Shema* may be chanted accompanied by music. This was in accordance with

Rabbi Judah Aryeh of Modena in his book *Kol Yehudah* (Voice of Judah), and in accordance with the rabbis of Safed and Tiberias and the sages (rabbis) of Rhodes and Roshed, see there. See also the praise of music in the book *Nefutsot Yehudah* by Judah Moscato in his first sermon called *Nora Tehilot*. Furthermore, I saw the last edition of *Pachad Yitschak* in manuscript, article *Shirah*, that in the year 1605 the service was concluded in the synagogue with music while saying *En Kelohenu, Alenu, Adon Olam*, and the like. The sages of Venice rose, Rabbi Judah of Modena, Rabbi Zorfati, Rabbi Leb Saroel, along with other rabbis, and rejected the complainers who wanted to abolish the music ("prevent the musicians").

All the evidence adduced and the views of the outstanding authorities cited, lead me to the principal conclusion that I see no prohibition on playing the organ in the synagogue . . . except that on the Sabbath and holidays a Jew should not play it, as is decided in *Orach Chayim* 338:1, this being prohibited lest he repair the instrument. However, in regard to the gentile (playing the organ in the synagogue on the Sabbath and holidays), *Ba'er Hetev* wrote ibid., note 3: "According to law, it is permitted to say to him, on the eve of the Sabbath, that he should play on the Sabbath, since the Jew himself is only prohibited to do so (to play the organ on these days) because of a *gezerah* (a precautionary prohibition, like a *seyag*, "fence"). The author of the *Magen Avraham* (Abraham Gumbiner) permits (a Jew) to tell the gentile to play on the Sabbath, except that he must not ask him to repair the instrument. In the land of David Ibn Zimra (Egypt), instructing the gentile to play on the Sabbath was prohibited as a matter of custom. In *Seder Eliyahu Raba*, permission is given to ask a gentile to repair the instrument on a Sabbath, but this is going too far. It is good to be heedful (cautious) and ask him on Friday to play the Sabbath. This is what my weak and inferior net brought up (i.e., "this is my humble conclusion").

Written and signed here in Verona on the last day of the month of Marcheshvan, year 5577 (1816.)

Jacob Chai Recanati of Pesaro, author and publisher of the book *Piske Recanati Haacharonim*, serving at present (as a rabbi) in the synagogue here in the Holy Congregation of Verona.

Responsum *Kinat Ha'emet* [The Zeal of the Truth] by Aaron Chorin, rabbi of Arad, Hungary

The zeal of truth and peace inflamed my heart and kindled in me the divine flame . . . to save the truth from the hand of its oppressors.

The subject I am discussing . . . is whether it is proper to pray in Hebrew when only the lips move, but the meaning of the prayer is not understood, or whether it is better to pray in the native language, which is understood?

Just by a glance, even without a thorough study of the views of the earlier and later rabbinical authorities by whose instruction, if followed, we shall live in this world and in the world to come, it is clear to everybody that the essence of the prayer is service of the heart. The service of the heart is the purity of thought, so the worshipper knows before whom, and what, he is praying. This being so, the reader of this "scroll" (responsum) will wonder and say: Why are you raising your voice ("crying out") in this matter? It is a simple, elementary thing (Lit. "Even little schoolchildren know the answer").

However, a few days ago I received a "flying scroll" (Zech. 5:1, 2; here: a communication). The author concealed his name, place (i.e., an anonymous letter) . . . and revealed to me the following: "Recently some men have arisen, among them understanding, wise men, upright in their ways, and built for themselves a gorgeous synagogue. However, this building is tantamount to the destruction of a building . . . because they pray there the *Pesuke Dezimra* (part of the morning service) in their native language, accompanied by a musical instrument . . . and thus they have strayed from the ways of our holy ancestors."

1. They abandoned our holy language and changed the wording of prayers which had been fixed by our ancestors.

2. Musical accompaniment of prayers is prohibited because: "neither shall ye walk in their statutes" (Lev. 18:3).

3. They transgress the prohibition: "ye shall not cut yourselves" (Deut. 14:1; this is traditionally interpreted to mean: You shall not form separate groups; see *Yevamot* 13b). Since many people of the congregation follow the custom of their fathers and pray in accordance with the traditional law, those who make the changes are in the wrong and are violating the above law (Deut. 14:1).

4. They breach the fence built by the sages by abolishing the silent prayer (*Amidah*) with the cantor continuing with the loud recitation of the *Amidah* immediately after the conclusion of the benediction *Ga'al Yisrael*.

5. They also complain about the wantonness of these men . . . for even the prayers which they say in Hebrew, they use the Sefardic pronunciation. They also read the weekly portion from the Torah without the traditional chant, which is based on the cantillation marks given on Sinai. He (the writer of the anonymous letter) pours out his wrath over them (the reformers) as do all who engage in calumnies: They open with praise, but conclude with disgrace.

Therefore, I cannot keep quiet and must speak up on this topic publicly . . . perhaps my words will reach the accuser, so he . . . will be ashamed because of his calumnies against the Jewish congregations and will be aware of the nonsense he has uttered. . . .

Judah Hanasi pronounced an important rule in his Mishnah (*Sotah* 7:1): The *Tefilah* (*Amidah*) may be said in any language. . . . The essence of the *Tefilah* is "wisdom and understanding," a man's words must be in consonance with his thoughts. His heart must understand and know what he is saying while praying, for what he is thanking, what he is seeking, and before whom he is speaking. . . .

The most outstanding halachic authority, *Magen Avraham* (commentary on *Shulchan Aruch, Orach Chayim* by Abraham Gumbiner) wrote in *Orach Chayim*, chap. 101, n. 5, citing *Sefer Chasidim* in brief . . . "It is better for a man to pray and to recite the *Shema* and benedictions in a language he understands than to pray in Hebrew without understanding it." . . . And he says there, in conclusion: "One who does not understand shall not pray because the (acceptability of) prayer depends on the heart . . ."

[Now Chorin quotes Maimonides, *Hilchot Tefilah*, chap. 1. Here Maimonides states that "when the Jews went into exile in the days of Nebuchadnezzar, they were mixed with Persians, Greeks, and other nations . . . and their children's language was a mixture of many languages . . . and they used corrupt language. . . . When Ezra and his court saw this, they introduced eighteen benedictions in a certain order (in Hebrew) . . . so that their prayer would be perfect like that of a man who uses pure (faultless) language."]

Now you see that if the men of that generation had been able to pray in the pure language of their land without mixing several languages, the Men of the Great Synod would not have needed to introduce the above measure. It was only due to the fact that the people of that generation were deficient in both Hebrew as well as the language of their habitation so that they had to learn the order, intention, and purpose of prayer, which had been ordained for them in one pure language, either the

language of their land or in Hebrew. The Men of the Great
Synagogue chose to arrange the prayer in Hebrew, but on
condition that they would learn it. The intention of the learning
was not to say it superficially, that is, by heart, . . . but that
they know the meaning of the words and of the content. . . .
The purpose of study was not to know the Oral Law by heart,
disregarding devotion. . . . However, because of our sins,
people do not bother to act in accordance with the ordinance
intended by Ezra and his court, i.e., not merely reciting them
with the lips but also with the devotion of the heart in order
that the pronouncements of his lips be in harmony with his
thoughts. However, most people merely pray by raising their
voice; therefore it is said, because of our sins: "She has uttered
her voice against me, therefore have I hated her" (Jer. 12:8).

All halachic authorities take the words "The *Tefilah* may
be said in any language" literally. The conclusion in chapter
Ketsad Mevarchin (*Berachot*, chap. 6) is in agreement with
Maimonides, *Hilchot Berachot* 1:6: "All the benedictions may
be said in any language, provided one says them as the sages
ordained them. If a man changed the formulation but mentioned God's name, His kingdom, and the subject of the benediction, he fulfilled his obligation even if he said it in a secular
language." Should you object that this is only so ex post facto,
but not a priori, my reply is: Those who understand Hebrew
certainly must not make an a priori change. But for a person
who does not understand Hebrew, it is certainly better to pray
a priori in a language that he understands, as I cited above from
Sefer Chasidim.

Anyhow, I say that we cannot replace the Hebrew of the
Eighteen Benedictions, the *Shema*, and the prayer pertaining
to the *Shema* by another language since these prayers are traditional (as Hebrew prayers), and it is easy . . . to follow the
ordinance, to learn the meaning of the words and the subject

matter. By changing it (into a foreign language), it is easy to
make the mistake of changing the prescribed formulation. . . .
The Men of the Great Synagogue arranged them in a pure,
easy, and intelligible language because Hebrew is the distinguished language, since God spoke in it to our fathers and
His prophets and gave us the Torah in Hebrew. . . . we hope
that our Sanctuary will be rebuilt and we will pray there in
Hebrew. Why should we unnecessarily forsake and abolish
that which has been transmitted by Ezra? Just because there
are one or two fools in town who do not want to listen and
study (Hebrew), should we forsake and abolish a proper
custom? . . . However, the *Pesuke Dezimra*, and the like, which
are songs and praises . . . which only one man in a thousand is
able to properly understand . . . and are said superficially without feeling and understanding . . . should not be said in Hebrew. . . . In truth, every sensible person should listen to the
advice of the *Chasid* (Judah), that it is better to say these songs
in the tongue of our native land. . . .

[In the next paragraph (pp. 19–20), Chorin complains about
the lack of decorum in our services, which leads to our disgrace
in the eyes of the gentiles. Therefore he demands dignity and
decorum in our worship services. He also states:] I remember
that I saw in a Midrash (I do not know whether it was in
Midrash Raba or elsewhere) that when the ministering angels
say a song (prayer), the person who rushes ahead or lags be-
hind, is pushed into a river of flames. . . . Indeed our sages
said: "It is better (to do) little with devotion than much without devotion." Better would be to shorten the text during
the workdays of the week than causing God's anger by a big
bulk of "nonsense" (hurried prayers) . . . and to recite them in
the native language. . . .

Even better than this is to say the *Pesuke Dezimra, Yigdal,*
and *Adon Olam*, and other lofty prayers on the Sabbath and

holidays accompanied by harp and song to inflame the heart of the worshipper. . . . Isserles already wrote in *Orach Chayim* 560:3 that for the benefit of a *mitzvah*, musical accompaniment is permitted. . . . According to law, the *sheliach tsibur* should be the greatest in wisdom and deeds in his congregation, but now all their strength is in their mouths. Only a foolhardy person says that musical accompaniment of the songs of praise in the synagogue is prohibited because of "neither shall ye walk in their statutes" (Lev. 18:3). This is so not merely because of the consensus of all the *poskim* (halachic authorities) that the peoples of Europe are not idol worshippers, since they believe in most of the fundamentals of the Torah, (but also because) . . . the last of the *poskim*, whom we follow, wrote that the consensus is that the prohibition of following the gentile laws refers to a law without reason. . . . However, a praiseworthy matter having an obviously pleasing effect, like the musical accompaniment, does not fall under the prohibition of "laws of Gentiles and Emorites" (i.e., idol worshippers). . . . Even today the custom of singing, at the reception of the Sabbath, the *Lechah Dodi* with musical accompaniment is customary in holy congregations. In an instance of a *mitzvah* like this, it is certainly permitted to use a musical instrument on the Sabbath and holidays, played by a gentile, as is made clear by the words of the *poskim* in *Orach Chayim* 338 and 339.

[Afterwards, Chorin explains that the prohibition of "Ye shall not make factions" does not apply to differing customs. There are many Jewish communities which have two synagogues, one of them following the Sefardic custom, the other the Ashkenazic. Against the objection that both Ashkenazic and Sefardic are still Hebrew and cannot be cited as precedent for permitting prayers in other languages, Chorin refers to Maimonides on the first chapter of Mishnah *Avot*, but without quoting the passage.]

In abolishing the *Amidah* to be said silently, they really change the Halachah that has been practiced since ancient times (see end of chap. *Yom Tov*, chap. 4 of tractate *Rosh Hashanah*). . . . In regard to the custom in Aragon, cited in *Bet Yosef* 591 in the name of Yitshak ben Sheshet, that the recitation of the *Musaf* by the cantor and congregation jointly, without the congregation first saying it silently, was done because most of the people are ignorant. This was done only for the *Musaf* prayer on Rosh Hashanah and cannot be cited, therefore, as a precedent for all the other days of the year. To avoid bothering the congregants, it is better to omit the prayers introduced by later authorities than to abolish the silent prayer or any established custom originating in the time of the Mishnah.

At times we have to break a law of the Torah because it is a time to work for the Lord (*M. Berachot* 9:55, interpreting Ps. 119:126). Now what excuse can we find, seeing that distinguished, learned men misbehave when the cantor repeats the *Tefilah*, (that is) they talk. . . . Most people increase their sins by (idle) talk. Therefore, their prayer is in vain. We cannot repair the damage or stem the tide. . . . And the children see the behavior of their parents, who sit . . . like people on street corners and in taverns drinking beer. The habit with which they grow up becomes their nature. . . . They are wise men in their own eyes and say: "We are experts and do not need the prayer of the cantor in order to fulfill our duty"; and we cannot protest against this.

Therefore, let us be grateful for this measure (innovation), which prevents the above evil. There is no more urgent time for it than this, ours, as Isserles wrote in *Orach Chayim*, beginning of chap. 232: "If the pressure of time demands it, the cantor should pray aloud together with the congregation."

Should you object: "A court cannot annul the decision of

another court unless it is greater in wisdom and number" (M.
Eduyot 1:5), then see Maimonides, *Yad, Laws of Mamrim* 2:7:
"If a decree was proclaimed, and they thought that it was
accepted by all the Jews (a requirement for the validity of
a rabbinical ordinance), and this was so for many years.
Yet after some time another *bet din*, court, saw that the decree
in question had not been accepted all over Israel, it has the right
to abrogate (the decree) even if it was a court lesser in wisdom
and number." We learn from the above words of Isaac ben
Sheshet that the institution of saying the *Tefilah* silently has
not been accepted all over Israel, otherwise the sages of that
time would not have refrained from leading the community of
Aragon on the right path. . . .

Re changing the pronunciation of the Hebrew from Ashkenazic to Sefardic: This is certainly acceptable since the sense
of hearing testifies . . . that the Ashkenazic pronunciation is
unsound (inaccurate). Thus wrote all the linguists of all
times. . . .

I testify that when Rabbi Nathan Adler of Frankfurt am
Main, rabbi in Moravia, stayed in Vienna for several months,
I was . . . often at the services in his *bet hamidrash*. He prayed
in the Sefardic pronunciation.

Re reading from the Torah without chanting, which embodies all kinds of noise and relieves the Torah of its dignity
. . . I bought a Torah scroll and introduced services where I
studied. On the Sabbath and holidays I read from it myself. I
never have read it with cantillation, which disturbs the devotion and does not have the "taste and smell" (spirit) of the
Torah. . . . Similarly, I do not change my voice in reading the
tochachah (curse; Lev. 26, Deut. 28) from loud to low,
because the words of the Torah are equally holy . . . and the
tochachah is just as holy and pleasant as *Shema Yisrael*. All
of them were given by God. . . .

The Jewish community has to take care of the dignity of

our religion lest we be disgraced any longer in the eyes of the gentiles as a result of our customs in our synagogues.

I saw among the accusations that your synagogue is closed during the week and open only on the Sabbath and holidays. You are not acting properly, though I see that your thoughts and intentions are good. [Now Chorin cites sources in support of their practice: Saadya, Maimonides, some sages; then he adds further reasons of his own for an infrequent attendance at the synagogue.]

Re praying with ten (*minyan*): This is not a daily obligation for everybody, and is not considered a *mitzvah*, as *Maharil* wrote in the *Laws of Eruvin*: "Were it that most people would pray in truth (with devotion) individually (at home), and that the fear of God be with them when going on the Sabbath and holidays to the synagogue, as is fitting!"

My brethren! You know that the *tefilot* were introduced in place of the *Tamid* sacrifices. Lest one neglect the *Tamid*, the sages ordained that every town having a population of 120 Jewish men should have ten (poor) idle men, recipients of charity and ready (=committed) to pray in the synagogue in the evening and morning. In regard to Rabbi Yochanan's statement: "When God comes to the synagogue and does not find ten men there, He immediately gets angry." In our time there is no anger. On the contrary, He says: "Who has required this at your hand to trample my courts?" (Isa. 1:12). This is so because the holiness of the synagogue had been desecrated by those attending it without the fear of God. You, who are praying with reverence and decorum . . . why should you cause, God forbid, God's anger saying: "Why did I come and there is nobody." Listen to me: If you are able to appoint ten men to pray daily in your synagogue, do it. . . .

   Arad, Hungary, 1818
   Aaron Chorin, Chief Rabbi
[In a postscript Chorin adds that he showed this letter to a

Sefardic rabbi, who, in turn, showed him a responsum which he bought in Vienna, written by David ben Zimra. In responsum 5, the author cites a responsum of Maimonides, written, in Arabic, to the Jews of France. In it he advises them to pray aloud with the cantor, and not to pray silently, and gives two reasons: "(1) The people will think that by praying silently, they had fulfilled their obligation. Consequently, when the reader repeats the *Tefilah* aloud, the people will engage in conversation, expectoration . . . and other activities even worse, a disgrace for us in the eyes of the gentiles who occasionally attend our synagogue. . . . (2) A man who cannot pray will see the others, who have already fulfilled their obligation, talking, and will not pay attention to the prayer of the reader, the result being that he will go forth without any prayer. . . ."]

Letter of Rabbi Moshe Kunitz to the Jewish congregation in Berlin

You asked the following questions:

"Re the synagogue which we established, we say the prayers as arranged by law, only a few details are different. These are:

1. The pronunciation of the prayers is Sefardic.

2. The cantor begins right after *Ga'al Yisrael* with a loud recital of the *Amidah*. The silent prayer is entirely omitted.

3. Several songs, praises, and exultations are accompanied by the organ, played by a gentile willing and engaged to do it."

Answer:

1. More than seven (of eight) parts of the prayer said by the Jews ascend to God in the Sefardic pronunciation, but less than one-eighth in the Ashkenazic pronunciation, because our

brethren are numerous (may God increase them) in Tunis, Tripolitania, Fez, Morocco, in all parts of Africa and Asia, in Europe in the cities of Turkey and Italy. All of these (people) pray in Sefardic. May you, too, be in their number, and may He harken and hear your prayer as He hears the prayers of our Sefardic brethren. This is not at all new even in our (Ashkenazic) lands. Not long ago the late Rabbi Nathan Adler prayed in his synagogue in the Sefardic pronunciation.

2. In regard to the silent prayer, see *Sotah* 32b: "Why was the silent prayer ordained? Not to shame the sinners (who confessed their sins in the *Amidah*)." In my book, *Ben Yochai*, I fully explained its foundations. There is nothing strange (wrong) in the eyes of the people in separating Jews from gentiles in this matter. This is especially so since, according to the Talmud cited above, the reason for praying silently is that the worshippers should not hear one another when confessing their sins. The confession in the places of the (Catholic) priests of the nations is silent and an eternal secret.

3. In regard to the musical instrument (organ) which you installed in the synagogue in order to attract our brethren who became estranged, and to stir the hearts of the women and children so they would love and fear God, as in the case of King Saul: "And it came to pass, when the minstrel played, that the hand of the Lord came upon him" (2 Kings 3:15); another favorable aspect is the fact that the player is a gentile. . . . There is no violation of the law in this . . . since it is a widespread custom in most places of Jewish habitation for a gentile to kindle and extinguish candles on the Sabbath in the synagogues. Similarly, many light *shevut* prohibitions had been canceled by the rabbis. There are later rabbinical authorities who permitted the use of musical instruments besides the prayer service for secular rejoicing. As known, they rely on the ancient French rabbis. And if you add to this the reason that

God is exalted by it, in that Jews who stayed away from our synagogues for a long time and almost vanished (as Jews) are once again attracted—that is, because of the organ they come back to the synagogue—you thus publicly sanctify God's name, and there is no greater *mitzvah* than this.

[After a paragraph of general character, in which he emphasizes, on the one hand, the importance of both Written and Oral Law, and criticizes, on the other hand, the opposition to the least reforms, Rabbi Kunitz says:] I advise you to open the synagogue every morning and evening, and ten idle men be appointed to pray there. Look and see your neighbors around you. Is there a house of worship open but once a week? The houses of worship of the nations are open twice every day . . . following the ancient Jewish way. . . . Now observe the law and do what is good in the eyes of the Lord. . . .

Vienna, Tuesday, twenty-fourth of the fifth month, 5578 (1818)

Moshe Kunitz of Ofen (Buda, part of Budapest)

SELECTIONS FROM אור נגה
Or Nogah
[The Light Dawned]
Part One, by Eliezer Libermann

Libermann lists eight accusations made by the Orthodox against the reformers:

1. They ordained that most of the prayers be said in German.

2. They abolished the silent prayer (i.e., the *Amidah* is only to be said aloud).

3. They omit the *Kedushah* of the morning prayer on the Sabbath.

4. They use the organ.

5. They introduced the Spanish and Portuguese pronunciation, which our forefathers have not known.

6. They read from the Torah without chanting. They do not call the men to the Torah by name.

7. They desecrate God's name by observing different practices; the Torah looks like two Torahs, and the prohibition of *lo titgodedu* (Deut. 14:1; interpreted as meaning: Do not make factions) would be transgressed.

8. They transgress the prohibition of Proverbs 1:8; 6:20, "And forsake not the teaching of thy mother," interpreted as meaning: You must not change the customs of our ancestors.

Libermann's reply to the above charges is essentially the same as A. Chorin's and of other early reformers. He uses the same passages from ancient and later sources that they and the Orthodox use. These sources are interpreted in accordance with a preconceived theology. This means that *eisegesis* is used very liberally. Among other sources he quotes Joseph Kolon, who says: "I have reliably heard that in the big city of Salonika there is a permanent cantor for women who do not understand Hebrew, and he fulfills his and their obligation by officiating in a foreign language" (p. 4). [After citing and interpreting many passages to prove that the prayers must be understood and, therefore, may be said in the vernacular, he continues (p. 9):]

All the above refers to Germany, where the Jews speak a good German and only very few of them know Hebrew. However, the situation is quite different in Poland. In this land, the Jews speak a faulty German mixed with Hebrew words (=Yiddish), but do know Hebrew. Therefore, it is better for them to pray in Hebrew, saying the prayers as ordained by the Men of the Great Synagogue, than to pray in corrupt German, or good German which they do not understand.

[In discussing the silent prayer, he first claims that he does not find pleasure in changing the customs of our ancestors. Then he cites four rabbinical authorities of the Middle Ages who hold that only a custom that is erroneous or senseless can be abolished. However, Libermann says that he often saw that great men in Israel, when they were pressed by time and had to go to a wedding or a banquet or the like, decided to say the *Amidah* only aloud. He cites *Magen Avraham* in support of this practice. Moreover, he accepts the view that the true reason for reciting the *Amidah* silently is to give the reader time to prepare his (loud) recital of the prayer (p. 10).

Among further authorities who ordained to say the *Amidah* only aloud, Libermann cites Maimonides (p. 12). David ben Zimra cites a letter by Maimonides addressed to the Jews of France advising them not to say the *Amidah* silently. The people would think that the silent prayer sufficed and would not listen to the loud repetition of the *Amidah* by the reader. Instead, they would talk, bring up phlegm, expectorate, etc. (p. 13). Other authorities of the Middle Ages recommend to say the *Amidah* silently only on Rosh Hashanah and Yom Kippur, but not on other days (p. 13).

The third objection, directed against the omission of the *Kedushah* of the Sabbath morning prayer, is nonsense. It was introduced by an unknown person. Among the sources cited is *Shulchan Aruch, Orach Chayim* 155 (p. 13). Libermann also cites Sefardic versions of the prayer service which do not contain this *Kedushah*.

Re the use of the organ, Libermann enumerates six possible objections and refutes them by citing traditional sources (pp. 14–15), along with his own interpretations and views. He also cites sources that permit the use in the synagogue of the same tunes (music) that are used in the churches, since the gentiles of our day are not idol worshippers. In many places, e.g., in most churches of Poland, no musical instruments are used at all. Had the use of musical instruments been a religious law, they would have to use them as they use the "holy water" (p. 15). Several biblical sources are cited to show that instrumental music had been used extensively. All the psalms were accompanied by instrumental music (pp. 17–18). Consequently, there is no reason to prohibit the use of the organ or any other musical instrument in our synagogues.

Libermann rejects the objection against the use of the Sefardic pronunciation mainly by the use of his own logical reasoning: All the great grammarians testify that the Sefardic pronunciation is grammatically more accurate. Subsequently, Libermann gives many linguistic details in order to prove the superiority of the Sefardic pronunciation (pp. 18–19).

Re reading from the Torah without chant, Libermann's argument is: Who heard Moses using or commanding the chant, etc.? In every country the Torah is read in a different way, in the way the people talk to one another. If the original traditional chant is a religious requirement, why is the tune different on various occasions, e.g., on Rosh Hashanah, Yom Kippur, Tish'ah Be'av? The implication is obvious (i.e., disregard the chant) (pp. 20–21).

Re the traditional requirement to call people to the Torah by name, Libermann cites halachic sources to the contrary (p. 21).

Against the accusation that the reformers transgress Deuteronomy 14:1, interpreted: "Do not make factions," Libermann cites talmudic and later sources. These sources permit differing customs and practices. This is particularly the case if there are two Jewish courts in one place, each having its own realm of authority. No objections have ever been raised against the various prayer customs (pp. 21–22). Consequently, the accusation of the Orthodox in this matter does not stand. Deuteronomy 14:1 cannot be cited against prayer reforms.

Libermann now proceeds to show that, according to the Talmud, we are permitted to change religious practices, even to permit practices that have been prohibited in the past. The first passage cited is *B. Chullin* 6b–7a. Here Rabbi (Judah the Prince) is cited as permitting vegetables of Bet She'an without tithing them, which was hitherto prohibited. When objections were raised against his new measure, he cited the verse 2 Kings 18:4, "Hezekiah . . . broke in pieces the brazen serpent that Moses had made, for unto those days the children of Israel did offer to it . . ." and continued: "Now is it at all likely that Asa did not destroy it? Or that Jehoshaphat did not destroy it?

Surely Asa and Jehoshaphat destroyed every object of idolatry in the world! It must therefore be that ancestors left something undone whereby he (Hezekiah) might distinguish himself; so in my case, my ancestors left room for me to distinguish myself."

This passage is, for Libermann, the basic source for the permission of making changes and permitting matters hitherto prohibited. He cites other sources too, but they are of considerably lesser value for his thesis of liberty to make changes (p. 22).

In the following paragraph (p. 23) Libermann pleads for daily services in the synagogue and cites sources to underline the importance of such services. This means that in this matter he opposes the reform practice of having services only on the Sabbath and holidays.

Then he continues: Though the *mitzvah* is to pray in any language which the worshipper understands, nonetheless it is proper to say some of the prayers in Hebrew, "as you really do." He urges that the children be taught Hebrew, the most important of all the languages. "You are wasting a fortune to teach them wisdom and the languages of other nations, why should they be denied the study of the precious language (Hebrew)? . . ."

Finally, Libermann urges that everybody in the synagogue should have a prayerbook, and this for two reasons: (1) A person who cannot pray and has to fulfill his duty by listening with devotion to the reading of the cantor, hardly can do this unless he follows the cantor by looking into the prayerbook. (2) Lest the words of the prayers be forgotten.] Therefore the proper way is that a person who has not yet prayed should pray with the reader word by word. A person who does not know to pray (in Hebrew) should have a prayerbook before him that has German and Hebrew in order to follow every prayer devotedly with the reader . . . (p. 24).

SELECTIONS FROM אור נגה
Or Nogah
[The Light Dawned]
Part Two, by Eliezer Libermann

[In the Introduction Libermann first criticizes the traditionalists who strictly adhere to old traditions and practices. Their eyes are blinded and, therefore, they cannot see the truth. He points out that it would be a sin to despise and deprecate secular wisdom and science. It is an important obligation to use the intellect, i.e., secular knowledge (science), in support of the true faith.] Just as faith alone without knowledge is not possible, as our sages said: "A brutish man dreads no sin, and an ignorant man cannot be saintly" (*M. Avot* 2:6). . . . thus, on the other side, knowledge and research are impossible without the assistance of faith. [Faith and research must go together (pp. 4–6).

This part of *Or Nogah* is a lengthy essay in which Libermann discusses the causes of disunity in Israel, a desecration of God's name. The disunity is caused by two groups, constituting two extremes. The one group adheres to everything that is old without examining whether it is right or wrong. They like the burden of customs no matter what the origin of a custom is, whether it was originated by an ignoramus or by women. The opposite group lacks faith altogether and is worse than the first one. They make derogatory statements against the sages of the Talmud, the eternal pillars of Israel. They deprecate every just matter that is an old heritage. They want only what is new. Both of these groups err and sin. Members of the first group cannot distinguish between truth and untruth, between good and bad. If they see that a man seeks God by making use of intelligence and wisdom, they consider him a heretic. In refuting their theology, Libermann cites passages from the Bible, from the Talmud, logic, and Kabbalah. Love, fear, and wisdom are the foundation of serving God without hypocrisy— so Rabenu Tam in *Sefer Hayashar*, sec. 5. Libermann's evidence from the Kabbalah is a passage in the *Zohar* (*Parashat Tazria*). Of his contemporaries he cites his friend M. Kunitz, rabbi of Ofen (p. 13).

Subsequent portions of the book are even more sermonic than the previous ones. Noteworthy is Libermann's advice that we should learn what is good from the gentiles, e.g., decorum during the worship service (see particularly p. 22). He supports his advice by citing from Rabbenu Tam's *Sefer Hayashar*, from Bachya's *Chovot Halevavot*, from Maimonides' *Mishneh Torah* (*Kiddush Hachodesh* 17:2, 5). On p. 32 he points out the importance of geography, world history, astronomy, geometry, anatomy, and logic for the proper understanding of our religious laws, and cites examples and historical incidents.

After citing *Magen Avraham*, chap. 199 (*Orach Chayim*), saying that today we must not reject any person (Jew) lest he completely separates from the Jewish community, Libermann says in the concluding part of his book (p. 51):] Every Jew's obligation to his Creator is to serve Him with all his heart and soul, to observe His laws. He must not stray to the right or left from the commandment He gave us through Moses. He must not transgress any of the Oral Laws imposed upon us by the holy sages of the Talmud, since both were given us by one

Shepherd. Though sometimes a matter (law) may be abrogated (suspended) temporarily, this right is given only to the sage (rabbi) of the city to decide it at his discretion (lit. "in accordance with his understanding"). We are extremely sorry to hear the news from far away that in most Jewish towns many Jews transgress a number of the prohibitions of the Torah. They desecrate the Sabbath, which is the foundation and root of our entire Torah and religion. The first warning of all the prophets concerned the observance of the Sabbath. There are also other matters which I do not want to mention not to desecrate the honor of our people. . . . These people cause other people to commit sins. . . . Let us return to God. . . .

SELECTIONS FROM אלה דברי הברית
Eleh Divre Haberit
[These Are the Words of the Covenant]
Published by order of the Orthodox community
[lit. the Righteous Court of the Holy Congregation]
of Hamburg (Altona, 1819)

[The title page gives the three topics of the book:

1. It is prohibited to change the "order" (=text, etc.) of the prayers, which is the order established (in the Orthodox tradition) in Israel.
2. It is prohibited to pray in any language except in Hebrew. Every prayer that is printed (worded) improperly— that is, not in accordance with our (Orthodox) custom—is unfit and prohibited to be used as a prayer.
3. It is prohibited to play any musical instrument on either the Sabbath or a holiday in the synagogue, even by a non-Jew.

In the Introduction, called "Proclamation of the Righteous Court of the Holy Congregation of Hamburg, May God Protect It," the above topics are repeated and elaborated on, presenting in detail the reasons for the necessity of the prohibitions. Among other transgressions ("sins") enumerated in the Introduction are: The liberals built a house of worship and called it a "temple," arbitrarily added some prayers and

omitted others; at the dedication of the temple women sang
in the choir; an organ was used; the silent prayer was abolished,
the reading of the prophetic portion on Sabbath was deleted,
etc.

This Introduction was signed by the three members of the
Orthodox *bet din* (court) of Hamburg.

The "Proclamation" is followed by a Foreword in German,
written in Hebrew letters, repeating what was said before in
Hebrew, and signed by the same men.

Following are the more characteristic and significant utterances by the responding Orthodox rabbis.]

1. *Letter by Meshulam Zalman Hakohen,*
rabbi of Fürth (pp. 1–2)

[In his brief letter, Rabbi Zalman expresses his agreement with
the decision of the Hamburg *bet din*. Expressing his deep sorrow, he urges his fellow Jews to pray and to beseech God to
put into their (i.e., the reformers') hearts the desire to change
their evil ways, that they repent and hold fast to the customs
of their fathers, since the custom of Israel is like the Torah.

After repeating the three areas of transgressions and briefly
expressing the reasons for his objections, which are, in a word,
the violation of old laws and customs, he again prays:] May
God pour His spirit, a spirit of grace and entreaties, upon these
men so that they may pray as in former times, to serve Him in
unity, so that there be peace, etc.

Fürth, 13 Kislev 5579 (1818)
Meshulam Zalman Hakohen

2. *Letter by Hirz Scheuer,* rabbi of Mainz (pp. 2–6)

No changes in prayers are permitted. This pertains not merely
to prayers established more than two thousand years ago by

the Men of the Great Synagogue, but also to later traditional prayers of both the Ashkenazim and Sefardim. By the least change, the originally intended meaning of the prayer would be altered. It is not permitted to change any custom, or to abandon it, unless there is clear proof that it had been introduced due to an error.

Prayers must only be said in Hebrew. It is impossible to translate them without losing something in their meaning and their original intent. These can be only expressed in Hebrew because of its brevity.

Mishnah *Sotah* 7:1, permitting one to pray in any language, had never been objected to. It applied to women of former times, since they did not understand Hebrew at all. Now, however, men as well as women know some Hebrew. They learn it from childhood. Mishnah *Sotah* cannot be cited as evidence since in those days most people did not understand Hebrew. For this very reason, Rav Ashi redacted (published) the Talmud in Aramaic. Whatever our interpretation may be, praying in Hebrew is the choicest *mitzvah*. According to law, a non-Hebrew ("foreign")-speaking Jew, who hears the prayer in Hebrew, fulfills his obligation, which is not the case with respect to other languages.

Changing the content and text of the prayers is the worst aberration from the Jewish faith, since the regular prayers constitute our basic service in place of the sacrifices. Changing the prayers would split Judaism into two religions.

Musical instruments should only be used at weddings and must not be permitted where no *mitzvah* is involved.

In Prague there are nine synagogues. In the largest one the Sabbath has been ushered in with music, but only up to *Bo'i Beshalom*, no further, i.e., before the Sabbath began. On Sabbath and holidays proper no musical instruments had been used there, and in the other synagogues they never had been used. On rare occasions, on the Sabbath before or after the wedding of rich people, musical instruments had been played in our congregation in the old synagogue up to *Bo'i Beshalom*, and as a result, men and women sat together mixed . . . so that they had to be rebuked. This evil custom was suspended over twenty-five years ago. It is known how sternly we are warned in this matter, and therefore in every Jewish community men and women pray in different (parts of the) synagogues . . . men below and women above, so that they would not look at each other, which would lead to levity and sin.

The conclusion, even for those who are inclined to be lenient, is that in our time . . . where there are many who publicly transgress the Sabbath, we must not permit anything (that might lead to a transgression though not a sin per se) in public. . . .

A final word: None of these three things can be permitted. A person who wants to show that these matters are permitted, will be held accountable (punished). . . .

> Mainz, 6 Kislev 5579 (1818)
> Hirz Scheuer

3. Moses Sofer (*Chatam Sofer*) (pp. 6–11)

[In attacking the "little foxes" (=reformers) he points out that a *takkanah*, an authoritatively established Jewish institution or practice, retains its validity even after the reason for the institution or (practice) has become invalid. This applies particularly to the contents of the prayers. Ashkenazim and Sefardim have to adhere to the texts of their respective traditional prayers, especially because the reason for these prayers did not become invalid. In such a case, not even the Prophet Elijah can invalidate a practice, as said by our sages in *Yevamot* 102b. Those who deny the validity of the Oral Law, established by our sages, are *heretics*.

The next attack concerns the omission of the prayers for the coming of the Messiah, the return to Israel, and the reestablishment of the Temple service as conducted there in former times.] Any prayer or expressed desire to return to the Land of Israel does not indicate disloyalty to our host countries. The Persian king did not have misgivings when Nehemiah, in spite of his high-ranking position in Persia, expressed his desire to return to the Land of Israel.

Since the destruction of the Temple we are like prisoners. The rulers of the nations in whose midst we live are kind to us. Therefore we have to pray for their welfare . . . and undoubtedly, they will be highly rewarded by God. . . . Nonetheless, it is not an evil (i.e., we are not ungrateful) if we hope to return to our land. If God is gracious to us, the other nations will praise Him too. If we are well off, they, too, will be well off.

However, these men (the reformers) do not hope, or believe whatsoever, in the words of the prophets in regard to the restoration of the third Temple, the coming of the Messiah, and in the utterances of our sages in the matter (see Maimonides, *Mamrim*, chap. 3).

As to the playing of musical instruments in the synagogue, this is prohibited. Our sages, who introduced the prayers, did not ordain the playing of musical instruments in the synagogue, though we originated the use of music in the Temple service. The reason is: Ever since the Temple of Jerusalem was destroyed, there is no rejoicing before Him. Although it is permitted, to some extent, to make people rejoice, e.g., bride and groom, since they are depressed by the *galut* . . . it is prohibited, however, in the synagogue, especially on a Sabbath. . . .

[Next he objects to the omission of the prophetic readings (*haftarot*), citing traditional sources (*M. Megillah* 4:2, etc.). Even more vehement is his objection to the use of any language other than Hebrew in a public worship service. The Mishnah (*Sotah* 7:1) permitting the reading of the *Shema* and the *Tefilah* (silent prayer) in any language is understood as permissible only when praying at home, but has no reference to the public service.

The fact that the common man does not understand Hebrew is no excuse for using the vernacular in the service. Everyone should learn the meaning of the prayers. If a person talks to a king of flesh and blood (i.e., a human king and not a Divine King), he has to speak the language of the king. And Nachmanides (beginning of *Ki Tisa* in Exodus) wrote that the holy language (i.e., Hebrew) is the language in which God speaks to his prophets. Our sages said that the world was called into existence through the Hebrew language. . . . It is God's language, and the Torah which He gave us was communicated in Hebrew.

Tuesday, second day of Rosh Chodesh Tevet, 5579 (1818)
Moshe Hakatan Sofer (= Rabbi Moses Schreiber)

4. Mordechai Benet, rabbi of Nikolsburg (pp. 11–16)

[First he attacks the new (Reform) prayerbook, which differs from all preceding prayerbooks by means of omissions and various changes contrary to our religion.

Both the Written and Oral Law originated with God. Those who rejected the Oral Law were base people, e.g., the sect of the Sadducees during the Second Temple, and later the Karaites in the days of Judah Gaon. As a result, their remnants are completely separated from the Jewish community, because without the traditional interpretation of the rabbis they cannot understand even one *mitzvah*.

Subsequently, Rabbi Benet lists the various omissions, among them those concerning faith, our redemption, and our hope for eternity. True devotion is possible only when the prayers are said in Hebrew.

A detailed opposition to the playing of the organ and other musical instruments in general in the synagogue-worship follows. Music interferes with devotion since it attracts the heart, causing pleasure. A dialectical argument follows in which Rabbi Benet tries to prove that the use of music in the Sanctuary of Jerusalem cannot be used as a basis for permitting music in our services. Concluding the issue, he states that the use of an organ on the Sabbath, even if played by a non-Jew, is a strict prohibition.

Near the end of his letter, Benet attacks Rabbi Aaron Chorin, rabbi of Arad. We must not accept any of his teachings because he has no facility at all (he is an ignoramus) in Talmud and Codes. Instead, all his endeavor is in the realm of "logic" (speculation, theology).

At the end of the letter, Benet makes an appeal for unity, pointing to the tragedies of Spain and Portugal as the result of disunity.]

3 Tevet 5579 (1818)

Mordechai Benet

Av Bet Din [Head of the rabbinical court]

Nikolsburg and the "Land" [=nearby communities]

5. Letter of the rabbis of Prague, members of the "Great Court" (p. 17)

[This is a short letter. At the outset, the rabbis bemoan the misfortune of the present generation, in which sinners and heretics have gained power. The rabbis also complain about the newly invented customs and about the fact that the reformers despise the Torah and the customs of our ancestors. They act as if every person had permission to pray as he wishes, though our ancestors prohibited us from making any changes in our prayers, especially from praying in any language other than Hebrew. Those who violate this tradition lack faith. Their intention is merely to acquire a higher reputation among the gentiles, who would then say that they (the reformers) are wiser than the other Jews. However, in reality, they are neither Jews nor Christians.

Playing the organ on Sabbath, even by a gentile, is a strict prohibition. As to those who play musical instruments in our congregation at *Kabbalat Shabbat*, the established custom is that the players must lay away the musical instruments half an hour before *Barechu* (beginning of the *Ma'ariv*, evening service proper).]

Concerning the "invalid" (=despicable) book entitled *Nogah Tsedek* (Light of righteousness), it is evil darkness, and one must not rely on it at all. We know the men who wrote it too well. It is all cunning lies, calculated to blind the eyes of the Jews, etc. . . . The judgment (punishment) of a person who transgresses the words of the sages is determined, and his prayer turns into sin.

Prague, 4 Tevet 5579 (1819)

The words of these great rabbis, members of the Great Court of the Holy Congregation of Prague

Eliezer Fleks
Samuel Segal Landau
Leib Melish

6. Second letter by Rabbi Mordechai Benet,
addressed to the Great Court of Hamburg (pp. 18–21)

[A Sefardic Jew from Izmir came to Nikolsburg with a copy of *Nogah Tsedek*. Rabbi Benet saw in it two responsa, one by Rabbi Shem Tov of Livorno and another by Rabbi Jacob Chai of Verona. At the outset Rabbi Benet makes the remark that they permit what is prohibited, and they will be held accountable (=punished by God).

The main topic is the use of musical instruments played by gentiles in the synagogue during services. This is, in Rabbi Benet's view, strictly prohibited, and he discusses this at length. However, he rejects the rest of the responsa in one brief paragraph merely by making derogatory remarks.]

Nikolsburg, 8 Tevet 5579 (1819)

Mordechai Benet

7. Letter from Rabbi Eliezer of Trietsch, Moravia, addressed to the Hamburg Court (pp. 22–24)

First complaint: The reformers of Hamburg built a house of prayer like that of the other nations. Further objections: This temple will be closed six days of the week and opened only on the Sabbath. They pray there partly in Hebrew, partly in the language of the gentiles. They also printed a prayerbook to suit them, changed the traditional text, and omitted the prayers for redemption. During certain prayers, they play the organ, relying on the book *Nogah Tsedek*, where an Italian rabbi permitted the playing of the organ on Sabbath by a gentile. However, the rabbi of Arad went much further.

This man, Aaron Chorin, is an ignoramus so far as Talmud and Codes are concerned, and one must not rely on his decisions. [After enumerating the changes Rabbi Chorin suggested, and showing that they are contrary to law and tradition, he declares:] It is crystal clear that they (who follow his instructions) are denying the fundamentals of our faith, the words of our prophets and sages, etc.

The very fact that an Italian rabbi and Aaron Chorin of Hungary had been asked to give their views, but not rabbis from Germany, Moravia, Bohemia, Poland, or the great rabbis of Hungary, proves that they (the questioners) were interested in falsification (distortion of law and tradition).

[Rabbi Eliezer strongly advises the Orthodox *bet din* to go to the gentile authorities asking them for support lest a new sect come into existence to which the gentile rulers are strongly opposed.] The gentile authorities in Hamburg are upright, they love law and truth. Choose wise and pious men, who shall go pleading (lit. "crying") with the authorities, so that "the house of the wicked shall be destroyed" (Prov. 14:11), "and the arms of the wicked shall be broken" (Ps. 37:17).

[He concludes his letter with a prayer to God for the destruction of those uprooting the roots of the religion.]

Triesch, 13 Tevet 5579 (1819)
Eliezer (rabbi) of Triesch

8. Letter from Rabbi Abraham of Breslau (pp. 24–25)

[This is a very brief letter confirming in a few words what the earlier rabbis said in detail.

In conclusion, he prays to God] that He may turn the hearts of the people who err so that they would listen to their (true) teachers, and that their sins be forgiven. . . .

Breslau, 20 Tevet 5579 (1819)
Abraham, son of the eminent rabbi Gedaliah Tiktin

9. Letter by Abraham Eliezer Halevi,
rabbi of Trieste, Italy (p. 26)

[Rabbi Abraham Eliezer Halevi considers the tragic news about the Hamburg reforms the worst since the exile from Palestine.] These wicked people took the place of their fathers. . . . God will not forgive them.

True, every person is responsible for his own actions, but

how much the more responsibility rests on the rabbis and sages,
who have the power to stand before the authorities, to stop the
damage and repair it, and to pursue the sinners till they return.
. . . I pray to God that He may have mercy over His people
. . . and plant in our hearts His love and fear, and gather in our
exiles into our land, so that our Sanctuary and glory may be
restored soon in our day.

    Trieste, 25 Tevet 5579 (1819)
    Abraham Eliezer Halevi

10. Letter by Akiba Eger, rabbi of Posen (pp. 27–28)

[The contents are the same as those of the above rabbis. Then
he adds:] The one who touches (neglects) just one of a thousand words (laws, requirements) of the rabbis of the Talmud
will cause the downfall of the entire Torah. A person who
questions the words of the Talmud certainly does not lay
tefilin and desecrates the Sabbath, since he would not know the
detailed requirements of the *tefilin* or of the Sabbath. The same
applies to all the other commandments, positive and negative. It
is a fundamental principle of our faith in the Written and Oral
Torah that it is possible to understand them only by accepting
the interpretations of the (traditional) rabbis, since the laws
are inseparable (you cannot accept some and reject the others).
A Jew who does not believe this is a *heretic*.

It is a shame that some Jews do not understand Hebrew.
It is a disgrace in the eyes of the non-Jews, since every nation
speaks its own language and loves it. . . . They (the Reform
Jews) teach their children French and Latin, but forsake the
holy language. . . .

We also have to pray for the rebuilding of Jerusalem, though
we live undisturbed among the nations . . . and must pray for
the welfare of the government as said in Jeremiah 29. Nonetheless, we hope and pray for the restoration of Jerusalem, not

for the sake of the pleasures and desires of this world, but in order to serve God in purity with the sacrificial cult in God's Temple. . . .

Playing the organ on a Sabbath or on a holiday, even if done by a non-Jew . . . is like praying with outstretched hand and falls under the prohibition: "Neither shalt thou set thee up a pillar" (Deut. 16:22). . . .

Akiba Gins of Eisenstadt, 27 Tevet 5579 (1819)

11. Letter by Aaron Joshua, rabbi of Rawicz (pp. 28–29)

[This letter concentrates on the importance of Hebrew prayer but offers nothing new.]

Rawicz, Friday, 3 Shevat 5579 (1819)

Aaron Joshua, son of Rabbi Dov Beer

12. Second letter by Moses Sofer (pp. 30–45)

[In this letter Rabbi Sofer exposes all the "lies" contained in the book called *Nogah Tsedek; Or Nogah*.

When Rabbi Sofer sent his reply to Hamburg two weeks before, he had not as yet seen the books *Nogah Tsedek* and *Or Nogah*, edited (compiled) by E. Libermann.

First he elaborates on the prohibition of playing the organ in the synagogue.] After the destruction of the Temple, we are not allowed to have other than vocal music in the synagogue. While there were musical instruments in the Temple, there was no organ there, perhaps because the word has a derogatory meaning (i.e., the word עֻגָב comes from the same root as the word עֲגָבִים meaning love, lust), just as there was a prohibition against bringing to the Temple Court water from a certain fountain that was called מֵי רַגְלַיִם "urine." The same applies to the synagogue.

More plausible to me is the explanation that according to a law of ancient idol worshippers the organ was used exclusively in the temples of idol worship, and it was therefore prohibited in the Temple of Jerusalem. If so, the use of the organ constitutes a prohibition of the Torah. True, they used the organ in one of the many synagogues of Prague, but stopped playing it before saying *Mizmor Shir Leyom Hashabbat* (Ps. 92). Moreover, after the organ broke down there, it was not repaired.

[Sofer was quite shocked to see, in *Nogah Tsedek*, p. 7, that the organ was to be put into the women's section of the synagogue.] It is known that women don't have the knowledge of playing the organ . . . and a gentile plays it. How then could they give such amazing advice, to have male players in the women's section of the synagogue, thereby setting the wick on fire (i.e., to cause sex-trouble).

[Rabbi Sofer points to erroneous analogies presented in *Nogah Tsedek*.] It has been a custom to hire a gentile for Yom Kippur nights to watch the candles lest fire break out and endanger lives. This led to the mistaken notion that it was permitted to tell the gentile to extinguish and kindle the lights on Yom Kippur. My teacher, Rabbi Nathan Adler, strictly prohibited the kindling of any light at *Ne'ilah* of Yom Kippur.

[An elaborate discussion about the necessity of attending daily services in the synagogue follows. Among others he cites a view that a prayer is answered only in the synagogue.

The next point of criticism is the view in *Or Nogah*, based on a traditional source (David ben Zimra, Responsa 5), that David ben Zimra's intention was to abolish the silent prayer and to only recite the *Tefilah* aloud, if this be possible without opposition. However, this is false testimony. There was such a custom in some places, contrary to the law in the Talmud, Codes, and books on traditions. This was not an established institution, but only a local and temporary one, etc. The author of *Nogah Hatsedek* boasts that he never read the Torah with chant. Rabbi Sofer now elaborates on the importance of chanting, claiming that it came down to us from Moses, etc.]

Though in ancient times the Torah was translated during the service into Aramaic, we don't do this now since people do not understand Aramaic. However, they did not translate it into the vernacular because it is impossible to render a truthful (fully adequate) translation, therefore it must not be done in the synagogue. Privately, we may translate it to any language and interpret it.

Praying in the vernacular is only occasionally permitted to individuals in the congregation. However, it is impossible to allow this on a permanent basis to the reader.

[In discussing the importance of the prayer for the gentile king and other officials, he points out that this does not mean that we pray for the downfall of other rulers in other lands, only for the downfall of the rebels in our land. In all our sermons we alert the people that honoring and respecting the king and authorities of the land is among the commandments of the Torah.]

The difference between the two types of fearing the king is obvious. All those (reformers) who do not believe in religion fear the king only because of his power lest he kill them. They fear and honor him in his presence only, but at home they despise him, his officers, and advisers. . . . But for the pious people (=the Orthodox), the opposite is true. . . .

[On p. 42 Rabbi Sofer states that Rabbi Libermann supports the haters of King David. He says one should not pray for redemption but, instead, for our peace among the nations. Sofer gives a number of historical events of persecutions and pogroms in various lands. The punishment started because of the sin of leaving God, getting close to the nations and not keeping separate from them.

According to Libermann, certain prayers should be omitted since we do not know their authors. Sofer (p. 44) points out that this is no valid reason and cites examples.]

Moses Sofer of Frankfurt on the Main

13. Letter by Mazal Tov, *chacham* (Sefardic designation for rabbi) of Modena (pp. 45–46)

[This is a brief letter endorsing the stand of the Hamburg *bet din* without giving specific reasons of his own. Noteworthy is his remark that he concurs with Eliezer Halevi, rabbi of Trieste.]

6 Shevat 5579 (1819)

14. Letter by the rabbis of Padua (pp. 46–51)

[The rabbis concur with the decision of the Hamburg *bet din*. Their detailed support does not include important or new aspects. They point out, among other things, that no man has the power to change the prayers; they must only be said in Hebrew, even by people who do not understand Hebrew. The rabbis of France objected to the custom of the women praying in any language other than Hebrew.

No two Jewish courts are allowed to exist in one place, since this would lead to a split, which is forbidden.

Holy and secular must not be mixed together, therefore we have to use Hebrew exclusively in our prayer. It is the language in which the world was created.

Playing the organ on a Sabbath, even by a non-Jew, is prohibited in places where this was a previously prohibited practice . . . (The ellipsis [three periods] is in the text and may have significance. It may indicate a [partial] disagreement in the matter with the Hamburg *bet din*).

The authors of the letter cite a traditional view permitting one to ask a gentile to play musical instruments at weddings; first, because according to a rabbinical authority (Avi Ha'ezri) it is permitted to ask a non-Jew to do something pertaining to a *mitzvah*; second, because there is no real rejoicing for bride and groom without instrumental music. In all of Israel, and almost everywhere in the exile, no musical instrument is used during the prayer service.]

   10 Shevat 5579 (1819)

Menachem Azariah Kastilnovo

Jacob, son of Rabbi Asher Luzatto

Israel Mordechai Kunyon

15. Letter by Moshe Ahagi, rabbi of Mantua (p. 52)

[This is a very brief letter expressing agreement with the Hamburg *bet din*. The only news in it is that Rabbi Moshe Ahagi wrote to the *chachamim* of Modena, Ferrara, Lucca, Venice, and Padua asking them for their support.]

   Mantua, 12 Shevat, 5579 (1819)

   Matsliach Moshe Ahagi

[A parenthetical note states that they (the Hamburg *bet din*) had already received the consenting responses of the *chachamim* of Venice and Modena, and that the rabbi of Venice requested to inform him about this.]

16. Letter by Rabbi Samuel of Amsterdam and Amersfoort (pp. 53–63)

[This lengthy letter contains more derogatory criticism than any of the others. Without the tirades, it would be a relatively

short letter. It does not add anything significant to the substance
of the previous letters.]

Amsterdam, 21 Shevat 5579 [1819]

Samuel (rabbi) of Amsterdam, Amersfoort, and the nearby
places

17. Letter by the rabbis of Livorno (pp. 63–68)

[The letter starts out with a tirade and continues in this vein.
Relatively few sources are given. The letter has the character
of a *musar* sermon, even quoting poetry. As to the essential content, it strongly supports the stand of the Hamburg
bet din.]

Livorno, *Beshalach* [the week in which Exod. 15:2 is read]
5579 (1819)

Solomon, son of Rabbi David Chayim Malach
Mordechai Nisim
Yitschak Korduyo Feriot
David
Jacob
Solomon Aryeh Abraham Nisim
Samuel, son of Rabbi Moshe Hakohen
Jacob Bondi
Benayah, son of Yehudah Koryot
Abraham Chayim Tofaya
Moshe Chai, son of Jacob
                    Rafael Milol

[Included with the letter by the rabbis of Livorno was a
short letter by Shem Tov, son of Rabbi Yosef Chayim ben
Samun, in which he concurs with the views of the above
rabbis.]

Date and place as above, except that it gives the day of the
week: Tuesday.

18. Letter by Moshe Toviyah,
rabbi of Hanau and its district (pp. 69–76)

[The letter expresses the same ideas, i.e., objections, as all the others cited above. The author emphasizes that assimilation to the non-Jewish surroundings is the primary reason for the changes: "We want to be like all the nations." The major part of the essay deals with the importance of Hebrew and the prohibition of the use of other languages for the prayer service. Secondary is a section dealing with the prohibition of the organ.]

Hanau, 24 Shevat 5579 [1819]

19. Letter by Rabbi Jacob of Lissa (pp. 76–82)

[He begins with derogatory remarks about *Or Nogah*. He says, among other things, that] he (Libermann) did not engage in this matter for the benefit of others, as this is not his custom. This was a business enterprise, to fill his bag with money, because this is what his soul desires. To him winning ten or twenty silver coins by playing cards or dice, as he did in Posen most of the nights he spent there, is equal to making money by printing a book. . . . If he utters some sensible words, they are probably stolen (i.e., they are plagiarism).

[The organ is prohibited not merely on Sabbath, but also on holidays and weekdays. Music is only permitted at weddings.]

In regard to the prohibition of changing the versions (texts of the prayers), we have to know a fundamental thing. It is known that the essence of religion and also the existence of the world depend on faith as their foundation. We are not at all permitted to only make use of the comprehension of our intellect, because the intellect often fails and is caught in the net of error. The intellect is merely a tool and help when combined with traditions of our fathers concerning Torah and customs.

Isaiah, addressing the men of his time, "Hear ye indeed, but understand not" (6:9), says that people should listen to tradition even if they do not understand it and must not base everything on intellect alone. It is not considered wisdom that you consider intellect alone. On the contrary, it is the lack of wisdom.

Even at the acceptance of His oneness (i.e., saying of the 'Shema') it is not said "*Understand* O Israel," but only "*Hear* O Israel," which is an expression of acceptance of the matters (commanded). We see that even the great scholars and philosophers were caught by intellectual error, as is known about Aristotle and his colleagues.

Not merely are we Jews commanded to adhere to our faith, and not to split up into groups, but the other peoples, too, have similar obligations. The rulers strictly watch over this. Permitting ourselves to change practices would lead to anarchy.

Just as we fully believe that God is the "Leader" of the world, thus we also believe that the king and the ruler is God's chosen one to exercise his rulership for Him. And just as we ask in all our prayers for the restoration of the Sanctuary, in order to be privileged to fulfill by it God's commandment, and to acquire higher wisdom . . . to gather there and conduct the sacrificial cult, thus we also pray in every prayer for the welfare of the kingdom and that it may endure, because it is also basic for leading a religious life and observance of the commandments. The essence of the matter is, there is no opposition whatever to the kingdom in any of our prayers. Its welfare is our welfare (lit. "Its peace is our peace").

An implication of the above said is that it is obvious that changing the versions (texts of the prayers) is bitter poison. . . .

And that which concerns the prayers to be said in Hebrew is likewise included in the above discourse.

[Now Rabbi Jacob demonstrates that it is impossible to

translate a Hebrew word accurately, since the word—he uses
the word *gibor*—has different meanings. . . .] For this reason
our ancestors realized that if permission would be given to
pray in other languages, false ("foreign") belief may be the
result, and the commandments may be wrongly interpreted.
Furthermore, since the study of the holy language is a *mitzvah*,
as Maimonides stated in *Avot* . . . praying in foreign languages
would have the result that Hebrew would be forgotten altogether. Besides this, they certainly had many other reasons
unknown to us. . . .

[At the end, Rabbi Jacob summarizes the three points
briefly.]

New Moon of Adar, 5579 (1819)
Jacob, residing (officiating) at Lissa

20. Letter by Rabbi Hirsch (of the family) Katzenellenbogen, rabbi of Wintzenheim in the upper district
of the Land Alsace, author of the Responsa *Sha'ar
Naftali*, and first (rabbi) of the Consistory of
Upper Rhineland (pp. 83–87)

Wintzenheim, March 17, 1819
[Facsimile of the seal] Le Grand Rabbiy et President
De Consistoire des Israelites de la Circonscription
de Wintzenheim
[The letter begins with a tirade. A few examples:] Robbers
came upon us, thieves of souls. . . . House of Israel! False
prophets increased in your midst. . . . They spread the spirit of
defilement over all the land. . . . My heart melted in me . . .
when I read the letter written to me by the head of your court,
dated 26 Shevat last. . . .
[The criticism corresponds to that of the other letters, i.e., it
concerns the changes in the prayers, the playing of the organ,

and singing in a foreign language.] They are worse than the Karaites and the sect of the Sadducees and Boethusians. . . . Hebrew is the language transmitted to us from the time of the creation of the world, since the world was created in using Hebrew (by God). . . . If one prays in Hebrew, he fulfills his obligation, even if he does not understand it. However, if he prays in other languages, he has to understand them. . . . According to Rashi a person fulfills his obligation even if he only hears the Hebrew prayer, though he does not understand it. . . . There is a good reason to read the *piyutim* (religious poems), even though they are not understood. . . .

Wednesday, 20 Adar 5579 (1819)

Naftali Hirsch Katzenellenbogen, head of the court ("chief rabbi") of the land and first in the Consistory of the Upper District of Rhineland

21. Second letter by Rabbi Eliezer of
Trietsch in Moravia (pp. 87–97)

[This letter of Rabbi Eliezer is mainly a sermon in which he repeats in a homiletical fashion his former criticism with some additional references to sources. For example:]

Azariah de Rossi, in *Me'or Enayim*, vol. 5, chap. 57, proves that at the time of the Second Temple the spoken language in Palestine was Aramaic; nonetheless Ezra and his court ordained that the prayers must be in Hebrew.

In the days of Antigonos (of Socho), Zadok and Boethus began with doubting the validity of the true tradition, and subsequently denied (the validity of) the entire Torah.

Even during the time of the Second Temple, when Israel dwelt in its land and had a king and (high) priest, they still prayed for the coming of the Messiah.

The belief in the Messiah is one of the thirteen basic beliefs,

according to Maimonides. It is also among the basic beliefs
according to Joseph Albo in his *Sefer Ha'ikkarim*. This basic
belief is fully explained by Don Isaac Abrabanel in his book
Mashmia Yeshuah, and *Yeshuat Meshicho*, and in his commentary on the books of Isaiah and Daniel. Omitting to mention
in the prayers the ingathering of the exiles and the redemption
seems to mean that they (the reformers) deny the belief in the
coming of the Messiah. . . .

It is known that God's punishments are "measure for measure." Therefore the calamity may be ascribed to the fact that
you did not properly honor the holy synagogue in your congregation. . . . In many congregations (and especially in Germany, as I hear) it is considered permissible to carry on idle
conversation in the synagogue, which is a bad thing and
sometimes results in yelling and quarreling, which is a serious
sin.

If this malady affected your congregation, you should know
full well that the anarchy (confusion) in your congregation
may be ascribed to this fact. Therefore men, women, and
children must be warned not to conduct idle conversation in
the synagogue at the time of the service.

[Subsequently Rabbi Eliezer emphasizes the importance of
warning and admonishing the people attending services. The
rabbi should begin his talk with a strong warning (*tochachah*)
against the bad qualities in man, especially against the un-
founded hatred for which our Sanctuary was destroyed and
which still persists among us.

Now he cites a passage from the book *Tomer Devorah* by
Moses Cordovero:] A man must love in his heart people. He
must love even the wicked because of the good qualities they
possess, and should not look at their blemishes. . . . There is
no Jew who does not possess good qualities, few or many.

They (the rabbis) shall warn against hating fellowmen, irrespective of nationality, because the non-Jews, in whose midst we live, are not like the non-Jews of former times. They believe in the Creator of heaven and earth and observe the "intellectual" commandments. It is known that such gentiles belong in the category "pious of the nations of the world," and they have a portion in the World to Come.

In spite of the fact that the Egyptians mistreated and oppressed us, embittered our lives and cast our sons into the river, God said (Deut. 23:8), "Thou shalt not despise an Egyptian, because thou wast a stranger in his land." This means that we must not remember the evil which they did to us; we must remember constantly only the good things they did to us. If this is so, how much the more is it incumbent upon us to always mention the good things of the nations, in whose midst we live and who do us only that which is good.

Never remind a person of the bad things he did to you, only the good things. . . .

Further warnings: Against the frequent "evil tongue" (gossip, calumnies); against envy, jealousy, hypocricy, bad (obscene) talk, thievery and robbery. The main thing is that the preacher should preach well and do what he preaches.

Another principle is the importance of "intention, devotion, of the heart." His intention must be pleasing to God.

[In the final paragraph, Rabbi Eliezer advises the great men (leading rabbis) of his time to admonish the dissidents in a gentle manner so that they repent and listen to them, and should not turn to a "tamarisk in the desert" (Jer. 48:6) in Hungary (i.e., Aaron Chorin) . . . so that they will be one nation with us. . . .]

21 Adar 5579 (1819)
Eliezer of Trietsch and its district
[This letter is also signed by three talmudists. Their letters were not printed in this book in order to make it easier on the reader

(i.e., not to burden him). The names of the three: Abraham Meir Turnimer, Sender Genzel, Eliezer Strasser.]

22. Third Letter by Moses Sofer (pp. 97–99)

[Inserted in this third letter by Rabbi Sofer is a letter of response by Rabbi Aaron Chorin, rabbi of Arad, in which he wrote that he erred and sinned in spreading false teachings. Now he has renounced everything and voided the responsum *Kinat Ha'emet*, printed in the book *Or Nogah, Nogah Tsedek*. According to the Torah a mere (declaration of) nullification suffices.]

I hurried and copied all the words of your decision. I sent them to the rabbi of Nikolsburg, and also signed my name to it . . . and also sent it to the rabbi of Trieste. . . .

Herewith I sent you a transcript of the letter written by the rabbi of Alt-Ofen (Obuda, a district of Budapest, Hungary) to Rabbi Aaron Chorin. (Note of the editor or publisher: Because of the honor of Rabbi Aaron Chorin, since he admitted his guilt and bent his head before the sages of our generation, we did not print this letter.) The teacher of Arad replied to this letter at unnecessary length; however, I give you here the text at the end of his words expressing his return (i.e., repentance) and admission (of guilt).

Moses Sofer of Frankfurt on the Main

This is the text at the end of the letter by the rabbi of Arad and his renunciation which he made "without feeling ashamed":

However, I have now heard that they made omissions in benedictions and prayers, that they do not pray for the ingathering of our exiled people, which is a basic belief and foundation of our Holy Torah; and they change the texts of the prayers. I apply to myself the verse: "And let this ruin be under thy hand" (Isa. 3.6). Therefore, I publicly declare: All my words in the letter *Igeret*

Kinat Ha'emet are null and void. Moreover, I shall not pass judgment in this matter nor give instructions, but it is up to the sages of Israel to pass judgment; and my opinion as against theirs be nought.

These are the words of the undersigned here in Arad, Monday, 13 Shevat, the weekly portion being (the one in which we read) "An altar of earth thou shalt make unto Me, and shalt sacrifice thereon thy burnt-offerings, and thy peace-offerings" (Exod. 20:21; the name of this weekly portion is *Yitro*).

Aaron Chorin

After he confessed and voided all his words said in the letter *Kinat Ha'emet* . . . I herewith sign with blessing. . . .

Here in Pressburg, Wednesday, 2 Adar 5579 (1819)
Moses Sofer of Frankfurt on the Main

SELECTIONS FROM צרור החיים
Tseror Hachayim
[The Bundle of Life]
by Rabbi Abraham Löwenstamm of
Emden (Amsterdam, 1821)

[This book, were it not for the illness of the author, would have been (in a shorter form) part of *Eleh Divre Haberit*. It repeats, on the whole, but in great detail and with additional arguments, the views expressed in the latter work, published in Altona in 1819. The book has nine chapters ("Responsa"):

1. Prohibition of the organ at the services in the synagogue.

2. Obligation of saying the *Amidah* silently.

3. Prohibition of changing the texts of the prayers.

4. A person praying in Hebrew fulfills his obligation even if he does not understand Hebrew.

5. The Ashkenazim are not permitted to change their customs by replacing them with Sefardic customs, and vice versa.

6. Saying the prayers and benedictions in other than the Hebrew language is prohibited.

7. The Torah has to be read with our customary cantillation and accentuation. The Ashkenazim are prohibited from using the Sefardic pronunciation, and vice versa. Calling a person to the Torah by his name and the name of his father is a requirement.

8. Prohibition of being in the synagogue or performing a *mitzvah* without a head-covering. Instances of prohibition in other cases: prohibition of men and women going together to, and sitting together in, the synagogue; prohibition of pronouncing the Tetragrammaton.

9. Every Jew must believe in the coming of the Messiah. This belief does not in any way contradict our love of the rulers of the land, which is everybody's obligation.

Since the book is primarily a repetition of the thoughts published a year earlier in *Eleh Divre Haberit*, a few passages should suffice. Whether the repetitions are conscious or accidental is beside the point. Noteworthy is the fact that Löwenstamm acknowledges his agreement with *Eleh Divre Haberit*.

In regard to musical instruments, Rabbi Löwenstamm says on p. 6: The organ is one of the most precious, beloved, and pleasant instruments that arouses the heart, lifts the spirit due to its pleasant tone. . . . However, when we go to a theater or concert we find no organ there. . . . On the other hand, the only musical instrument played in the churches is the organ, except for rare occasions, such as honoring the king and the like, when big church concerts are being arranged. However, at the regular weekday or holiday services only the organ is used in the churches.

It is quite amazing that the organ, a most precious instrument, is banned from the house of the king and every orchestra, while in the churches it is the only admissible instrument. . . . The reason for this can only be that at the foundation of the Christian religion the organ was chosen for some reason not known to us any longer and reserved for church use only, while its use for secular purposes was prohibited. . . . Regarding the argument stated in *Nogah* that many churches in Poland and elsewhere do not have an organ (implying that it is not a required instrument and has no Christian religious significance), the explanation is this: The organ is a very expensive instrument and not every church can afford to buy one; also, it is not a conditio sine qua non for the churches, just as the readers in the synagogue of villages and small towns are congregants, while in big congregations expensive cantors are employed. . . . Löwenstamm's conclusion is:]

1. The organ is prohibited in the synagogue by the Torah, whether it is played by a Jew or a gentile, on weekdays as well as on the Sabbath.

2. Other musical instruments, if played by gentiles, are likewise prohibited by the Torah.

3. Musical instruments, except the organ, may be played on weekdays, but are prohibited on the Sabbath by the Talmud, even in the Sanctuary (of Jerusalem), and much more so in the synagogue.

[On pp. 17–18 Löwenstamm concludes that, although a knowledgeable reader (cantor) is able to fulfill the duty of saying the *Amidah* for people who do not understand Hebrew, even according to Rashi, a reader who is not knowledgeable cannot do this. However, the Ashkenazim are customarily eager to hire a cantor who sings well but do not care whether he understands Hebrew well. Both together (i.e., having both of these abilities) is a very rare and unusual combination. Therefore, we have to say the *Amidah* silently. Since the reader does not fulfill the duty for others, we do not have to care too much whether the reader is learned or not. If we would care much for this, we would lose the ancient sanctified custom of engaging a good singer.

On p. 20b he offers parables explaining why we must not change the prayers:

1. A physician administers medicine to a patient. Standing next to him is a man who knows nothing about medicine but, being a simpleton, does not like the doctor's actions. Nonetheless he cannot question the doctor's measures, since he knows nothing about medicine. Even if the physician were to explain to him his reasons, he would not understand them. Therefore, he must not change the doctor's orders and has to rely on them.

2. A high official of the king instructs an ordinary person, who has only had contact with people like him (i.e., ordinary people), how to formulate his petition to the king. Can he object and demand a different formulation?

Similarly, since our saintly ancestors, sages and prophets ordained the prayers for us, how can we change them? Or how can we omit even one of them?

Löwenstamm devotes a full chapter (pp. 62–68) to the question of wearing a hat. The problem is: In our days, standing before the king with the head uncovered is an expression of reverence. Are we, therefore, permitted to pray, to enter the synagogue, or to perform any *mitzvah* without wearing a hat? Should this be prohibited? Furthermore, is it permitted not to wear a hat at home or while performing secular tasks?

Löwenstamm first cites *Mishneh Torah, Tefilah* 5:5: "(While praying), a man must not stand with his head uncovered and with his feet uncovered (barefooted) if the custom of the people of that place is not to stand before great men except with shoes." Löwenstamm states that the clear implication of this passage is that the custom here refers to the feet only, but the head must always be covered when praying. He then quotes *Shulchan Aruch, Orach Chayim* 91:3: "Some say, one must not pronounce God's name with the head uncovered; and some say we must object to people coming to the synagogue without a head covering. Straw hats are considered as a head covering, but placing the hand on the head is not. However, if another person places his hand on someone's head this, is, by implication, an acceptable head covering."

On p. 63 Löwenstamm says: A special friend of mine showed me a written statement in their (the gentiles') laws, that one of their great lawgivers commanded them to pray or prophesy only bare-headed. When I saw this I said that praying or the doing of anything holy without a hat is a definite prohibition of the Torah, which states: "neither shall ye walk in their statutes" (Lev. 18:3).

In discussing the wearing of a hat when engaged in secular activities, Löwenstamm cites *B. Nedarim* 30: "Men sometimes cover their heads and sometimes don't." This clearly implies a permission. Other passages cited indicate that it is a *mitzvah* to wear a hat even when not engaged in prayer or another religious deed. Thus *B. Kiddushin* 31a: "Rav Huna, son of Rabbi Joshua, would not walk four cubits with uncovered head. He said: 'The *Shechinah* is above my head.'" A similar passage is found in in *Shabbat* 118b.

After a lengthy discussion, Löwenstamm states:] Standing without a hat is contrary only to piety, but walking four cubits without it is prohibited by law. However, now, after the Jews accepted the custom of piety as a law, violating the custom, wherever it had been accepted, is arrogance and heresy. . . .

However, if a man's livelihood is in jeopardy by being different from other people at work, leniency seems to be all right . . . especially since we find many instances where permission (i.e., leniency) was granted out of financial consideration even on the Sabbath, provided that the prohibition concerned is of rabbinical origin. Likewise no stringency is in order if we would be ridiculed by gentiles, as we find that although the wearing of sandals (shoes) on Tish'ah Be'av is prohibited by law, the *Tur* and Isserles in *Orach Chayim* 554:7 permitted it for Jews living among the gentiles except in the

Jewish street. But at home, where one has no dealings with
gentiles and no fear of monetary loss or ridicule, to stay without
head covering is definitely prohibited. . . .

However, walking four cubits without a hat is definitely
prohibited by talmudic law. . . . Since a person sitting without a
hat cannot be careful enough and might walk four cubits
without a hat, therefore . . . every man should make for himself
a small skullcap and wear it under his hat (I saw many great
men doing this for reasons of health; therefore, doing this,
everyone can say "I am delicate"). Then he can remove his
hat when standing or doing business with gentiles. . . .

I was asked whether men and women may go together to the
synagogue. My answer: This is prohibited. *Sukkah* 51a speaks of
the important measure of separating men from women in the
Jerusalem Temple. . . . our custom to have the women's section
above and the men's section below has good talmudic foundation. . . . Daily experience proves the veracity of the Talmud.
The custom of our ancestors is like the Torah, don't depart
from it.

I was also asked. Is it permissible to pronounce the Tetragrammaton letter by letter? (p. 68).

God forbid! . . . The majority of the rabbinical authorities,
among them the sages of the Tosafot and Rabbi Obadiah of
Bertinoro, hold that the punishment for a person pronouncing
the Tetragrammaton is limitless. . . . Another proof for the
clear prohibition for the pronunciation of the Tetragrammaton
is the fact that it has no vocalization of its own in the entire
Bible. If it stands alone, it is vocalized with the vowels of
Adonai, and if it stands next to *Adonai*, it is vocalized *Elohim*.
. . . However, if we were permitted to pronounce it, it would
have to have a vocalization of its own so we know how to
read it.

Anyhow, it is clear that a person pronouncing the Tetragrammaton errs and commits a grave sin, and according to the majority of the sages will not live in the World to Come. . . .

[In the last chapter, "The End of Days" (pp. 70–81), the question is raised:] Must every Jew believe in the coming of the Messiah, in the return of our captives (to Israel), and the restoration of the crown of Jerusalem and the Temple to its pristine glory? Does this belief not contradict our obligation to love our ruler and host-land, which is obligatory for both Jew and Gentile alike?" (Löwenstamm uses the word "patriotism.") Are we permitted or obligated when praying . . . to omit the expressions of hope and supplication for our redemption, since this might be considered a violation of our obligation of loving our king; or are we prohibited to make any changes in the respective prayers?

The answer: A Jew who does not believe in the coming of the Messiah, in Israel's return to their land, the restoration of the Holy City, and the Temple, is not a Jew. Moreover, I say that he is not worthy at all to be called a human being. This belief does not, in any way, contradict the love of the individual person for his king and country. Therefore, we are not allowed to omit from our prayers even one single letter pertaining to the Messiah and the Holy City. . . .

[After a long, elaborate discussion, giving both the Christian view of the Messiah (Jesus) and at much greater length the traditional Jewish position, supported by prophetic and later sources, Löwenstamm states (p. 75b):] The conclusion is that as long as there are pious and nonpious Jews on earth, and gentiles who do not believe in the Jewish faith at all, redemption (Messiah) has not come. . . .

Not merely are Jews prohibited from rebelling against their rulers, concerning which God adjured them by a serious oath, but they must also pray for full peace for their king and country. . . .

But even after the great and awesome day of the Lord will come . . . even then we are not permitted to stretch out our hand and assist ourselves. . . . Even then we'll have to remain completely quiet and not deviate from the orders of the ruler . . . until every nation and ruler take us . . . to the house of Jacob's God, due to their good will and great love for us . . . with lips full of blessing and with hands dripping myrrh of love and peace and place the crown of royalty upon the head of our Messiah. . . . We long only that they send us with the desire of their soul to Jerusalem . . . and appoint David, our Messiah, king. However, if they do not want to do this out of their full desire, then, even if we see that we have the power to go to Jerusalem by force, we are not permitted to do anything of our own lest we break the oath imposed upon us by the God of our fathers. . . .

SELECTIONS FROM חת״ם סופר
Chatam Sofer
Responsa by Moses Sofer (1762–1839)

Choshen Mishpat, resp. 197
[*Chatam Sofer* prohibits a *shochet*, under the threat of excommunication, from reading secular books. In his free time he must read in the holy books, the Torah and the Talmud.] Now, if you find that he transgresses what I just said, then his *shechitah* (i.e., the animal he slaughtered) is *nevelah* (nonkosher) and he must not function as a reader (in the synagogue), and he is like a lion in the woods and like a braying donkey. . . . Appoint a pious rabbi who does not read secular books and who does not speak a foreign language (but speaks Yiddish) . . . since this is like putting an *asherah* (idol) into the Temple of God. . . . Maimonides borrowed from the books of the Greeks . . . and apologized that he did it lest the people of God seek wisdom in the books of others (non-Jews).

Chatam Sofer, Responsa, pt. 6, resp. 84 (Cf. Chamiel, *Sinai*, 28), question addressed to *Chatam Sofer* in 1819 by Rabbi Baruch ben Meir of Hamburg.
Points of complaint:
   A number of years ago heresy spread among some higher-class people in our Jewish community. They willfully trans-

gress God's commandments. They publicly desecrate the Sabbath, and we have no power to stop them. . . . They established for themselves a house of worship for Sabbath and festivals only as was recently done in Berlin. . . . In addition, they printed a prayerbook for Friday night and Sabbath only, in which they made many changes. . . . Of the *Birchot Hashachar* (morning benedictions) they only printed *Elokai Neshamah* in the language of the peoples (i.e., German) in their letters (i.e., not in Hebrew letters as done in Yiddish). [Then other omissions and prayers said in German are listed.] They also use tunes of gentiles played on the organ. Though they read from the Torah, they do not read the *Haftarah*, the prophetic portion. Instead, they employed a teacher who preaches sweet words mixed with gall (lit. "wormwood") directed against the words of our sages. Afterwards, the cantor reads a newly invented version of the *Musaf* prayer, not in accordance with either the Ashkenazic or the Sefardic custom. They omit the prayer for our return to our land. It is obvious that they do not want the Redeemer to come so that we may return to Zion. . . . They (the reformers) went forth to lead the pious astray towards the practices of the nations. . . .

We sent to the congregational leaders who were appointed since the French (Napoleonic) war by the government to proclaim in all our five synagogues the prohibition against praying from that prayerbook. We also prohibited them from praying in other than the holy language. We also prohibited any change of traditional custom.

We found it necessary to present our words to the (gentile) *authorities*. However, the arrogant people of our generation (=Reform Jews) complained about us (lit. "acted as informers") that our decision was unlawful. Moreover, they went to the gentiles and desecrated His Holy Name. Recently a book entitled *Nogah Hatsedek* was printed in Dessau without the con-

sent of the congregational leadership. In it a view of the rabbi
of Leghorn (Livorno) is cited permitting the organ. Also
printed in it is a reply by Aaron Chorin, rabbi (lit. *"av beth
din,"* head of the Jewish court) of Arad, Hungary, which he
sent to Berlin. In it he permitted everything. . . . He also permitted one to pray in the language of the nations, and that the
organ be played on Sabbath by a gentile. He also permitted one
to read from the Torah without chanting. . . . Since the gentile
authorities here are men of reason and knowledge, they instructed us to bring evidence from the noted sages. . . . Therefore we are asking you . . . to write us a reply (responsum) as
early as possible stating your consent in three matters:

1. No man has the authority to change the traditional text
of the prayers.
2. One must only pray in the holy tongue.
3. Playing the organ on Sabbath, even by a gentile, is prohibited. . . .

Hamburg, Friday, 7 Kislev 5579 (1818)
Baruch, son of Meir, head of the *bet din* of the congregation
of Hamburg.

Chatam Sofer's Reply (*Chatam Sofer*, Responsa, pt. 6, resp. 84).
Re your complaint that the temple of the reformers is closed
during the week and is only open on Sabbath: I wish it would
be closed on Sabbath, too, since they changed the liturgy that
has come down from the Men of the Great Synagogue, from
the sages of the Talmud, and from our sainted fathers . . . and
also omitted the reference to the coming of the Messiah, the
restoration of Zion and Jerusalem . . . and employ Christians
to play the harp and the organ . . . on the Sabbath, which is
prohibited to us; and most of their prayers are in German.
Praised be God Who, in His great mercy, showed us favor

before the gentile authorities, instructing the leaders of the Jewish community (Hamburg) to solicit the opinion of the sages, among them my opinion, about the above way of worship. My opinion:

It is well known that Daniel prayed three times daily. . . . Also the priests, performing the (sacrificial) service, prayed the *Amidah*, etc., . . . and for the restoration of David's dynasty, even though they were under the Hasmonean rule and that of Herod. . . . The Mishnah of Judah Hanasi and both *Talmudim* contain an abundance of laws about the daily prayers . . . which have been said for almost two thousand years without any objection. Now little foxes, the "darkies" (scum) of the diaspora (Reform Jews), rose to cause destruction and make changes, though "no court can annul enactments of another court unless it is greater in number (of its members) and in wisdom" (M. *Eduyoth* 1:5). Even if the reason for an institution does not hold any longer, the institution is not invalidated. This is especially true with respect to the prayers which have been said by the entire Jewish people. . . . No court can be larger in number (than the court that ordained the prayers) as the (highest) court is limited to seventy-one members.

[*Chatam Sofer*, in giving this view, cites Maimonides, *Mishneh Torah, Mamrim,* 2:2. The *Rabad* (Abraham ben David of Posquières, ibid.) claims that if the reason for an enactment is not antiquated, not even the Prophet Elijah can invalidate it. However, he differs with Maimonides in the case of an enactment which became antiquated, in which case the enactment can be invalidated even by a smaller court. Here, however, we have two reasons for the continuance of the traditional prayer service:]

1. The reason for its continuance has not become invalid. . . .

2. Even if the reason would have become invalid, and the Halachah would be in accordance with *Rabad*, a vote of the sages of our generation would be necessary . . . (which would result in the rejection of the reforms).

If they (the reformers) would say that the reason for the reestablishment of David's dynasty and of the Temple service has become invalid, since we now live peacefully among the nations, with regard to this I have already said (see above) that prayers for the rule of Judah (David's dynasty) were said all during the (Jewish) rulership of the Second Temple. . . . Therefore, such prayers would not offend our king and our princes. . . . In fact, even they hope to possess the city where their Messiah (Jesus) is buried (Jerusalem). Nehemiah was second only to the king in matters of honor and great wealth, but still sad about the desolation of the Jewish land. And the king did not resent it. . . . We are like prisoners since the destruction of the Temple. By God's grace we are treated kindly by the gentile kings and authorities, . . . and we have to pray for their welfare. . . . Nonetheless, it is not a sign of ungratefulness if we hope to return to our land. . . . all the nations and kingdoms know that we pray and hope for the coming of our Messiah . . . but never resented it. However, these men (reformers) either do not hope for, or do not believe in, the words of the prophets in regard to the rebuilding of the Sanctuary and in whatever the sages said in the matter. . . .

I say that they flatter the gentiles saying: "We are like you." They (the reformers) throw thorns into their eyes in taking a Christian to play in their temple as Samson, the prisoner, played in the temple of the Philistines against his will. We have to fear that the gentiles will say that the Jews are mocking us. . . .

Furthermore, if they say that the playing of the Christian is as if done by a monkey (i.e., to be disregarded as an integral part of the service), the result would be hatred between us and the gentiles. . . . even though some rejoicing (by music) is permitted in behalf of bride and bridegroom, yet in the synagogue no rejoicing (by music) is allowed, especially not on the Sabbath. . . .

As to their omission of the prophetic portion, this is contradicted by an explicit Mishnah (*Megillah* 3:5) and cannot be abrogated. . . .

The same holds true with respect to the use of non-Hebrew in public worship service. This is totally impossible. The statement of the Mishnah (*M. Sotah* 7:1) that the *Tefilah* (silent) prayer can be said in any language. . . . this can be done only occasionally . . . but a permanent reader must not use a foreign language in a public service . . . for an accurate translation into another language is impossible. . . . As to the objection that ordinary people do not understand what they say in Hebrew . . . it is better to introduce the requirement of learning the meaning of the prayers than introducing that they be said in a foreign language. . . . the holy language (Hebrew) is the language that God speaks (Nachmanides, beginning of *Ki Tisa* in Exodus); and our sages said that the world was created by using the holy language. God gave us the Torah in Hebrew, therefore we cannot talk to Him in our ordinary (non-Hebrew) language.

Therefore, what you said with respect to the holy synagogue is law. . . . It is a law that it is prohibited to use their (the Reform) prayerbooks, which are written in a foreign language. The text has to be Hebrew and the versions have to be old (i.e., traditional), as printed long ago. The organ must not be used, certainly not on a Sabbath . . . and I agree to prohibit (the above innovations) to every Jew. . . .

Pressburg, Tuesday evening, second day of the New Moon, Chanukah, (1818) 5559.

Chatam Sofer, responsum addressed to Akiba, rabbi of Posen
(Responsa, pt. 6, resp. 86)
[First, *Chatam Sofer* makes reference to a copy of his responsum
to the (Orthodox) congregation of Hamburg dealing with
the practices of the new congregation (Reform), to the books
נוגה הצדק *Nogah Hatsedek* and אור נוגה *Or Nogah*, which
he abbreviates א'ו'ן' *Aven*, meaning "sin."

Though he had already stated his view about the prohibition
of the organ in the synagogue in his letter to the Hamburg
congregation, he has since found a further reason to prohibit
the organ.] After the destruction of the Temple, in com-
memoration of the sorrow, only vocal music (singing) is allowed in the synagogue, but not instrumental music as this is
more pleasant. There was no עוגב *ugav*, (traditionally understood as meaning organ) in the Temple, perhaps because this
word has a sexy etymology (love, lust, posterior). . . . However, it was allowed in private homes, as correctly said by David
in Psalm 150:4 "Praise God with . . . organ. . . ."

A more likely reason for the prohibition against the organ in
the Sanctuary is the fact that the ancient idol worshippers used
this instrument exclusively in their temples, even before our
Sanctuary was erected. King David used the organ in his
private home just because the idol worshippers prohibited its
use in private homes and used it only in their temples.

[*Chatam Sofer* was appalled to read in *Nogah Hatsedek*,
p. 7, that the organ should be placed in the women's (section
of the) synagogue.] It is known that women do not have the
wisdom (skill) to play the organ. It is very difficult to push
the (pedal of the) instrument, and (therefore) a Christian man
plays it. . . .

[*Chatam Sofer* then justifies the employment of a gentile on
Yom Kippur night to watch the candles:] If fire breaks out,
lives would be in danger. This is misunderstood by some people,

and they ask the gentile to extinguish and kindle lights on Yom Kippur. . . . Though it is possible to (excuse) those who have the candles lit at *Ne'ilah* time by gentiles, I do not permit it. . . .

[*Nogah Hatsedek*, p. 25, . . . claims that we do not have to pray daily with a *minyan* (quorum of ten men). *Chatam Sofer* cites many passages from Talmud and Codes that praying daily with a *minyan* is required by law.

Chatam Sofer discusses at length the requirement to say the *Amidah* twice, once silently and once aloud. . . . Among the many details, it may be of interest that Sofer cites Sefardic practices, among them one by Maimonides, that in Moslem countries people are very particular in not spitting and talking during the prayer service, etc.

Sofer stresses the prohibition of separation, that is, of having different practices in one place (town). This includes customs.

Sofer criticizes the *Nogah Hatsedek*, p. 24, for the author's negation of the chanting which, in reality, goes back to Moses.

The Targum (Aramaic translation of the Torah), and translation in general, is discussed next. The (reading of the) Targum (in the synagogue) had been abolished because the people did not understand Aramaic.] But why is the Torah not translated in their language (the language of the land)? Because it is impossible to make a precise translation that truly expresses the intention of Scripture. . . . And such a translation in the synagogue would be equivalent to telling lies. At home, one may translate the Torah into any language. . . .

The above respondent urges one to say the silent prayer in Hebrew, but songs should be sung in pure German. I say, though there is not much calamity in singing such songs, however, if they do not understand the words of the *Shema* and the *Amidah*, why do they not order the people to learn and to understand Hebrew. Behold they did learn the languages of the gentiles.

[Sofer flails his (Libermann's) support of David's haters in advising against praying for redemption, and only praying for our peace among the nations, citing Jeremiah 29:7, but forgetting about Isaiah 62:7.]

If he must complain, he should complain against the One Who made him a Jew. . . .

[Sofer concludes the responsum with a tirade against Libermann.]

Chatam Sofer, responsum addressed to Abraham Eliezer, rabbi of Trieste (Responsa, pt. 6, resp. 89)

[*Chatam Sofer* agrees with those who prohibit the customs of the *New Sect* (=Reform). They permit the organ on the Sabbath played by a gentile organist.

However, the organ is an "Emorite" (heathen, non-Jewish) law (practice) in the house of idol worship. The word *ugav* (organ) may come from עֲגָבִים (*agavim*) (= love, lust, posterior) and therefore not permitted, just as *urine* is not permitted. And just as it was not permitted in the Sanctuary (of Jerusalem), so it is not permitted in the synagogue.

No instrument is permitted in the synagogue because of the words of Scripture: "How shall we sing the Lord's song in a foreign land?" (Ps. 137:4). This prohibition refers to the use of instruments. Singing, however, is permitted.

The following appears in the same source:] A rabbi, Daniel of Shimonta, had a question: A pregnant widow weaned her child three months after birth and wanted to remarry. I (the questioner) said, she must wait twenty-four months, as is the law. But the rabbi of Arad permitted her to marry immediately and expressed his readiness to perform the ceremony. Our ancestors were fools in this respect, why shall I be a fool?

[*Chatam Sofer* agrees with the questioner and adds:] Should there be some extenuating circumstances to permit it, the

matter lies in the hands of the great sages of our generation.
[Then he adds:] If we had the power over them (the Reform
Jews), my opinion would be that we ought to separate them
from us. We should *not intermarry* with them. They are like
Sadducees, Boethusians, Anan (founder of the sect of the
Karaites), and Saul (-Paul). They have their (religious practices,
i.e., their sinful religious conduct and are heretics), and we have
our (true Jewish) ways. All this seems to be true theoretically
(lit. "from the viewpoint of [theoretical] law"), but not in
practice (i.e., in reality we cannot declare them as being a
separate sect) since we do not have the royal permission and
edict. Besides, my words are in vain. Anyway, I wanted to comply with your wish and wrote to the congregations of Hamburg, Prague, and Brod to solicit the opinions of the great men
of the time and send their opinions to you.

SELECTIONS FROM לב העברי
Lev Ha'ivri
[The Heart of the Hebrew]
by Akiba Joseph Schlesinger
(Ungvár, 1864)

Lev Ha'ivri, p. 18a

. . . Once a rabbi was employed who preached his sermons in German. Our rabbi said: "I was told that he was a learned and pious man." The *gaon*, Rabbi Meir Ish Shalom, replied: "This is the way of the evil inclination. Now they elected a learned, pious man who preaches in a foreign language. Later they will elect an inferior man speaking German." And at the end he said in his holy language (Yiddish), "Kummt ays ein goy ayfzunehmen als rav" (Finally, they will employ a goy as rabbi). One great man present at this conversation said: "It is unbelievable how our rabbi hated that learned, pious man who used the foreign language." . . . And I said, when I saw that he died at half of his life span, that this was the result of the vehement curses uttered by the righteous of that generation. However, in truth, when I paid attention to the matter, I saw that most of the rabbis using a foreign language were truly pious and had erred, in that they were misled or coerced in this matter (i.e., preaching in a foreign language), and did not reach old age. Some of them were killed, others remained childless. The children of some went the wrong (sinful) way. . . .

Lev Ha'ivri, p. 18a

It once happened during the life of Rabbi David Deutsch (rabbi of Neustadt, father-in-law of Rabbi Meir Ish Shalom [Friedman]), some prominent men decided that they wanted to have their children taught the language and writing of the nations (i.e., of the non-Jewish environment). To this end, they hired a teacher who knew the foreign language (of the land). When the rabbi, of blessed memory, heard this, he remained silent. At the *Minchah* service on the Sabbath he bought all the *mitzvot* (the right who should be called to the Torah), and he himself went up to the Torah. The teacher was standing close to the *bimah*. After he (the rabbi) had said the blessing over the Torah, he said in a loud voice: "Moses, our teacher, handed us down this Torah scroll from God's hand. Rabina and Rav Ashi handed us down the Oral Law from him. Now this arrogant fellow came to uproot two Torahs. May he be uprooted! I am sure that the child who is under his tutelage will become a sinner." Hereupon a deadly fear befell these family heads (who hired the teacher). Immediately, on the following day, they sent the teacher back to the place from whence he came. He then traveled to Neutra and presented to the (non-Jewish) court there false accusations against the above rabbi. The court acquitted him.

Lev Ha'ivri, pp. 21 ff.

[Commenting on *Chatam Sofer*'s words: "Be heedful of changing (i.e., you must not change) your name and your language," Schlesinger says:]

Sofer does not refer to the family name but to the first name . . . e.g., if his first name is Aaron, he should not be called Adolf. . . . "Our ancestors were redeemed from Egypt for four reasons, one of them was: Because they did not change their names" (*Vayikra Raba*). . . . In another version of the above Midrash the reading is: "Because they did not change their *language.*" The wording in *Sefer Mitzvot Gadol* 50 is: "You must not follow the ways (lit. "laws") of the gentiles, neither with respect to their clothing, nor with respect to their customs. [After quoting a few biblical verses, Schlesinger continues:] "Accordingly, Israel must be separated from the gentiles in clothing, in custom, and in speech. . . . [Reference is made to Sofer's Responsa, *Choshen Mishpat*, resp. 197, to Jacob Emden and other rabbis. Then he quotes P. Talmud *Shabbat* (I.4; 3c ff.) where, among the eighteen prohibitions issued against the gentiles shortly before the war against Rome in 70 C.E. was also the prohibition against their language, i.e., we Jews must not speak their language.] These eighteen prohibitions cannot be annulled even by a court greater in wisdom and larger in membership (which are the accepted prerequisites for the annulment of an older ordinance), because for these our ancestors risked their lives. Accordingly, not even the Prophet Elijah and his court can abrogate them (Tosafot, *B. Avodah Zarah*, 36 a, s.v. והתנן).

Among the prohibited languages are *not* Hebrew, Greek, Aramaic, and Arabic (derived by *eisegesis*). . . . Accordingly, the Torah was given to Israel in these four languages as interpreted in *Sifre, Berachah*, on the passage, Deuteronomy 33:2 (the critical ed., like other texts too, has "Roman," not "Greek"; see *Sifre* on Deuteronomy, ed. Horowitz-Finkelstein, [Berlin, 1939], p. 395; see also ed. Friedman, ad loc. p. 142b). Syriac and Persian are included in Aramaic, as we are informed in Tosafot, *Bava Kamma* 83. . . . Our sainted ancestors, who were forced not to speak Hebrew, changed the language of the nations into Yiddish. . . . Thus we have to understand Rabbi Sofer's command that we must not change the language (i.e., replacing Yiddish by another language), since our Yiddish is, from the viewpoint of Jewish law, just like Hebrew. And thus

I heard and saw (a citation) in the name of the holy Isaac Luria that he used no secular language on a Sabbath, but talked in our language (Yiddish). . . . The language agreed upon by the Jews and used exclusively by them has the holiness of the holy language (Hebrew). Therefore, Rabbi Sofer ordained that the Jews must not change their language in our time, and this refers to our Yiddish. Since the Jews do not use among themselves the language of the nations, they do not transgress the above eighteen prohibitions. Translating the Torah into the language of the nations entails many sins: Transgression of positive and negative commandments. . . . Translating the Torah is prohibited by law as stated in *B. Kiddushin* 49. Exceptions are only the Aramaic translations by Onkelos and Jonathan ben Uziel. See *Shulchan Aruch, Even Ha'ezer* 38:25. See P. *Megillah* 6, the reason for the permission of translating the Torah into Aramaic and Greek. . . . The truth why we translate the Torah into our Yiddish is, perhaps, that it is not a specific language of the nations, but only a corrupt language. It offers, so to speak, merely hints and explanations, which constitutes no translation, since this is not done in a language accepted and used by an entire (foreign) nation. . . . However, to teach and to translate in a manner which is not noticeably Yiddish is not permitted by anybody. . . . Mordechai (ben Hillel) relates in *Megillah*, chap. 1, that Rabbi Joel prohibited the translation of the Torah for a proselyte into the language of the priests (non-Jewish ministers), which we call *Hochdeutsch* (High German, i.e., good literary German). . . . Our Mishnah (*Sotah* 7:1), which permits the use of foreign languages in certain instances (including the *Shema*, silent prayer, grace after the meal, etc.) does not contradict the eighteen prohibitions, since the foreign language he is using (and to which the Mishnah refers) is Yiddish. Or perhaps we have to explain it (the Mishnah) as did Rabbi Jonah: Occasionally (i.e., exceptionally) it is permitted. . . . According to *Magen Avraham*, chap. 590 (of *Shulchan Aruch, Orach Chayim*) it is permitted only if he cannot speak Hebrew. . . . All of you, who are using a foreign language, and all who are making any change in the ways of Israel . . . while the judgment of the wicked is twelve months (in Gehinom; see *B. Rosh Hashanah* 17) the (punishment of) heretics, sectarians, and informers . . . and those who deviate from the ways of Israel . . . (is that) they descend to Gehinom and will be punished there for many generations. . . . [Now he flails secular knowledge, which is studied in a foreign language.] You see that reform is real heresy and apostasy, which may come to realization by establishing a seminary, God forbid. Or to that which happened in Württemberg, where the prominent men took council, acted as informers to the government till they came to power, just as in our generation they intend to establish a seminary here to separate Israel from God by force. . . . Investigate the condition of our brothers, the Jews, in Germany, etc. . . . Amalek did not cause as much harm to the Jews as the harm intentionally done by this evil family (the reformers). May God save us from their hands and avenge the blood of his servants before our eyes. . . . They lead the children of sainted ancestors away from the heritage of their fathers toward sectarianism and heresy; and (may He avenge) the sin committed against the Jewish children whom they eternally killed in school with their murderous sword. Land, O land do not cover their blood! "For the oppression of the poor, for the sighing of the needy, now I will arise, saith the Lord" (Ps. 12:6).

Did the (Jewish) people of Württemberg believe a few years ago that this enemy would gather so much power that it would be necessary to make a law prohibiting one to enter the synagogue, called temple, wearing a *talit* and *tefilin*; and that the other synagogues would be closed, due to the activity of informers, by gentile courts. . . . many die . . . and their children cannot say *Kaddish*. At the time of Bar Mitzvah, the blessings over the Torah are written for them in foreign characters, because they don't know Hebrew or Jewish letters. . . . God will not forsake His people, but the future generations will throw stones upon the graves of these bad people. . . . How many rabbis did they ordain, who cause people to sin. . . . Vienna, Breslau . . . Everybody who supports this foreign (non-Jewish) matter, his soul is not the soul of Israel, as stated in the holy Zohar: They are the *erev rav*, the "mixed multitude" (who left Egypt with the Jews and caused all the trouble that followed the Exodus), and they will be identified before the Redeemer will come. . . .

SELECTIONS FROM שומר ציון הנאמן

Shomer Tsiyon Hane'eman

[The Faithful Guardian of Zion]

A periodical, Tuesday, 21 Mar-Cheshvan 5607
(Altona, 1846) p. 206

Letter from the sages of Jerusalem (pp. 20a–20b), transcript
from *Kinat Tsiyon*.
[This is a reply to a letter from Germany, printed and signed
by 116 rabbis, entitled *Shelome Emune Yisrael* (The perfectly
faithful of Israel). It is a letter complaining against the decisions
of the Brunswick Convention of the liberal rabbis. It also warns
the faithful not to yield to enticement but to remain firm in
their traditional beliefs and practices.] You must not listen to
the man who wants to change or abrogate the least detail, or to
permit that which is prohibited, or a Jewish custom—a custom
is like the Torah. Even if he brings unrefutable proof to substantiate his view, one must not listen to him . . . for he mocks
the words of the sages and is called a heretic (*min*) about whom
we pray everyday: "The heretics shall have no hope" (*leminim
al tehe tikvah*). These men arrived at this state because of their
haughtiness. They think they are wise men thoroughly understanding the Talmud and are smarter than the former sages. . . .
These men are like the men of Sodom. . . . they are like the
Karaites, who left the Jewish faith in the geonic period. . . .

It is your duty to strengthen the faith of the Torah of the chosen Jewish people. . . .

5606 (1846)

(The letter is signed by seven Sefardic sages in Jerusalem.)

Responsum about the innovations of the reformers in matters of the synagogue by Abraham Sutro, rabbi of Münster (1784–1869); issue 144 (Altona, Friday, 5 Shevat 5613 [1853]), p. 287. [Rabbi Sutro replies to a friend (not named) on questions concerning reforms and changes in the prayer service of the synagogue.]

1. Is it permitted to use the organ in the synagogue, especially on the Sabbath, since you heard that Reform rabbis permitted it? [Rabbi Sutro, referring to his book, *Milchamot Hashem*, prohibits it. He also cites *Betsah* 36 and interprets it as the source of prohibition.]

2. Is it proper to call a person to the Torah by a "card" (handing him a card) without calling his name? Know that the real intent of these reformers is that no name of a Jew should be mentioned any longer. Thus it is said in *Megillah* 21: "Monday and Thursday and on Sabbath *Minchah* three men read," and unquestionably, they are called (to the Torah) by name. . . . The widespread and universal custom is to call a person "so and so son of so and so." . . . See how our early rabbis endeavored to decide how to call to the Torah the son of an apostate since he cannot be called up by the name of his father, who converted (to another religion). Therefore, he is called up by the name of his grandfather. . . .

They (the reformers) also do not know what is known to people who are knowledgeable in regard to the events of the times in many prisons, and especially in Siberia, the severe punishment for the rebels and murderers is that their names are not mentioned any longer, but they call them: first, second,

third, lest they be remembered. My friend, look at the stupidity
of these fools (reformers). In their opinion hereby the men
called to the Torah are elevated, but, in reality, they utterly
degrade them, so that they be considered as people without
names and base people. In reality, we have to be sad about this
imbecilic people, but we are guiltless. . . .

3. . . . the teachers and the officers have the practice of
silencing the people when they pray aloud and with devotion as
did our forefathers. In this, too, they (the reformers) err and
cause others to err, because this is the way of the idols . . . of
the mourner whose dead (relative) lies before him. They do
not recite (aloud) even the *Shema*, which you have to hear.
These fools resemble the dead while still alive . . . only the
Shemoneh Esreh must be prayed silently. . . . And . . . who has
eyes to see will see and discern and will not listen to the whispers.

Responsum in matters of the Synagogue by Abraham Sutro,
rabbi of Münster (1784–1869); ibid (Altona, Friday, 12 Iyar
5613 [1853]), p. 305.
In this periodical (issue 144) it is shown and proven that we
have to sing and pray aloud in the synagogue . . . and the
practice in all the synagogues has been to say the *Shema* together (aloud). This is in contrast to the reformers, who put
the hand upon the mouth of the congregation lest their voice
be heard. . . .

I also was asked whether the playing of the organ was permitted in the synagogue; whether men and women were permitted to sing together in the synagogue. This, too, I mentioned in my book *Milchamot Hashem*, p. 111, saying that this
is a strict prohibition, since it is established for us: "The voice
of a woman is *ervah*" (nakedness, i.e., arouses men sexually)
(*Berachot* 24a). And in *Sotah* 48a Rav Yosef said: "When men
sing and women join in it is licentiousness. When women sing
and men join in it is like fire in tow. What is the practical

implication (i.e., the practical difference between the first and second case)? We must abolish the latter before the former."

But even without this, a Jewish woman's entering the men's section of the synagogue is an act of arrogance and lewdness, since in the Sanctuary as well as in all the synagogues a special section has been made for the women separating them from the men's section. . . . And all the intention of the reformers is to remove the veil of modesty from the faces of the chaste Jewish girls in order to make them like unashamed, lewd women. Now see how far the lewdness of the reformers has gone: In all other synagogues, the women are on a higher level (gallery). A curtain and a fence separate them from the men's section lest they look at each other. However, now in many new synagogues not only did they remove the fence, but they (the reformers) lowered the honor of the women to the lowest level. Not even a curtain separates them. Behold, it is known to knowledgeable people that the Pope in Rome commanded and warned that women and virgins must not sing in their theaters and circuses, since this appears to be an act of lewdness. Now, what the Pope prohibited in theaters, a place of entertainment and jesting, the reformers permitted in the synagogues a place of holiness and reverence.

[At the end of the above letter Rabbi Sutro strongly objects to reading from the Torah without chanting] . . . they do not read the Torah but announce it like the wood choppers and water drawers announce their merchandise in the markets and streets. . . . I praise our Jewish brothers in Holland and France who made no changes at all, not in the synagogue, nor in the laws of the Torah. . . . One who transgresses an explicit prohibition of the Talmud, transgresses the injunction of the Torah: "Thou shalt not turn aside from the sentence which they shall declare unto thee" (Deut. 17:11), as is stated in *Berachot* 19b. . . .

It is a definite prohibition to travel on a Sabbath by train. . . .

SELECTIONS FROM דרך יבחר
Derech Yivchar
[The Way to Choose]
Responsa by Chayim Bezalel Panet, rabbi of Tasnád (1803–74)

Responsum 1, against the "wicked"
[Rabbi Panet points out in this responsum that a man who talks to the public has to use the language of his people so that he will be understood. Therefore, he has to use the language that everybody understands—Yiddish, in spite of the fact that it has German roots. However, if one would speak in pure German, most people would not understand him. Then he attacks those who "waste their time" speaking the language of the (non-Jewish) peoples and studying secular subjects. He then flails the *Prediger* preachers claiming that they are igno-ramuses in Talmud and Codes, and are only smooth talkers. Therefore, they are unworthy as rabbis since they lack the required knowledge. Their smooth talk has no beneficial effect on the people. On the contrary, men of this "sect of the choir-temple desecrate the Sabbath, eat pork and other abominable food." These preachers have "no fear of God," therefore their words bear no fruit.]

We know that many of these preachers received secular education. They ate from their bread and sacrifices which are an abomination to us. . . .

We know of a man, who was appointed educator in a place

262

where a choir-synagogue was built, what happened to him: He ate for many years in a house of gentiles. . . . The essence of the matter is: It is better to attend the house of worship (church) of the non-Jews and listen to the sermons of their ministers called *Geistlicher* than to enter a choir-synagogue and to listen to the sermon of those preachers. . . . in their words there is hidden heresy that many people do not notice. . . .

Responsum 80, to Rabbi Jeremiah of Ujhely
[He refers to a letter from the (Orthodox) rabbi of Csongrád(?).] First he joins in with other persons' objections against establishing a seminary (in Budapest ?) whose task would be to destroy the foundation of our religion.

Then he complains about the *ame haarets* (ignoramuses) who are called "rabbis" or "preachers," but do not know Talmud and Codes, etc., and are only smooth talkers. . . . Yet, thank God, even in this generation there are great learned sages. For this reason these preachers, who mislead the people, cannot raise their heads against them, because the great men of our time would hit them over the head and ridicule them as they would point out to them, face to face, their ignorance in Talmud and Codes. Even in other fields of wisdom they are nothing in contrast to the Orthodox sages of Israel. For this reason they want to establish a seminary so that the Torah be forgotten by Israel, thinking as the generation of the flood. . . .

SELECTIONS FROM לפלגות ישראל באונגריא
Liflagot Yisrael Be-Ungaria
[To the Divisions of Israel in Hungary]

by Leopold Yekutiel Judah Greenwald, pp. 64–65

The Synod of Orthodox rabbis in Nagymihály, Hungary (now Michalovce, Czechoslovakia), 1865, made the following resolutions, binding for all Jews throughout the world:

1. With the exception of Yiddish, sermons must not be delivered in a foreign language.

2. Entering a synagogue and praying there is prohibited if the *bimah* is not in the middle of the synagogue.

3. Constructing a tower on the synagogue is prohibited.

4. Wearing special clothing (gowns), similar to those worn by the functionaries of other religions, is prohibited to cantors and other functionaries of the synagogue.

5. The partition between men and women in the synagogue must be made in accordance with the old tradition. That is, the men must not be able to see the women. A railing-type partition is prohibited.

6. Listening to a choir, or saying amen after the conclusion of their singing, is prohibited.

7. Entering into a choir-temple (liberal synagogue) is prohibited. Doing so would be worse than entering into a temple of idol worshippers.

8. Weddings may not take place in synagogues.

9. It is prohibited to change any Jewish custom or any traditional synagogal practice.

These resolutions were signed by seventy-one rabbis, corresponding to the membership of the Jerusalem Great Sanhedrin. This synod was called by the initiative of Rabbi Hillel Lichtenstein of Szikszó, Hungary.

SELECTIONS FROM מהר"ם שיק
Maharam Schick
Responsa by Moses Schick (1807–1879)

Orach Chayim, responsum 37 (Reply to a man, whom Schick does not know)

Re your congregation, which split in two, the new group being the *Neologen* (liberals): Now the *Neologen* repented and also abolished the choir on Yom Kippur. They only left the *bimah* stand at the front of the synagogue (instead of moving it to the middle as required by the Orthodox) because the people who have their seats in the middle would lose their seating if the *bimah* were moved back to the middle of the synagogue. Do we still have to consider them as *Neologen* and reject them? Is the meat of animals (including fowl) slaughtered by their *shochet*, whom they had prior to their repentance, still prohibited. . . ?

It is true that nothing stands in the way of repentance. Maimonides, end of chap. 3, *Laws of Repentance*, after explaining in detail that the wicked and heretics have no portion in the World to Come, wrote: "All are accepted if they repent." However, this refers obviously to God, who knows the thoughts and the hidden matters, or if there is clear evidence in the matter. On the other hand, we human beings, having limited vision, certainly must not rely on this. This is also the case elsewhere. See *Shulchan Aruch, Choshen Mishpat* 34, end. . . . The evidence for this is the *Mishneh Torah, Avodah Zarah* 2:5: "We do not accept (certain) sinners, even if they repent." The seeming contradiction of Maimonides' views in the matter is resolved by *Lechem Mishneh*, as we suggested above, i.e., that God, not man, will accept them if they repented with heart and soul. . . .

In our case, many congregations and pious Jews are unable to read the minds of the *Neologen*. My conviction is that in truth, they did not repent. . . . They are just waiting for the right opportunity to come. In the meantime, they are on the alert and gather strength. They are presently silent, because it is known that the group (*chevrah*) of Keepers of Faith, and the executive committee, watch out to thwart the plans of the wicked. . . . It was due to their (i.e., *Chevrah of Keepers of Faith*) endeavor that God gave us a victory, in that the emperor, judges, and the *Landtag* (legislature) endorsed and confirmed the laws of our, i.e., Orthodox, organizational statute. This is the reason why the *Neologen* are now silent. Therefore, every Orthodox Jew has to watch out not to fall into the net of the *Neologen*. . . . B. *Makkot* 6a states that a person who joins the sinners is, according to the Torah, like the sinners. Therefore, God-fearing people must keep afar from them. Their *shochet* is prohibited as before. Beware of making peace with them. . . .

Moses Schick of Brezova

Orach Chayim, responsum 70 (addressed to his disciple, Wolf Sofer, rabbi of Sengrot)
[The question concerns a decision of Rabbi Hillel Lichtenstein which prohibits one to preach in German. The questioner cannot find proof for this decision. It bothers him since the people only understand German. He also points to many similar problems decided by Rabbi Hillel Lichtenstein.

Schick admits that he has not seen the decisions of Rabbi Lichtenstein, but says he has received many questions concern-

ing them; with some of which he concurred, while with others
he disagreed.]

It is evident that since the Jews changed their ways and
acquired secular knowledge and speak the languages of the
gentiles, they have been learning less Torah. Many young men
forgot it altogether, and they abandoned the *mitzvot* and
piety. . . . There are many heretics and sinners. All of them
started their wickedness by learning foreign languages and the
wisdom of the gentiles. . . .

Our sages said in *B. Sanhedrin* 45: The cloth which was used
by the executioner to strangulate a person sentenced to death,
and the stone which was used to kill the condemned person are
prohibited for any further use and must be buried. Similarly, it
would be appropriate to bury everything that killed and stran-
gled the Torah, the *mitzvot*, and piety. Rabenu Asher wrote
to Rabbi Israel of Toledo concerning philosophy: "Thank God
that He saved us from it!" (Rabenu Asher, Responsa, sec. 55).
Do not cite evidence to the contrary from men who acquired
secular wisdom and remained pious. The minority does not
disprove our contention which holds true for the majority. . . .

If the deeds of a man are sincere and done out of faith, and
his intention is good, then I could find no reason to prohibit
him (referring to the use of German) in a place where people
do not want to listen to anything but German. Furthermore, if
he does not preach in German, they would replace him by another, unworthy rabbi, etc. I could not find a prohibition for a
God-fearing man to preach in German. [Now Schick quotes a
passage from the *Shitah Mekubetset, B. Baba Kamma* 3, citing
Meiri, which supports his view, but continues:] This was my
opinion in matters of preaching in German. But numerous colleagues opposed me, and I am compelled to accept their words in
reverence and trepidation, etc. [This means that Schick retracted
his former opinion, permitting pious men to preach in German,
because of the pressure brought upon him by his colleagues.]

Orach Chayim, responsum 71
(Huszt, 28 Tamuz 1866), addressed to Rabbi Mordechai Leib
Klein, Miklós, Hungary
[The question: What should Rabbi Klein do under the following circumstances: He has to support his family, wife, and ten little children as a teacher of the congregational *bet hamidrash*. Now reforms have been introduced in the synagogue of the congregation. The *bimah* is at the eastern end; there is now a choir with its members dressed as is customary (i.e., they are wearing robes). All this was done at the teacher's displeasure. Nonetheless, he did not resign from his job as of yet. Although he has to attend the services occasionally, he allowed himself to stay there in order to support himself and his family, and for the sake of peace within the family, which is very important. Should he not attend the synagogue, he would have to wander about (looking or begging for another job), and would have to neglect his study of the Torah. There are also health reasons, i.e., he is weak (ailing). Now he heard that many rabbis proclaimed a prohibition in print against the (i.e., such a) synagogue and choir, and that this prohibition is worse than eating pork. There is a doubt whether in this case martyrdom is required (i.e., he must rather die of hunger than continue in his job, as is required in certain instances, see *B. Sanhedrin* 74a–74b). In the opinion of the teacher, martyrdom is not required in this case, neither is it as serious as eating of pork.

The answer:] I have already given my opinion in writing briefly as well as in detail, elsewhere, concerning the synagogue and choir. The essence of the matter is that everyone who changes a Jewish custom and imitates the deeds of other nations, transgresses many prohibitions. [Now Schick quotes Maimonides and *Mecholat Hamachanayim*, where the possibility of required martyrdom is considered.] However, I already wrote that martyrdom does not seem to be required in this case. I also explained that the prohibitions are directed against those who make the reforms and like them. However, a person who prays there in his innocence because he has no other synagogue to which to go, or for another reason, does not transgress the above prohibitions. Nonetheless, the Torah prohibits him to pray there because it is prohibited to join the sinners, and we have an interpretation in the first chapter of *Makkot* that a person who joins the sinners is like the sinners. Even if a person does not pray there, but merely stands or sits there when others pray with the choir, in which case he might not be considered an active participant (lit. "joiner"), behold it is said in *Yoma* 70 that "seeing a *mitzvah* is a *mitzvah*." . . . This implies that seeing a sin is a sin. . . .

. . . Now let us see whether the above matter is as serious as eating pork. We read in Mishnah *Avot* (2:1) "Be heedful of a light precept as of a weighty one." . . . Here it is obvious that even if going there is merely a rabbinical injunction, it is still prohibited, for a man, even in order to support himself and his family, may not transgress a rabbinical prohibition, except in an instance where his life is in jeopardy. See *B. Sanhedrin* 26, Tosafot. . . . Furthermore, it is a decided Halachah that the extinguishing of a fire on a Sabbath is prohibited even if he (the owner) loses all his possessions and will become a public charge.

The reformers stretch the concept: The commandments are given to live by them (Lev. 18:5), i.e., not to die by them (B. *Yoma* 85b), and therefore permit everything claiming that otherwise their lives are in danger. They transgress the Sabbath and holiday prohibitions, the prohibition of taking interest and other laws of the Torah. . . .

[Schick cites *B. Eruvin* 21b:] Akiba was in prison, but had no water to wash his hands before eating and said: "Better that I die than to transgress the words of my colleagues." Akiba acted thusly because the time (i.e., special circumstances) prompted him to be stricter than normally required by law. We have to

act likewise today due to the needs of the times because the reformers strive to make the Torah and the *mitzvot* to be forgotten. . . . This is similar to a time of persecutions, except that
there physical force was threatened, but now they (the reformers) lead God's people astray by deceit. In this instance martyrdom and the abandonment of material goods are required.

I wrote all this as a reply to your question so far as the law
is concerned. However, I do not understand the matter itself.
According to your letter you receive your salary for teaching.
Why do you have to go and pray with the congregation? . . .
They know that you do not agree with them and do not want
the choir. Are they asking you to be a hypocrite? . . . In my
opinion, Jews are not inclined to cruelty, that is, to take revenge
on a pious man who teaches Torah, just because he does not
follow their ways. . . . The children of Israel are merciful. . . .
Certainly, because of this (merciful nature) they will not stop
supporting you as they did hitherto.

. . . I advise you to say openly to those who pay your salary
that it has now become clear to you that the reforms are prohibited for the Jews. God forbid that you transgress a weighty
or light prohibition because of sustenance. Even if you have to
go begging, you must not sell the right way for money. . . . You
must not pray in the synagogue with the choir. Even if you have
to travel to a place nearby or a place far away (in order to
make a livelihood) do it. . . . Make this public and don't be
ashamed. However, ask the leaders not to make the one matter
dependent on the other, since you are permitted to teach in
the *bet hamidrash* as before, they should not act unjustly and
take revenge. However, you and your family should be prepared to withstand temptation even if you will lack bread, in
case they do not want to support you as a teacher. God does not
forsake those who trust him in truth. . . .

Moses Schick of Brezova

Orach Chayim, responsum 304 (Huszt, Friday, 4 Nisan 5632 [1872]), addressed to Chayim Sofer, rabbi of Munkács.

[Schick confirms the receipt of Rabbi Sofer's letter in which he complains about the wicked, who desecrate God, who publicly rebel and reject the belief in the Messiah, the Kingdom of the House of David, and the restoration of the Sanctuary.] You suggest that they be excommunicated and their sons not be circumcised. I gave you my opinion on this matter once before and am now repeating it. . . .

I am surprised that you forgot that excommunication is prohibited by the law of the government, which we have to observe. . . .

I do not know whether circumcision should be denied to the sons of the sinners even if this would not be contrary to state law. . . . True, occasionally it is permitted to transgress a law of the Torah as a "fence of the law" (i.e., to protect and strengthen a law). . . . However, in this instance it is doubtful that denial of circumcision would serve as a "fence." . . . They are denying the roots of our religion, reject the entire Torah, abhor circumcision. They will be glad if they will have a good reason and excuse not to circumcise their sons. Therefore, I do not believe that denying circumcision would serve as a "fence." . . . In the case before us, in which they deny (implicitly) the validity of circumcision, and are ashamed only to say it explicitly, in denying them circumcision, we would merely support their desire.

Another reason for the above-said: According to the halachic authorities (given by Schick) only the greatest men of the generation or the leaders, appointed and recognized by the people, can ordain a "fence." . . . Who gave us authority to issue such an ordinance for another country? . . .

It seems that, according to law, we must not intermarry with them (i.e., the liberal, nonobservant Jews) because of the consideration of bastardy (i.e., nonobservance of certain laws has the effect that the resulting children are bastards). . . .

You were surprised about my reply to your view that we must not consult a physician who attends liberal synagogues. Since we are not permitted to excommunicate people, what is the source for your prohibition? Furthermore, you should have said: "Those who pray there and accept their (the liberals') texts of prayers and associate with them (should not be consulted)." I do not know why they should be rejected just for attending liberal synagogues. . . . A building in which there are no idols, or objects related to it, is not prohibited, even if people commit sins and heresy in it. The act of entering the synagogue itself is not prohibited unless we fear that the person entering would follow them (the heretics of the synagogue). However, even if we do not fear that a Jew would join them . . . it is still a *mitzvah* to keep four cubits away from the heretics. . . .

Moses Schick of Brezova

Orach Chayim, responsum 305, addressed to Abraham Samuel Binyamin, rabbi of Pressburg
[First, Schick chides the great Orthodox sages for their silence "on the day of battle" against the sinners (reformers).] . . . in contrast, Ezra and his followers expelled the Samaritans from the Jewish community, prohibited their bread and wine, like that of the gentiles of the land. . . .

Now heretics, evil rabbis banded together, attacked the Torah . . . and printed sinful legislation (protocols). . . .

Although we cannot excommunicate them due to a prohibition by the government, nonetheless, I do not know why we should not publicize the truth regarding the judgment (punishment) of these men, since they denied the divine origin of the Torah, as many of their utterances and heretical books testify. This being so, they are not Jews, but are worse than non-Jews,

as often explained by Maimonides. . . . They are not trustworthy
in regard to any ritual and law of the Torah, even less trustworthy as teachers and rabbis. . . . What they slaughter is
nevelah (nonkosher), as stated by Maimonides, *Laws of Shechitah*, 14. They are unfit to be witnesses and judges. Their
divorces and marriages are, of course, invalid, as written by
Maimonides, *Laws of Testimony*. Since they are like complete
gentiles, their daughters and sons are prohibited for us (i.e.,
for marriage). . . .

Just as the daughters of the apostates are prohibited for us
to marry, the same law applies to these heretics (reformers).
Even though in *Niddah* 33b the ruling is that the daughter of a
Sadducee is permitted to a Jew, Maimonides explains in his
Mishnah commentary, *Chullin*, chap. 1, that Sadducees and
Karaites are not like heretics (i.e., they are better than heretics=
reformers). They were made equal to heretics in many respects
only because they caused harm. This applied to the former
(talmudic) times, the reason being that they were afraid of the
sages of Israel, as explained in *Niddah*, loc. cit., and did observe
the Torah. However, after the Sadducees and Karaites had
been rejected as adherers of our religion, their daughters were
prohibited even after accepting the Jewish faith because of the
possibility of bastardy. . . . How much the more so should
these heretics (reformers), who left the (traditional) faith
and created a sect for themselves, be treated. . . . Their descendants may be bastards, and we are not permitted to
intermarry with them, even if they return and accept the true
(Orthodox) faith.

Since we have made it clear that their legal status is like
that of the gentiles, it is prohibited to worship in their houses
of worship. . . . wicked people are not members of the *minyan*,
but they recite the *Kaddish* and *Kedushah* (which is permitted only if there is a *minyan*). . . . Even if there are ten

kosher (observant) Jews, their reader is (halachically) not a reader, since he is not considered a co-religionist and cannot serve as our agent (representative).

This is the legal status, according to the Torah, of the wicked just discussed. Why should we not publicize this so that the ignorant people who still hesitate should fear for their souls and keep away from them? Therefore I beg you to alert the great rabbis to decide what to do to give strength to the Jews who want to hold fast to the Torah, and to thwart the counsel of the wicked. . . . This publication will do much benefit. It will also alert the great rabbis of Germany. Every rabbi who agrees with the letter of the pious Jews, shall sign it. . . .

Moses Schick of Brezova

Orach Chayim, responsum 306 (Month of Ab, 5637–1877) addressed to Isaac Beer Bamberger, rabbi of Würzburg Germany

. . . I have heard that you rendered a decision that if the Reform Congregation of Frankfurt am Main swears (guarantees) before the Orthodox community that they do not want to separate themselves in regard to every matter of the Torah, it is permitted to be with them within one community.

Truly, I do not know why you said this. In my opinion it is clear that this is prohibited to us by the Torah, by the Hagiographa, by our sages, and by consensus. And this is also supported by experience. Moses said on the occasion of Korah's rebellion: "Depart, I pray you, from the tents of these wicked men, and touch nothing of theirs, lest ye be swept away in all their sins" (Num. 16:26). . . . Our sages learned from this incident that we have to remove and excommunicate the wicked. . . . Thus we are commanded to be separated from them. . . . And Korah did not worship idols. He only rejected some parts of the Torah, just like the reformers of our day. I have no doubts that if excommunication would be permissible today, you would excommunicate them. . . . I am profoundly surprised why you permitted to join them. . . . Our sages said that they are like non-Jews. We are warned by the Torah to be separated from them more so than from the gentiles. It is permitted to accept certain sacrifices from the gentiles, but not from the apostates . . . and from those who publicly desecrate the Sabbath and from the heretics. . . .

The above prohibition is expressed also in the Hagiographa, Ezra 4:3, "Ye have nothing to do with us to build, etc." *Orach Chayim*, end of chap. 153, rules that whatever was forbidden with respect to the Temple of Jerusalem, is also forbidden with respect to the synagogue.

It is likewise prohibited to have a common cemetery with them, since we have the ruling that a wicked person must not be buried next to a righteous (Orthodox) person. You cannot observe this ruling in a common cemetery without much quarrel.

Furthermore, it is a matter of experience and consensus that those who associate with them do not become sinners. However, the following generations do become sinners. Prior to the last Passover a prohibition was printed, signed by more than two hundred rabbis, and it said: "Even if our opponents insist that we will have peace, we do what we want to do, and you do what you wish to do. Employ any rabbi you so desire, but let us be one group (community)." Do not listen to them. . . . I also received word from *Chatam Sofer* to stay afar from them as much as possible, and we must not be with them in the same community.

After I clearly stated my view, I beg you to change your mind. . . . Please admit the truth, lest innocent people stumble and God's name be desecrated by you. . . .

Moses Schick of Brezova

Yoreh De'ah responsum 169 (Huszt, Sunday of *Nitsavim*, 5638 [1878]), addressed to Rabbi Meir Kalisch
[Rabbi Kalisch informs Rabbi Schick that he rebuked the people of his community who had assumed gentile names. These individuals claim that it suffices to use their Jewish name when called to the Torah. This is nonsense, Rabbi Kalisch says, since changing the name is prohibited by the Torah. The proof text is Leviticus 20:26, "I will set you apart from all these peoples so that you may be mine," which is cited by Maimonides, *Laws of Idol Worship*, chap. 11. This verse is interpreted, according to the *Sifra*, just as we are prohibited to imitate gentiles in any respect, such as regarding clothing and other customs, how much the more so does the prohibition concern the acceptance of their names.

In his reply Rabbi Schick first relates an incident that occurred in Jargin, his former community: When he submitted the list of names registered with him to the official authority in charge, he got angry and said: "It is not proper that the Jews assume gentile names. . . . Other nations, Hungarians, Frenchmen, etc., do not change their names. They take pride in their names, whereas the Jews are ashamed of their names and change them, and assume the names of the gentiles. This is a disgrace." Rabbi Schick asserts that he was unable to give him a good reply and said, therefore, that the reason for this was the exile, i.e., that we have to live among the foreign nations.

This reply was weak, indeed, and Rabbi Schick continues, even though our ancestors had to suffer more under the yoke of the exile, they did not change their names. They were not ashamed of their Jewish names. On the contrary, they were proud of them. Today, however, although the yoke of the diaspora has eased, and the Jews are not despised by the gentiles, they change their names and language in order to resemble them. The Jews today do not want to bear the names of their ancestors. This is astonishing, since B. *Yoma* 38b states that we are prohibited to assume the names of the wicked because "the wicked man's name rots away" (Prov. 10:7). The Jews who assume gentile names show that they place the gentiles above the Jews. The "new" (i.e., modern) Jews despise their ancestors and martyrs and, at the same time, glorify the gentiles by giving gentile names to their children. One of the very reasons for our ancestors' exodus from Egypt was the very fact they did not change their names.

Whether the gentile (i.e., family) name should be entered on the bill of divorcement is a controversial issue, Rabbenu Tam prohibiting it (Tosafot B. *Gittin* 34b), and his decision is scrupulously adhered to in Poland. On the other hand, Rabbi Moses Sofer requires the entry of the gentile names in a bill of divorcement (in addition to the Jewish names) for a very good reason (see *Chatam Sofer, Even Ha'ezer*, resp. 118).

Rabbi Schick concludes his responsum with a remark that all his life he has warned his children not to transgress the prohibition of assuming gentile names, and they heeded his warning. Finally he suggests that others should follow his example so they will be blessed.]

Moses Schick of Brezova

Yoreh De'ah, responsum 331 (Yergin, 28 Shevat 5605 [1845]) [Sent to Tsvi Hirsch Lehren and to Rabbi Eliahu Abraham Prinz, whom he highly praises for printing their attacks against the blasphemies of the Karaites (reformers).] I am also ready at any time to smash and break the molars of the sinners to the limit of my strength. . . .

Last June various men assembled in Brunswick . . . and called it a convention of rabbis from Germany. The Satan also joined them, and they vehemently attacked God's Torah and the Oral Law. . . . They blasphemed God . . . denied the coming of the Messiah . . . made arrogant statements against our sainted Men of the Great Synagogue . . . among them the Prophets: Haggai, Zechariah, and Malachi. . . .

. . . They originated the nonsense printed under the title *Protokolle der ersten Rabbinerversammlung.* . . . They were not rabbis but Karaites, dressed in the garb of rabbis. . . . they did not reach the status of rabbis. . . . At night they went to bed with nothing, and in the morning they opened their eyes and were rabbis. . . . Some of them became known by their publications as heretics. . . . He who rejects the Oral Law is a heretic. . . . According to Maimonides they are like full gentiles with respect to trustworthiness. It is prohibited to eat the food they decide to be kosher. Their books are books of sorcerers, heretics, and it is a *mitzvah* to *burn* them. . . . they shall go to Mount Gerizim, to sectarians and Karaites. . . .

. . . What they said in specific, i.e., permitting to marry gentile girls, is a lie, since this is prohibited by the Torah. They remain gentiles until they convert to Judaism. . . .

What is true in this particular case applies to every instance they decided or are going to decide. . . . it is null and void. . . .

Moses Schick of Brezova, servant (=rabbi) of the Congregation Yergin, near Pressburg.

SELECTIONS FROM יהודה יעלה
Yehudah Ya'aleh
[Judah Shall Go Up]
Responsa by Judah Aszod (1830–1905)

Orach Chayim, responsum 3, addressed to Abraham Beck, rabbi of Holitsch.

The men of your congregation decided to change the location of the *bimah* against your will. They acted improperly and against the law as already decided by the author of *Chatam Sofer* (Rabbi Moses Sofer). . . .

[After discussing whether the placing of the *bimah* in the middle of the synagogue is a law or merely a custom, Judah interprets Maimonides' words to mean that the matter is a matter of law, not of custom. The reason given by Maimonides is that people would hear the reading or the preaching better if the *bimah* is in the middle of the synagogue. However, according to *B. Sukkah* 51, even without this reason, its place is in the middle of the synagogue.] It seems to me, too, that the real reason is that the reading of the Torah resembles the receiving of the Torah on Sinai, where the Israelites surrounded Mount Sinai, and the Torah was in the middle above them. . . .

[Afterwards Judah discusses the reason for the change in his time. He explains that in the Tabernacle, as well as in the Sanctuary, there were two altars:] A gold altar, which was the altar for the incense. It was used only in the morning and the evening, and just for a short period. Its place was at the *parochet*, i.e., front end of the Tabernacle (and Sanctuary). However, the copper altar, which was used all through the day and night, stood almost in the middle of the Tabernacle. . . . The *bimah*, made for the reading of the Torah, which has to be studied day and night, is comparable to the copper altar, the altar for the burnt offering. . . . the Torah takes the place of the burnt offering . . . it should be in the middle, just as the navel is in the middle of the body. . . .

However, the reformers, since they do not want to study the Torah constantly, compare the reading of the Torah and its study to the incense, not to the burnt offering. Therefore, they place the *bimah* for the Torah-reading in the front, comparing it to the golden altar, . . . lest everybody have an equal part in it (i.e., not everybody should hear it well), which would be the case if the *bimah*, like the copper altar, would stand in the middle. . . .

I urge you to strive with all your might to effect a change of their mind so that they would not carry out the above change. Also see to it that no other changes be made. . . .

Judah Aszod

[The responsum is followed by additional reasons of no great significance, advanced by the son of Judah Aszod.]

Orach Chayim, responsum 4

[Rabbi Aszod scolds the Jews who print the translation of the Talmud in the languages of the non-Jews because "a non-Jew who studies the Torah is guilty of death" (*B. Sanhedrin* 59a). He also gives another reason: "thou shalt not give a stumbling block before the blind" (Lev. 19:14). In addition, he quotes *B. Chagigah* 13a: "Rabbi Meir said: One must not communicate the words of the Torah to a non-Jew, as it is written (Ps. 147:-20): 'He hath not dealt so with any nation; and as for His ordinances, they have not known them.' " Tosafot, ibid., argues and cites, instead, Leviticus 19:14, but resolves the difficulty.]

Those new teachers who preach in German started the calamity by printing their sermons, including the sayings of our sages. [And now, who can object to them, and to whom would they listen if they go on printing extensive translations including the Talmud?]

The prohibition of teaching Torah to the gentiles applies only to the Oral Law, which was given orally and only to the Jews. But the Written Law was certainly handed down to everybody, etc. [Subsequently, he refers to a controversy in the matter.]

Orach Chayim, responsum 6, addressed to the rabbis of Germany and to Rabbi Hirsch Lehren of Amsterdam.
[The responsum is directed against the liberal rabbis convened in Brunswick and the changes of religious practices made there. Some of his principal complaints are: The rabbis of Brunswick intend to abrogate the Oral Law; to change and reduce (the number and content of) the laws of the Torah arbitrarily, including prayers. He compares them to Zimri, who committed a lewd act with a Midianite woman (Num. 25:6 ff.). A further complaint: They abuse all our customs.]

Another sin committed by the liberal rabbis assembled in Brunswick is that they printed their decisions in order to cause the people to sin. . . .

This is not a time to be silent. . . . Do all in your power . . . to restore the crown of the Torah to its pristine state. . . . These treacherous people forgot that a (Jewish) court cannot abrogate even insignificant customs or laws introduced by another court, etc. Even an assembly of great sages cannot do this. . . . [As an example, Judah cites Jonathan Eybeschuetz, who prohibited the drinking of nonkosher wine ("wine in general," i.e., not prepared by Jews).] This prohibition cannot be voided under any circumstances. It would be proper to excommunicate the rabbis assembled in Brunswick for all their sins, but we have to observe the royal law which prohibits this. We trust that God will exert beneficial influence on the governmental authorities in the matter. . . .

The above mob also decided to abolish the *metsitsah* (sucking of the blood after circumcision). Omitting the *metsitsah* does not merely endanger the child's life, as said in the Talmud, but violates also a *Halachah Lemoshe Misinai* (a certain type of ancient Sinaitic oral law). According to Maimonides the reason for the *metsitsah* is to weaken a man's excessive sexual desire.

[Subsequently, Judah chides the above rabbis for abrogating the *Kol Nidre* prayer. Then he scorns their arrogance for permitting one to marry a non-Jewish woman on condition that their children would be raised as Jews.] According to Jewish law such a marriage has no validity at all, and her child is like her (i.e., non-Jewish). In my opinion, they soon may permit one to commit incest. . . .

They also deny the belief in the coming of the Messiah. . . .

The decisions of the above convention are void, they are like a broken sherd. . . .

Semnitz, Sunday, 12 Tevet 5605 (1845)

Judah Aszod

Orach Chayim, responsum 35, addressed to the leaders of the Congregation Würzburg, headed by Chayim Kraus.
[The leaders of this congregation complain about a modern rabbi in their town and Rabbi Aszod repeats four of his transgressions:]

1. The rabbi wrote something in German on Rosh Hashanah in the presence of witnesses.

2. He publicly announced and wrote to the heads of the Jewish congregation that the Men of the Great Synagogue, because of the spirit of the time, abrogated the sacrificial cult and replaced it by prayers and pleasant songs.

3. He wanted to entice his congregation that they consent to abolish the second day of the holidays legislated for the diaspora (the lands outside Palestine).

4. He personally shaves his beard with a cream during the intermediate days of the holidays.

Now you want to know whether you are permitted to keep him or are obligated to dismiss him. . . .

. . . According to the law of the Torah he is unfit to render a decision on the basis of any one of his four transgressions. He cannot serve as a rabbi at all because he is a heretic. . . . Maimonides said, *Sanhedrin*, chap. 4: "If a man is unfit to serve as a judge or to render a decision in a matter concerning religion because he is ignorant or unworthy, but received the authorization by error . . . such authorization is invalid." . . . accordingly, the rabbinical authorization of this man must be revoked. It is prohibited to accept his decisions, and his rabbinical diplomas, if he has any, are null and void. . . .

Judah Aszod

Orach Chayim, responsum 36, addressed to the heads of the congregation in Weissenberg.

[Judah replies that the complaints contained in the letter he received are legitimate. The essence of the complaints is that the sinners trample on the *Shulchan Aruch*, on the laws and customs contained in it. In replying Judah points out, among other things, that according to the Talmud (*Sanhedrin* 110), except for synagogue customs, no custom whatsoever can be changed, even after the reason for the custom became invalid.]

A custom overrides a law (*Shulchan Aruch, Choshen Mishpat*
232:19). . . . It is also prohibited to change customs of the
synagogue as the reasons for them are still valid. . . . Who
dares to violate the customs of the *Shulchan Aruch*, which were
accepted and confirmed above (by God) and below (by men),
in the Land of Israel and abroad more than three hundred years
ago. . . . If there are knowledgeable men in the group of
sinners in your congregation, there is even more lawlessness
there. . . . And if they speak without knowledge, a thousand
ignorants do not count as one man. If there would be a vote,
they would not count. . . . Regarding the group of sinners,
even if many rabbis are among them, every change of the laws
and customs of the *Shulchan Aruch* they want to make, is
invalid. . . . Every pious man must keep away from them. . . .

The sect of the innovators effected the closing of your synagogue and school by the non-Jewish authorities. Before matters are restored, you will fulfill your duty by praying privately
without *minyan* of ten men. I wish my words would be printed
in Hebrew and translated into a foreign language, perhaps they
would awake. . . . Yet even if this will not help, God will
punish them. . . .

Judah Aszod

Orach Chayim, responsum 37, addressed to the leaders of the
congregation in Gyula (Hungary).
[The leaders of the congregation in Gyula complained that the
(new) rabbi omitted certain prayers and altogether changed
the liturgy of Rosh Hashanah. The rabbi, too, complained to
the secular authorities that the congregation would not permit
him to preach again. Judah Aszod said:] I saw the sermon he
preached on Rosh Hashanah and felt very distressed over the
suffering of this generation. . . . They appointed a rabbi who
is ignorant, lacking the fear of God and Torah. . . . Had he had

a trace of reverence, he would not have desecrated God's name
so profoundly. . . . Even Yom Kippur does not atone for this. . . .
He has no portion in the World to Come. . . . He was appointed
by the gentile authorities, against the will of the congregation
and the sages. It is prohibited to rise before him or to honor
him in any manner. . . . As soon as the complaints about him,
which had been lodged by great men, reached me, I instructed
my disciple, Rabbi Deutsch, rabbi of Ipolyság, to publish
in all the newspapers that he voids the writing (document) he
gave him, and that his *semichah* is null and void. . . . According
to the reply of Rabbi Deutsch, he never gave him a *semichah*,
and the preacher Back (or Bock) deceived you. . . . *Shulchan
Aruch, Yoreh De'ah* 246:8, rules that if a rabbi does not walk
on the right path, though he may be a great scholar and everybody may need him, it is still prohibited to study Torah with
him, and even the more so to rely on his decisions. . . . I advise
you to send literal copies of this letter to the outstanding rabbis
asking them to do their part. As soon as you will receive three
more letters from three famous rabbis, the emperor and government officials will, undoubtedly, approve the decision of the
rabbis to eradicate the evil from your midst. . . . The three rabbis
should be the rabbis of Pressburg, Ujhely, and Grosswardein.
Do not publish this letter before you have received their letters
of consent. . . .

Judah Aszod

Orach Chayim, responsum 38, addressed to Rabbi Beck, Holitsch
The question is whether the wedding ceremony may take place
in the synagogue. It is a good omen to have the marriage ceremony under the sky, as is our old custom. See *Shulchan Aruch,
Even Ha'ezer*, end of chap. 61.
    I am afraid that having the marriage ceremony precisely in
the synagogue constitutes a transgression of a law of the Torah:

"Ye must not follow their laws" (Lev. 18:3). True, Rabbi Jacob Levi relates that in Mainz it was customary to have marriage ceremonies in the synagogue. However, who can tell that at that time and in his place the gentiles had their weddings in their churches?

What is most painful is the fact that by making reforms they are wasting precious time to find proofs for changing a custom, to abolish or to uphold it, and neglect the occupation with Torah and important Halachot.

I beg you to use all your power to prevent any change in your place, in accordance with the established principle that custom voids law. The sages allowed many matters which are contrary to law to stand in order not to void a custom, as is known. How much the more so is it that they upheld a custom which is like a law. . . .

Judah Aszod

[Afterwards, Rabbi Aszod suggests to give eleven reasons to the authoritative person for having the wedding in the open.] (1) *B. Kiddushin* 52: Women were not allowed in the Temple Court (of the Sanctuary), etc. (2) She might menstruate because of the fright. . . . (3) Wedding under the sky is a good omen. (4) In the synagogue, men and women would mix. (5) When she is menstruating, she does not go to the synagogue, women's section. (6) It is prohibited to change a custom. (7) A wedding resembles the giving of the Torah. . . . (8) It resembles the sanctification of the moon (which is to be done in the open). (9) A reason for our custom may be to compensate for the sin committed by the Jews when they made the golden calf, when they permitted publicly committing incest. . . . (10) To publicize the joyous *mitzvah*. . . . (11) To permit the wedding in the synagogue only falls under the prohibition in Leviticus 18:3 (see above). I have more good reasons, but it is time to be brief.

The Above

Orach Chayim, responsum 39 addressed to several men, whom Aszod does not name.

Re your request asking me to give you the Torahitic view in regard to a synagogue which newcomers to a certain town want to tear down, in consonance with the spirit of the time, and want to replace it by synagogues resembling the temples of other religions ("choir temples"). They also introduced their ways (tunes) of singing, their type of clothes, etc., so that many men of other religions testify that these synagogues are exactly like their temples. You want to know whether such a synagogue is permissible. . . .

[Aszod forbids the new synagogues resembling churches, their mode of singing, the clothing of the cantors, and even more the change of customs. All this is contrary to the religion of the Torah as clarified in the *Shulchan Aruch*.]

Experience tells us that what is happening there are indications of innovations called reforms and are as such contrary to our religion. . . . The Orthodox Jews must prevent the building of such a synagogue and must refrain from praying in it. . . . We must not make any change. . . .

I wrote a responsum to the congregations of Weizen and Jormato, because they wanted to build a tower (steeple) on top of the new synagogue. I inform you that this is prohibited by the Torah (Lev. 18:3). . . . If seven-eighths of them permit a matter, and one-eighth Orthodox Jews prohibit it, and they are right, it would be a desecration of God's name to follow the majority rule. . . . See what I wrote to the congregation Weissenburg. . . .

Judah Aszod

SELECTIONS FROM בית הילל
Bet Hillel
[The House of Hillel]
Responsa by Hillel Lichtenstein (1815–1891)

Responsum 13, on Azriel Hildesheimer (Halberstadt, 1820–
Berlin, 1899) addressed to Rabbi Meir Auerbach, Jerusalem
[After some introductory remarks, Rabbi Lichtenstein criticizes, in derogatory terms, Azriel Hildesheimer, who wants to
establish a school in Jerusalem. He is characterized as a man]
of deceit, a liar, out for only monetary gain, wrapped, so to
speak, outwardly in a garb of righteousness which outwardly
justifies his deeds, like a pig that stretches forth its hoofs . . .
so that many are caught in his net. . . . I only publicize this so
that this "abominable troubler" who intends to destroy the
Jews . . . in that all he intends to do is to uproot the Torah,
the fear (of God) . . . and to increase faithlessness and heresy
in Israel. The city and its surroundings, which before were like
the Garden of Eden, have been left after him as a wilderness,
destroyed by foreigners.

[Quoting Chayim Sofer, author of *Machaneh Chayim*, etc.,
he continues:] "May God have mercy over His land because
הרשע הילדסהיימער the wicked man Hildesheimer is the
horse and the wagon of the evil inclination (יצר הרע), his
strength and success have not come in a natural way, but the
demon of Esau rides on him. All the sinners who rose over a

period of many years (or: a hundred years) did not accomplish as much as he did in destroying religion and faith. . . . were it not that God left us a small remnant, all of Hungary would have turned to heresy by him and his evil agents. . . . "'You must write a letter (to the rabbis) so they know that God will not forgive them if they do not join in a great assembly to excommunicate the man . . . who wants to set up an idol in the Holy City . . .'" (end of quotation from Chayim Sofer).

In regard to the matter proper, i.e., establishing (Jewish secular) schools . . . this is just like willfully taking Jewish children . . . to the priest so that he teach and sway them to deny God and His Torah and all the principles of our faith, and sprinkle upon them that water . . . so that they would no longer be called Jews. . . . He who does this is a worse enemy than Pharaoh and the wicked Haman, because they tortured the body only, but the others are murderers of the souls as the sages said: "Worse is the man who causes a person to sin than the one who kills him." And such wicked people commit considerably worse wickedness than the enticing priests, called missionaries, since the latter rarely succeed and have to spend much money in the process . . . but as for these men who are ensnaring many souls, my heart aches for their corpses. . . . Now everyone who has brains in his skull clearly sees the heresy and foolishness . . . of that "abominable wicked man who causes this wickedness" . . . he destroys them so that they would not have eternal life. . . .

Now "my brothers and friends" assemble and be one nation . . . and do everything in your power to exult the Torah and the fear of God, and do not be afraid of "these tails of smoking firebrands" (Isa. 7:4) (because they are the agents of the devil . . .). . . .

Hillel Lichtenstein of Vécs, rabbi here (in Kolomea).

(Responsum 39, addressed in 1863 to an unnamed rabbi in an unnamed city
[Rabbi Lichtenstein complains that] the Jews of the diaspora learned to speak the pure language of their respective countries. So did their leaders, and the devil of every nation cleaved to them. As a result, they interpret the Torah in a blasphemous manner at variance with the Halachah; they are hypocrites, liars, twisting the words of our Holy Torah anyway they want to. . . .

[Then he attacks the *Prediger* (preachers), whose intention is to follow non-Jewish ways] It is prohibited to keep peace with them. . . . They are worse than their sinful ancestors because they were known as wicked people by everybody, but these (leaders of our day) dress themselves in the garb of the rabbinate, are considered to be pious men. . . . And this is not even enough for them, they also want to be considered Chasidim, mystics . . . to bless Israel and give them amulets. . . .

[Later he speaks about an individual rabbi, Azriel Hildesheimer (see Greenwald, *Letoldot Hareformatsia*, p. 73), without mentioning his name,] whose reputation was that he was a fully righteous man. But woe to us, because the damage which he wrought in our country (Hungary) is unbelievable. Thank God that he saved us by leaving us. But woe to us, because these evil beasts (like Hildesheimer) are not like other evil beasts, which are gone when they leave, since when he was to leave us, he still remained here. He did not want to leave the place until a sinful rabbi speaking a foreign language was appointed. . . .

A foreign language must not be mixed with our Torah, and no one speaking it shall enter our camps, since our camp must remain holy. . . .

SELECTIONS FROM מלמד להועיל
Melamed Leho'il
[It Teaches to Be Useful]
Responsa by David Hoffmann (1843–1921)

Part 1, responsum 16, (pp. 11–19)
Question:

In a city (not named) the officers of the congregation decided to install an organ in the synagogue. The rabbi of the congregation tried the best he could to prevent this, but did not succeed. Therefore, he wishes to choose the lesser evil and permit the use of the organ on weekdays, e.g., for weddings and on the birthday of the king. Consequently, they would not desecrate the Sabbath. Moreover, he is afraid that if he resigns because of the organ, another rabbi will take his place who would not only permit the organ, but would introduce other reforms (lit. "great calamities"). Therefore, the rabbi asks whether he should remain there and permit the use of the organ on weekdays.

Answer:

[Before answering the question, Rabbi Hoffmann surveys the literature on the subject in great detail. In doing so, he concentrates on the responsa published in *Eleh Divre Haberit* in 1819, when the problem became acute in Hamburg, where, in addition, many other reforms were introduced in spite of the strong opposition of the Orthodox *bet din*. All the Orthodox authorities responding to the question agreed that it was prohibited to play the organ in the synagogue on the Sabbath and on holidays, even if the organist were non-Jewish. However, they did not agree on the question as to whether playing of the organ on weekdays was prohibited. Examining the above responsa, Hoffmann found three opinions:

1. Some of the respondents prohibited the organ on Sabbath and holidays, but made no decision with regard to the weekdays. This may mean that the organ is permitted on weekdays; but it may also mean that the matter was doubtful in their minds, and they did not want, therefore, to render a decision one way or the other (the rabbis of this category are found on the following pages of *Eleh Divre Haberit*: the members of the Orthodox *bet din*, at the beginning of the book, the others on pp. 1, 23, 25, 28, 29, 50).

2. Some of the rabbis explicitly permitted the organ on weekdays (the *bet din* of Prague, p. 17; ten rabbis of Livorno, p. 67, who also permitted the organ on the intermediate festivals, but the organ must only be played by pious Jews).

3. Some rabbis prohibited the use of the organ in the synagogue on the Sabbath as well as on weekdays. The foremost authority in this category is *Chatam Sofer* (Moses Schreiber), p. 9 (others on pp. 5, 18, 61, 76, 81, 85). Hoffmann also lists in this category Rabbi Judah Aszod, a later authority who cites his teacher, Mordecai Benet, though he explicitly prohibits the organ for the Sabbath only.

Hoffmann now cites several later authorities who prohibit the organ for the Sabbath as well as for the weekdays, referring to the biblical injunction: "neither shall ye walk in their statutes" (Lev. 18:3).

Hoffmann then remarks that the ordainees of the Hildesheimer Rabbinical Seminary (of which he was the head)

receive a document, together with the rabbinical diploma, stating that the organ is prohibited because of the above injunction
(Lev. 18:3). Accordingly, it is prohibited on weekdays just as
on the Sabbath. This is also the opinion of Rabbi Samson
Raphael Hirsch (Commentary on Leviticus, loc. cit.)

After having cited the above opinions, Hoffmann investigates
four aspects of the problem before giving his own opinion.
These aspects are:

1. Was there a musical instrument similar to our organ in the
Sanctuary of Jerusalem? After discussing the opinions of a
number of rabbis, he also states that the famous composers
Meyerbeer and Bartholdi declared that the organ disturbs the
pleasant melody (Hoffmann does not give the source for this
information). Weighing the literature on the topic, Hoffmann
says that apparently there was no organ in the Sanctuary.

However, even if there was an organ, it was not better than
the *matsevah*, pillar (altar). This was beloved in the days of our
early ancestors but became an object of hatred (and was
prohibited) later because it became an object of idol worship.

2. Re the organ in the Prague Jewish community. Those who
permit the organ in the synagogue cite as evidence the fact that
in a synagogue in Prague there was an organ, and nobody
objected. Hoffmann quotes from *Eleh Divre Haberit* (p. 5)
that Prague had nine synagogues, but only in the biggest one
was there an organ, and the music accompanied the reception
of the Sabbath (*Kabbalat Shabbat*). However, the music ended
before reciting Psalm 92. But after the organ went bad, it was
not repaired. (The rabbi of Prague wrote to Rabbi Hoffmann
that the organ was not in the Altneuschul, but in the Meisel
Synagogue.)

Hoffmann now explains, by way of a conjecture, why the
organ had been installed in Prague. There is a prayerbook
printed in 1678 in Amsterdam. In this book a song (poem) is
printed before *Lechah Dodi* and the heading says: "A nice

song by Solomon Singer, played in the Meisel Synagogue in Prague on *ugav* (organ) and lyre before *Lechah Dodi*." The text of this poem indicates the reason for permitting the use of musical instruments to receive the Sabbath. The poem praises the Sabbath, connecting it and Israel symbolically with bride and groom, emphasizing joy and pleasure. This may mean that since it was permitted to play music in honor of bride and groom, similarly, the rabbis also permitted to play music in honor of Queen Sabbath and her mate, Israel.

[Hoffmann now cites a conjecture by Rabbi Abraham Emden in *Tseror Hachayim*, p. 6b, saying that perhaps this synagogue and organ were built before the gentiles used the organ in their services. In fact, we heard, this synagogue was standing there since the times of the Second Temple of Jerusalem. Since it was built without violating a law, the prohibition of adopting gentile laws did not apply, and therefore remained unchanged. However, when it went bad, it was not kept any longer because at that time the organ had already been used exclusively in the temples of the gentiles for their services, and is therefore prohibited for us.]

[Hoffmann doubts the validity of this conjecture and suggests, instead, another conjecture. It is more probable that the Jews in Prague believed that the organ was given in the Torah as one of the musical instruments of the Temple, and he cites a rabbi's view in support of this conjecture. The Jews of Prague thought that its use was permitted since we did not take it over from the gentiles. Since they later abandoned the organ, this proves that they erred when they installed it.]

It is inadmissible to cite as evidence the custom of one single congregation and shut the eyes before all the other congregations. We have not heard of another instance before the time the reformers ("destroyers") gained power. [Hoffmann adds at the end of this section another, less plausible, conjecture.

3. Prohibition of the organ because it is one of "their laws."

Hoffmann points out that the Hebrew term *Chukotehem* (lit. "their laws"), as used here, does not mean "idol worship" but "foreign cult." This is done lest we think that the organ, used by Christians, is an object of idol worship and therefore prohibited. Then he discusses the explanations of a number of halachic authorities who claim that the organ is prohibited because it is an instrument of a foreign cult, and it is a prohibition of the Torah.

4. Prohibition of the organ because its use constitutes an imitation of the heretics (reformers). Hoffmann states that even if we could say that the organ is not an instrument of idol worship (or foreign cult), it still cannot be permitted because its adoption would be an imitation of the heretics.] It is known that the reformers ("destroyers") began their law-breaking activity with the adoption of the organ. In connection with it, they publicly desecrated the Sabbath, changed the prayers, rejected the belief in the coming of the Messiah, and committed other abominations, in spite of protestation by Orthodox rabbis. Now, if we permit the organ, the reformers will say: "We introduced the organ by force, and now the Orthodox rabbis approve of it." Soon they will permit other prohibited matters, which are, in their opinion, contrary to the spirit of the time. . . . It will not take a long time and, in connection with the organ, women-choirs will be heard in the house of worship. . . . They testify by their changes, that they deny the promises of the prophets saying that the *Shechinah* will return to Zion and the sacrificial cult to Jerusalem. . . .

[Hoffmann disagrees with a rabbi who prohibits the organ because of mourning for the destruction of the Temple in Jerusalem. For this reason, other instruments are also prohibited, though they are permitted at weddings and in honor of the king.]

[Conclusion: It is clear that the organ cannot under any

circumstances be permitted even on weekdays. However, if a rabbi permits the use of the organ at weddings and in honoring the king under compulsion or because of a need, relying on some authorities who prohibit it on the Sabbath only, and has the excuse, i.e., that it is not used in the worshipping of God. . . . because of this sin I do not intend to renounce his rabbinical diploma which I issued to the student. However, he must publicize why he gave the permission lest others learn from him to permit it altogether. Whenever such a case comes before us, we have to scrutinize it very carefully]

Wednesday, second day of the New Moon of the First Adar, (1897) 5657.

[In the postscript, he adds two more negative opinions, but does not discuss them.]

Part 1, responsum 29 (pp. 28 ff.)
Question:

In our *minyan* there are one or two men who publicly desecrate the Sabbath, not merely by working but also by smoking. They do not even make *Kiddush* and *Havdalah*.
Answer:

[Hoffman cites halachic authorities who hold that a man publicly desecrating the Sabbath cannot be considered a member of the *minyan*. He also cites an authority believing that every transgressor is a member of the *minyan* as long as he had not been excommunicated. However, this authority (Yaviz) does not explicitly say that a man desecrating the Sabbath publicly also counts as a member of the *minyan*. It is possible, therefore, that he would not count him in this instance as a member of the *minyan*. Hoffmann also quotes authorities stating that a man who is publicly wicked cannot be counted as a member of the quorum (three) for the grace after the meal. Now Hoffmann quotes other authorities stating that this (exclusion of sinners) applies only to a man who sins merely to vex the pious. Today, however, they do not transgress the law for this reason. According to another authority and in another instance, witnesses have to testify against a person that he desecrated the Sabbath in the presence of ten Jewish men in order to take action against him.

The implication of all this is that, according to the law, a man who publicly desecrates the Sabbath is not to be a member of the *minyan*. However, today the custom is to be lenient in Hungary, and how much the more so in Germany. Hoffmann now cites an incident where a member of an Orthodox congregation whose store was open on the Sabbath was prevented from reading the service. Then he went to another Orthodox synagogue, where he was permitted to do so. When the man responsible for this leniency was questioned about the matter, he replied: "This has been the custom in this synagogue for many years. Since the rabbis of this synagogue were illustrious men, they must have had good reasons for upholding the lenient custom." Since these reasons were not transmitted, Hoffmann conjectures that they may have relied on responsum 23 in the New Responsa *Binyan Tsiyon*. Accordingly, people desecrating the Sabbath in our time resemble, somewhat, an infant captured by gentiles (and growing up among them, without knowing that he is Jewish. Such a Jew is not responsible for his transgressions). This comparison is justified, because most of the Jews in our country desecrate the Sabbath, but have no intention to deny the principles of our faith.] And thus Rabbi Meshulam Zalman, in the name of the author of *Sho'el Umeshiv* (Josef Saul Halevi Natanson), informed me. He wrote that the Jews of America are not disqualified for desecrating the Sabbath, because they are like infants captured by the gentiles. Later I found a similar explanation in the *Notes of Rabbi*

Akiba Eger on Yoreh De'ah, chap. 264. [Then he cites some works with contrary views.] May it be as it is, he who is lenient in including such men into the *minyan* has a basis to rely on. However, if a person is able to go to other services without shaming a man and pray with pious people, this is certainly better than relying on the lenient decision.

There is still another reason to be lenient. In our time, they are not called "public desecrators of the Sabbath," since most people do it. Certainly, if most of the Jews would be innocent, and only a few would be arrogant in committing the transgression, he (the transgressor of the Sabbath) would justly be considered a heretic in regard to the Torah and a doer of an abominable thing highhandedly and as one who turns his back to the Jewish community. However, since most of the Jews are sinners, their transgressions turn into their advantage. The individual Jew thinks that this is not such a great sin and does not have to commit it in privacy. On the contrary, the pious ones are called today separatists, and the sinners follow the normal path (lit. "the path of all the land").

Part 1, responsum 41 (pp. 53–54)
[Rabbi Barbash, a native of Russia, now resident of Seden, Germany, received permission to travel to Russia to his family and children. Since the trip may take seven days, he might have to travel on the train on a Sabbath. In his letter of inquiry, addressed to Rabbi Hoffmann, the learned questioner cites several sources which indicate that he is permitted to undertake the trip.

One of the decisive questions in the matter is whether the trip is undertaken for the sake of a *mitzvah* or not. If the purpose of the trip is a *mitzvah*, leniency may be in order. The presently intended trip is certainly being done for the sake of a *mitzvah*: for raising them (his children), giving them a Jewish education,

and supporting them. Subsequently he cites the opinion of Rabbenu Tam, who holds that every trip is considered a trip for the
sake of a *mitzvah*, with the exception of a vacation trip. The
lenient views which Rabbi Barbash cites pertain to travel by
boat and wagon, since there were no trains in former times.

Rabbi Hoffmann, in his answer, supports Rabbi Barbash's
conclusion, though he rejects some of his proofs. He adds
supplementary proof permitting Rabbi Barbash to undertake
the journey. Most interesting is his reference to a number of
early authorities (*rishonim*) who maintain that no man has the
right to object to a lenient custom in this matter (of travel on
the Sabbath).]

Part 1, responsum 63 (p. 85)
Question:
The cantor of the local synagogue (place not given) is using
a tuning-fork in the synagogue, claiming that he could not sing
otherwise. I was told that in Russia this causes no concern even
on the Sabbath, and all the members of the choir are using it
on the Sabbath. My question is: Shall I object to the matter?
Answer:
[In my humble opinion we must prohibit the use of musical
instruments on Sabbath, even where a *mitzvah* is involved,
especially in our time, when most German (Jewish) congregations commit a sin by using the organ (see chap. 16). I have
already shown that according to some talmudic opinions, the
use of musical instruments on the Sabbath is a prohibition of
the Torah. Even though this opinion was not accepted, nonetheless the prohibition was considered by our ancestors to be
a serious one. However, since there are rabbis (i.e., Orthodox
rabbis) who permit the use of the tuning-fork (Hoffmann
names them), I say that in such a case where the cantor cannot
sing well otherwise, it is not necessary to raise objections. Better

if he does it in his innocence (i.e., while unaware that it might be a sin) than doing it presumptuously (knowing that a sin might be involved). . . .]

Part 2, responsum 80
Question:
  Is it permissible to have the circumcision performed by a heretic (nonobservant or Reform Jew) if no pious *mohel* can be found, or shall the circumcision be postponed until a worthy *mohel* can be found?
Answer:
  [Hoffmann first cites the decision of Moses Isserles in *Shulchan Aruch, Yoreh De'ah* 264, saying that a Jew who rejects the entire Torah is like a gentile. Therefore, if such a Jew performed the circumcision, some "blood of the covenant" must be drawn later (by a pious circumciser, i.e., the ceremony of circumcision has to be repeated, though not completely).
  Next, Hoffmann cites Rabbi Ozer's opinion saying that a *mumar* (heretic or reformed Jew) who himself is circumcised is, according to the *Shulchan Aruch*, admissible. His conclusion is that a *mumar* is preferable to a woman in regard to circumcision.
  Subsequent opinions cited, among them that of Akiba Eger, seem to be even more lenient. They admit a *mumar* in a case of need a priori (without asking for a second, symbolic, circumcision). In reality, this is not a leniency; it would be more of a leniency to postpone the circumcision from the prescribed eighth day to a later date just to wait for a pious mohel. Hoffmann cities a responsum of Rabbi Eger regarding a question whether an expert *mohel*, who publicly desecrates the Sabbath, was admissible. In his reply, Rabbi Eger says, among other things, that if this *mumar* commits the transgressions in

the presence of ten *mumarim*, this is not considered a public transgression (public transgression is only the one committed in the presence of ten observant Orthodox Jews). In conclusion, he advises that such a man should not be honored and entrusted with circumcision unless no other *mohel* is in town, or in an instance of emergency.

It is possible that admitting a *mohel* who publicly desecrates the Sabbath is called a case of emergency because if he be rejected, arguments might be the consequence. Anyhow, we do not have to investigate and clarify whether this *mohel* desecrated the Sabbath by performing in the presence of ten Jews a kind of work which is prohibited in the Torah. "But with the discreet is wisdom" (Prov. 11:2), i.e., it is wise not to investigate the man involved. So far Akiba Eger.

Emulating Rabbi Eger's lenient tendency in the matter, Hoffmann says that we cannot categorically declare that everybody who is called a heretic is a complete heretic like a *mumar*, who rejects the entire Torah, and we have to judge him, therefore, favorably, at least in considering his circumcision to be proper in a case of emergency; although according to the above authorities a circumcision performed by a *mumar*, rejecting the entire Torah, is also acceptable in an instance of emergency.]

SELECTIONS FROM אוצר נחמד
Otsar Nechmad ("Nichmod")
[Precious Treasure]
by Leopold Yekutiel Judah Greenwald (1899–1955)

Is it proper to have the wedding ceremony in the synagogue?
(pp. 47 ff.)
The question (name not given):

I have seen throughout my lifetime that here in this country
wedding ceremonies performed by Orthodox rabbis are held
in the synagogues, and nobody objects. To my greatest sur-
prise, I saw today a new book: *Responsa of Maharab*, chap. 34,
where the author relates: "It happened at the wedding of his
son, a very pious man who did not permit one to have a wedding
in the synagogue, in spite of very cold weather and danger (to
health). He did this because Isserles cites a view in *Even Ha'ezer*,
chap. 61, that the wedding be held under the sky for a happy
omen: the children of the new couple may multiply like the
stars of the sky. *Chatam Sofer* likewise strongly objected to the
rabbi who arranged weddings in the synagogue. Although Isserles, *Yoreh De'ah* 391, stated that weddings have been arranged
in the synagogues, the (above) author cites *Tiferet Yisrael*, who
claims that Isserles' text has a printer's error. The evidence:
Isserles cites as his source the words of *Hagahot Maimuni*,
and there the reading is: בית הנישואין *bet hanisu'im*, abbreviated as *b.h.* ב"ה The printer erroneously resolved it

בית הכנסת *bet haknesset.* He also cites *Shoel Umeshiv* that, by arranging the wedding in the synagogue, the reformers would be strengthened. . . . My question is: Did the great rabbis of our country not know this? Are all erring and changing the proper Jewish custom? What is your opinion?

[Answer:

When I came to the United States from Hungary and was elected rabbi here (in Columbus), I was confused, because no marriages are performed in the synagogues of our land (Hungary) due to the decision of *Chatam Sofer* and his great disciples, though they did not consider what Isserles cited: According to some authorities weddings must be performed solely under the skies. The fact is that great, pious rabbis perform marriages in the house of the bride for several reasons. If the couple do not want the wedding under the skies, they would not insist. . . . However, no pious rabbi ever performed a marriage in the synagogue. What I saw in New York, i.e., that a hole (skylight) is made in the roof of the synagogue, so the wedding be under the sky, believing this settles everything, is a mistake . . . because the requirement to have the wedding under the sky is secondary, since other prohibitions are extent, if the marriage is performed in the synagogue.

At first, I succeeded in having the wedding in their court-yards and homes. However, later, I could not withstand the trend (pressure) . . . and arranged weddings in the synagogue, but I watched out not to desecrate the sanctity of the syna-gogue. I ordered that the women go to the women's section. I did this after I investigated the law and arrived at the conclusion that weddings are permitted in the synagogue a priori. This in addition to the reason that to do differently is almost impossible in this country, since many uninvited guests would come to the courtyard of the synagogue, whites, blacks, children . . . and would disturb our joy with their mockery. Weddings in hotels are even worse, since they eat there and feed the guests non-kosher or questionably kosher food.

Then Greenwald criticizes the author of the *Responsa Maharab* for publishing his book.] He wants to show in it that he is more pious than many great pious rabbis. . . . He obviously did not see the texts of Isserles, of *Chatam Sofer*. . . . He apparently wrote without thorough study of this matter, as is quite obvious in regard to all the other matters included in the book. . . . This refers to the prohibitions of synagogues that do not have the *bimah* in the middle, to the synagogues in which the cantors wear special clothes as is customary in other religions, though according to their opinion "this is a more serious prohibition than eating pork" (Moses Schick, *Orach Chayim* 71). The author did not care for all this and prayed there.

[Greenwald now cites sources showing that in the Middle Ages and later weddings had been performed in the synagogue. He also rejects the explanation that ב״ה *b.h.* originally meant *bet hanisuin* and not *bet haknesset*, and cites good evidence that at the time of *Maharil* (Jacob Levi, 1365–1427), before and after, weddings were held in Germany in the synagogues. . . . Other sources state that in our time we do not care for the custom of having the ceremony under the skies as we do not care for Karo's and Isserles' advice to have the marriage ceremony only at the time of the growing moon as a good omen.]

No early source states that the wedding ceremony has to take place under the sky (see, e.g., *Machzor Vitry*, p. 588). *Tosafot B. Sukkah* 25b, s.v. *en simchah*, cites the custom to have the marriage ceremony under the sky but only in case there are many people . . . "and a house would not hold them." Similarly the *Tur* (Even Ha'ezer) chap. 62 . . . "occasionally, when there are many people, the marriage blessings are recited under the sky."

[Greenwald brings further sources indicating that weddings

under the skies were unknown in Cracow in Isserles' time. An interesting incident: Isserles once officiated at a wedding ceremony on Sabbath night (resp. 125). Could he have ordered to take the candles on the Sabbath to a place outside. . . . *Bet Shemuel* (Samuel ben Uri Phoebus, seventeenth-century), *Even Ha'ezer*, chap. 30, n. 9, states: "We are customarily arranging divorces and weddings in the synagogue." . . . Thus it is clear that in former times, and later (seventeenth-century), wedding ceremonies were held in the synagogues . . . and in Cracow as late as 1883.

The question to be investigated is why the great rabbis of Germany and Hungary changed the custom and moved the *chupah* (wedding ceremony) from the synagogue to another building, to a courtyard, or to the synagogue court?

According to *Mecholat Hamachanayim* (Israel David Margoliot Yafeh), the *chupah* was removed from the synagogue as a "fence" (precautionary measure). . . . In *Mahatil's* time the bride was led by the women to the threshold of the synagogue, and no woman, except the bride and bridesmaids, entered the synagogue. In those days the bride was very young; today, however, she is an adult and sometimes menstruating; men and women enter with her. Therefore, the rabbis ordained as a fence against incest and separation of menstruating women from the holy place, that weddings should not be held in synagogues. (Greenwald does not accept this reasoning.) Isserles, chap. 88, permits menstruating women to enter the synagogue in principle, even though he writes that this is not the custom in our land. . . . *Magen Avraham*, ibid., permits a menstruating woman to enter the synagogue a priori for a joyous occasion pertaining to her son or daughter. . . .]

[Greenwald's conclusion, based on statements by *Chatam Sofer* and others, is that the true reason for prohibiting weddings in the synagogue is because the Christians require that

weddings be arranged in churches. (Greenwald refers erroneously to a convention of Catholic priests in 1540, in Mantua and
Byzantium, where, among other laws, the law was issued that
marriages must take place in the church, otherwise they have no
validity whatever.) King Charles (Emperor Charles V?) consented that this be the law. Ever since, this has been the law of
the Catholics. The Protestants did not accept this law, and the
marriage can be performed by a judge, without a minister,
and in a place other than the church. Some great Jewish
sages, in opposition to the Catholic law, moved the *chupah*
from the synagogue, since for us the marriage is valid even
without the services of a rabbi. If someone insists on having
the wedding in the synagogue in a country where this (Catholic) law is in force, the prohibition of not following their laws
(Lev. 18:3) applies. However, in our country, the United
States, where most of the people are not Catholics, and even
among them only one in a hundred has his wedding in his
church, the matter is analogous to the instance cited by
Magen Avraham in the name of Joseph Kolon, *Laws of Purim*,
end of chap. 690, "If matters change from what they used to
be in former times, it is permitted to change the custom in accordance with the time." Therefore, it is certainly proper to
arrange weddings in the synagogue, since the consideration
of *Chatam Sofer, Laws of the Gentiles* . . . is not present. . . .]

It is clear that in our country the consideration of following
"their laws" does not apply, and we have to follow the early
institution, as testified by *Chatam Sofer,* that our ancestors
ordained the law to bless bride and groom in a holy place. . . .
but a warning must be issued that the place of the women is
the women's section. . . .

SELECTIONS FROM היכל יצחק
Heichal Yitzchak
[The Tent of Isaac]
Responsa by Isaac Halevi Herzog, (1888–1959)

Vol. 2, responsum 27 (p. 103)

Question:

Is it proper to permit the wedding ceremony to take place in the synagogue?

Answer:

Eve after Sabbath, *tazria* (in Leviticus) 5702 (1942.)

Addressed to: Rabbi Benzion Meir Chai Uziel, Chief Rabbi of Israel.

I received your comments . . . in matters of having the wedding ceremony in the synagogue.

In Poland, where I was born, in Lithuania, and, to my knowledge, in all the countries which were part of Russia until the First World War, the weddings were performed under the sky. . . . generally the intention prevailed to have it in the courtyard of the synagogue or nearby.

When my father and I came to England we found that the weddings there were performed in the synagogue. Though my father did not like this, he had no power to change it, since this has been a custom there for many years. I myself found the same custom in Ireland when I was appointed as a rabbi in Belfast. I had no power to change it, but did not permit the playing of music during the ceremony, neither the harmonium nor the piano.

However here in our Holy Land we do not have this evil custom, thank God. . . . Not merely the Ashkenazim are prohibited to change their custom of having the wedding under the sky, but we have to object strongly that the Sefardim, who do not care for it (having the wedding under the sky), and have the weddings in a building, lest they hold weddings in the synagogue.

I do not want to discuss the matter at length, since this was done by Chayim Medini in *Sede Chemed*, article: *Chatan Vekalah.* . . .

I add to all this that it is prohibited to kiss small children in the synagogue (*Orach Chayim* 98). At a wedding it is impossible to prevent reprehensible kissing. Not merely husband and wife kiss each other, but also relatives and friends, men and women, resulting in transgressing in the synagogue the actual prohibitions concerning close contact with menstruating women, and with persons to whom the incest prohibition applies. Abroad I always have issued a warning both in writing and orally against kissing. Sometimes they listened to me, but many times they did not, and I felt very bad about it.

The great sin of mixing men and women is also present. Though it was possible in the good old times to arrange that only the mothers enter the synagogue, or, in their absence, the bridesmaids, as stated by *Maharil*. However, today it is impossible to make restrictions in this matter, and the important measure of separating men from women, introduced in the Second Temple, became void, and thus the synagogue is being desecrated.

Thank God that I had the good fortune to settle in our Holy Land. . . . Now they come to make innovations (reforms). We have to stand up with all our might against these

changes. "The Torah comes forth from Zion," and the diaspora
has to learn from the Land of Israel, and we must not learn
from the reforms introduced in Western Europe, which we
regrettably could not prevent.

If the intention of the people is to add to the wedding ceremony the aspect of holiness of the surroundings, it is fitting to
have it in the courtyard of the synagogue. It is also possible to
erect a sort of a building in the courtyard of the synagogue,
open above the *chupah*, so that it be under the sky. . . . The
Sefardim do not have to do this, but still should erect a special
structure in the court of the synagogue like the wedding building that formerly existed in every "Jewish" town; see *Choshen
Mishpat* 163. Under no circumstances must the *chupah* be
in the synagogue proper.

Yitzchak Isaac Halevi Herzog

[This responsum is reprinted in *Noam*, vol. 12, p. 358, in abbreviated form. At the end of the responsum, reference is made
to a related responsum: *Noam*, vol. 8, p. 284, "Responsa Be'er
Mayim Chayim."]

SELECTIONS FROM שרידי אש

Seride Esh

[Survivors of the Fire]

Responsa by Yechiel Jacob Weinberg (1885–1966)

Vol. 3, responsum 18, (pp. 41–42) Friday of Sabbath *Shirah*, Berlin (no year given), to Rabbi Mordechai Borer of Geilingen. Question:

A Reform rabbi officiated at a wedding. Now the man wants that an Orthodox rabbi should write a *ketubah* for him and asked whether a new wedding ceremony would be needed, since the wedding ceremony might not have been done in accordance with the law. Or perhaps one should be lenient since gossip might result concerning their only daughter and the previous cohabitations, etc.

Answer:

See *Chatam Sofer*, no. 100, referred to in *Pitche Teshuvah Even Ha'ezer* 42, note 11: A rabbi officiated at a wedding and appointed the sexton (as the second witness). Later they found out that the sexton was a relative (i.e., not admissible as a witness). The conclusion there was that legally there was nothing wrong, since there were many unrelated people present, though the rabbi invited a relative.

Accordingly, in our case . . . there were the sextons and the cantor, therefore why should we worry? Anyhow, . . . you may

say to him, with the words of *Chatam Sofer*, "It is a good thing
and no harm is done if the husband weds her discretely again
in the presence of two qualified witnesses," and in the presence
of the sexton. You may tell him that this is needed for the writing of the *ketubah*, since this was not done properly at the time
of the wedding . . . However, the husband should not be told
that the first wedding was invalid lest gossip be spread about
that rabbi, and also to avoid the belief of husband and wife that
they have conducted a life of lewdness.

                                        Yechiel Jacob Weinberg

Vol. 2, responsum 154 (p. 374)
Fifth day of Chanukah, 5720 (1959), Montreux.
To: Mr. Meir Lewinger.
Re your question whether it is permitted to read the Torah
in a synagogue where the *bimah* is not in the middle. Further-
more: What was the Orthodox practice in Berlin?

I do not know what their practice was, since in Berlin the
place of the *bimah* had only been changed by the liberal Jews.
They also use the organ on the Sabbath and holidays with a
women's choir. A prohibition had been issued against praying
in these synagogues by the great rabbis of our generation because of the many prohibitions involved: prohibition of transgressing the Sabbath, listening to the (singing) voice of a
woman, imitating the laws of the gentiles, desire of assimilation
and actual assimilation among the gentiles.

Re the question whether it is halachically permitted to read
from the Torah in a synagogue which has no organ but the
bimah is not in middle, behold Maimonides, in *Hilchot Tefilah*
11:3, wrote: "The *bimah* is placed in the middle of the house . . .
so that everybody can hear." *Kesef Mishneh* (a commentary
by Joseph Karo) wrote, ad. loc., that this is not a requirement,
but a matter that depends on place and time. The author of the
Shulchan Aruch omitted this law, because in his opinion this is

only a custom. However Isserles, in *Orach Chayim* 150:5, transmitted Maimonides' text. The source is given in *B. Sukkah* 51b, *Yerushalmi*, ibid. 5:1, Zohar, *Shelach* 164b.

[Weinberg now cites references from *Chatam Sofer, Meshiv Davar*, Judah Aszod, etc. Clearly, it is prohibited to change the customary place of the *bimah*, a custom which has been observed for many generations. Moses Schick wrote that not having the *bimah* in the middle is prohibited as a non-Jewish law.]

Although having the *bimah* anywhere but in the middle is prohibited, nonetheless it is not prohibited to pray there, and even less so to read the Torah publicly there. On the contrary, there is a *mitzvah* involved in giving the people the benefit of reading the Torah. The worshippers who come to pray with the congregation committed no transgression. Only the builders of the synagogue and the leaders who made the change acted against the law. I never heard that the rabbis prohibited one from praying in a synagogue which has no *bimah* in the middle (Note: Now I was informed that in Hungary the rabbis prohibited one from entering a synagogue which does not have the *bimah* in the middle. This, however, was done at the time of war against the stream of assimilation. The removal of the *bimah* from the middle of the synagogue was among the first signs of assimilation, which is not the case where the Satan of assimilation does not dance.) I know that in the town of Kiberti in Lithuania, near the German border, a synagogue was built and the *bimah* was placed near the holy ark to the displeasure of the sages. Nonetheless, the rabbis did not refrain from praying there when they happened to be there (in the above town).

It is only as a "fence," lest to strengthen those who displease the sages, and lest they say: "The sages permitted it," that I am advising you, or another Torah reader, not to pray there permanently and to state the reason publicly, that they refrain from praying there because the *bimah* is not in the middle.

However, you definitely must not refrain for this reason from attending public services.

Yechiel Jacob Weinberg

Vol. 2, responsum 107 (p. 256)
Iyar 5698 (1938)
To Rabbi J. Raphael, preacher in Zwickau, Saxony.

The children of a Jewish father and a Christian mother are considered non-Jews. For this reason, as a matter of principle, it is prohibited to give them a Jewish education. However, since the children of (Bar Mitzvah) age intend to embrace Judaism, and the father intends to convert the little children upon reaching majority, it is permitted to give them instruction in Judaism in reliance on the future conversion.

The age of adulthood is thirteen years for boys and twelve for girls, if they are Jewish. However, for non-Jews, the mental maturity is also taken into consideration. Therefore, it is permitted to give Jewish education to non-Jewish children before they reach the age of adulthood, since they, in agreement with their father, want to convert to Judaism. To be sure, first the mature children, who are also mentally mature, should be converted before the lessons may start.

The conversion to Judaism for women is done by three (rabbis, i.e., a *bet din*). She has to obligate herself to fulfill the commandments in their entirety. She also has to immerse in the *mikveh* (see *Shulchan Aruch, Yoreh De'ah* 268: 3 ff.). I suggest that you seek out an experienced Orthodox rabbi to carry out the act of conversion.

Yechiel Jacob Weinberg

Vol. 2, responsum 11 (p. 21), addressed to Rabbi J. Königshofer, Dresden

Re the synagogue with the organ: I have already expressed my opinion that, according to law, it is not prohibited to pray in a synagogue where the liberals pray with organ music on week-days. Praying with organ music is prohibited, but this does not make the place unfit to prohibit it for people who pray there without the organ. People say that there is a ban against it. However I searched thoroughly and found no ban concerning this matter in any book.

Therefore, it is certainly permitted to pray in a building adjacent to the (main) synagogue. However, in a matter like this, the specific conditions and circumstances have to be considered, too. We fully discussed this orally.

Re curtain and fence in the women's section: Maimonides wrote in his Mishnah Commentary, *Sukkah* 5:2: "The place of the women is above the place of the men lest the men gaze at the women." Tosefot *Yom Tov*, ibid., wrote the same. However, in the *Laws of the Lulav* 8:12, he (Maimonides) wrote: "Lest they mix." This is also the reason in Tosefta *Sukkah* 4:1, and Rashi concurs. Therefore, in Poland and Lithuania they are not so strict, because the people there constantly look into the prayerbook and do not lift up their eyes. However, in Germany they are strict on good grounds (one has to follow the stricter local custom, cf. *M. Pesachim* 4). . . . You have to consider the place and time. If it is possible to correct matters, it is certainly a *mitzvah* to do so. However, we should not engage in a big argument and disturb pious people just to make the *mitzvah* more beautiful, dignified. . . .

[After this opinion, Rabbi Weinberg briefly touches on another topic: Rabbi Königshofer should remain in his pulpit if at all possible, and he adds:] I spoke in Breslau to the leaders of the congregation on your behalf. They said: if I know that your sermons would make a deep impression, they would be willing to appoint you (as a rabbi). I did not want them to bother you with trial sermons and the like, so you have to wait. . . .

Yechiel Jacob Weinberg

Vol. 2, responsum 6 (p. 12)
Eve of Shavuot, 5692 (1932)
Addressed to: Rabbi J. Stranski, Nachod.
Question:

May a man who is married to a gentile be counted as a member of the *minyan?* Rabbi Stranski points out that according to *Orach Chayim*, chap. 58, 11–12, a sinner may be a member of the *minyan* as long as he had not been excommunicated. According to the *Peri Megadim*, this only refers to a man who committed a sin to satisfy his "appetite" (desire). However, if a man transgressed the law in order to vex others, he cannot be a member of the *minyan*.

Answer:

At first thought we might say in our case that the man in question commits the sin in order to satisfy his appetite and may be a member of the *minyan*. However, it is pointed out in the Responsa *Zichron Yehudah* that this was so only in former times, when excommunication was possible. Therefore, as long as a man was not excommunicated, he could be a member of the *minyan*. Today, however, excommunication is prohibited by state law, therefore we have to consider the reason, the intent, of our law, and not the formality. This means that every person who transgresses a law, making himself liable to excommunication, is called "excommunicated" inasmuch as he is to be discounted from the *minyan*. Therefore, a man married to a gentile woman, who, according to the law, ought to be excommunicated as a "fence" for the law, is to be considered as being lawfully under a ban, and his inclusion in the *minyan* is prohibited. *Zichron Yehudah*, ibid., chap. 48, renders a decision that calling him to the Torah is likewise prohibited. See also Responsa *Peri Hasadeh* 3:3 and the Responsa *Tsevi Tif'eret*, chap. 39, in great detail.

Yechiel Jacob Weinberg

SELECTIONS FROM נועם

Noam

[Pleasantness]

the Israeli Responsa Yearbook

Vol. 1 (1958), pp. 70 ff. Rabbi Joseph Eliahu Henkin, "About the Conservative Reform on Marriage"
[The conference of Conservative rabbis (ראבּיים) which convened in 1935 decided to introduce a new practice: At the time of the wedding a document ("power of attorney") should be issued authorizing an agent to write and hand over a *get*, a Jewish bill of divorce, to the wife (now a bride) in behalf of her husband (now her groom) after she had received a civil divorce. Such a practice had been proposed and printed five years earlier and called "Suggestion (Plan) for the Benefit of the *Agunot* (הצעה לתקנת העגונות)." The printed text includes the condition that this suggested procedure would be translated into reality only if the great rabbis gave their approval. However, these rabbis did not give their consent to this reform; nonetheless, the Conservatives transformed the plan into reality.

Rabbi Henkin declares that the Conservative measure is tantamount to permitting a married woman to marry another man and has no basis in the Halachah. This reform is contrary to both the Torah and the Halachah and is to be rejected.

Of interest is Rabbi Henkin's concluding statement: If a man and a woman are married only by the secular authorities and live together in a Jewish environment for thirty days, they are also to be considered as married from the viewpoint of the Jewish law.]

Ibid., pp. 283 ff.
[Rabbi Joseph Eliahu Henkin goes on to attack the new Conservative *ketubah*, marriage document, in which bridegroom and bride obligate themselves "to recognize the *Bet Din* of the Rabbinical Assembly and the Jewish Theological Seminary of America . . . to summon either party at the request of the other, in order to enable the party so requesting to live in accordance with the standards of the Jewish law of marriage throughout his or her lifetime. We authorize the *Bet Din* to impose such terms of compensation as it may see fit for failure to respond to its summons or to carry out its decision."

Rabbi Henkin first refers to the negative reaction to this Conservative reform by Orthodox rabbinical organizations. These organizations declared that the innovation was prohibited and the Conservative *bet din* is liable to destroy the sanctity of marriage and of Judaism. Among Rabbi Henkin's arguments against this novel section of the *ketubah* are the following:]

The obligation to observe the laws of the Torah applies to every Jew, no matter whether they attach their signature to a document or not. We know that many Jews do not observe the laws, and their signed paper of obligation to comply with the law is worthless. Moreover, if the *bet din*, supported by the civil government, has the power to enforce a divorce, the signatures of bride and groom are unnecessary. On the other hand, if according to Jewish law no sufficient reason for a divorce exists, the divorce enforced with the help of civil authorities is invalid, since according to Jewish law a *get meusseh*, enforced divorce, is invalid. Likewise, a blank and unspecified obligation, referred to in the Conservative *ketubah*, is also invalid.

[At the end of the article, Rabbi Henkin expresses the suspicion that the Conservatives, by their *takkanah*, innovation (in this case), intend to publicize and advertise their *bet din*. Although the leaders of the Conservatives claim that the purpose of their deviation from the tradition is intended to save whatever can be saved from among those who utterly neglect their Judaism, this dangerous path is liable to blind the eyes of the people. They will continue on their evil path due to the enticement and improper persuasion by the Conservative *bet din* and leaders. This is an abomination. Every pious person should flee from this as from the fire.]

Vol. 3 (1960), pp. 131 ff. Rabbi Benzion Fuerer, On teaching the girls Torah.
Question:

Do the men in charge of religious education act properly in teaching girls the Written as well as the Oral Law?
Answer:

M. Sotah 3:4 reads: "Hence Ben Azzai says: 'A man ought to give his daughter a knowledge of the Torah so that if she drinks (the bitter water) she may know that the merit (that she had acquired) will hold her punishment in suspense.' Rabbi Eliezer says: 'Every man who teaches his daughter Torah is as though he taught her lechery.' The Gemara: 'Do you really mean lechery?' (No). 'It is *as if* he taught her lechery.' "

[Next, Maimonides is quoted (*Laws of Talmud Torah* 1:13): "A woman who studied Torah receives reward, but not the same reward as a man since she is not commanded to do so. Everybody who does something (meritorious) which he is not commanded to do, does not get the same reward as a person who is commanded to do it, but a lesser one. Even though she receives reward, the sages commanded that no man should teach his daughter Torah because most of the women do not have the proper attitude when studying, but, due to their inferior intelligence, interpret the Torah improperly (in a foolish manner). The sages said: 'Everybody who teaches his daughter Torah is as if he taught her lechery.' This refers to the Oral Law; but as to the Written Law, he must not teach her a priori (in principle). However, if he taught her, it is not like teaching her lechery."

Now a lengthy discussion follows in which many halachic authorities are cited. Among these are *Shulchan Aruch, Yoreh De'ah* 246, repeating Maimonides' view, to which Isserles adds: "Anyhow, the woman is obligated to learn the laws pertaining to women." *Ture Zahav*, ibid., holds that women may study a priori the simple meaning of the Written Law, but not in depth.

The biggest obstacle to Rabbi Fuerer's attitude in the matter is Rabbi Eliezer's view (see above), which he forcibly interprets away:] In his (Rabbi Eliezer's) generation the negative view in regard to the study of Torah by women referred merely to the obligation concerning it. This was a generation of knowledge. . . . The daughter acquired her education without intentional (formal) study. . . . (Formal) study in those days did not add to the education of the daughter but detracted from it. Thorough study is more difficult for women than for men. . . .

Though in the generations referred to above, the study of the Torah by women did more harm than good, it is clear that in our generations as of late the study of the Torah by women does more good than harm, for two reasons:

1. Today the question is not whether a girl should study Torah or not even Torah (i.e., nothing at all). The question today is whether she should study Torah or other (i.e., secular) subjects. The insatiable hunger for knowledge took hold of every person, men and women. Who can stem this mighty tide? When the Gemara interpreted Rabbi Eliezer's words to mean

"Teaching the daughter Torah is *as if* she had been taught lechery," we must say that if the girl of our time does not study Torah, she studies lechery (nonsense, secular subjects, etc.) proper. . . .

2. Whether the matter is or is not in accordance with our spirit, it is a fact that today the woman teacher has taken the place of the man teacher of former times. This teacher transmits the Torah to both the boys and girls of the elementary school. If we do not teach the daughter Torah in school (teachers' college), the liberal teacher will inherit the place of the pious (Orthodox) teacher, and she will teach the children of the elementary school the falsified Torah.

Moreover, when Isserles said: "Anyhow, the woman is obligated to study laws pertaining to the woman," this means that the sages prohibited only the study of the Torah for the sake of (theoretical) knowledge, but not the study for the sake of knowing the observance of the commandments. The knowledge on which the deed depends is necessary and welcome. This being so, the observance of the commandments by the children depends on the knowledge of the teacher, since she is the one who transmits the knowledge of the Torah in the elementary school. It is obvious that all the laws are the same for her (i.e., she has to know all the laws), whether they apply to her as a woman or as a teacher of boys.

This appears to be the considered opinion of the great sages of the last two generations. This attitude regarding teaching girls has been positive, not only with respect to the Written Law, but also with respect to the Oral Law, like Mishnah, (other) laws, etc. . . .

Vol. 4 (1961), p. 13 Section *Sha'ar Halachah*, ed. Rabbi Gershon Arieli.
Question: Is it permitted to assume gentile names?

Answer: Translating the Hebrew name into a foreign language is not prohibited. However, changing the Jewish name into a gentile name is definitely prohibited.

Vol. 5 (1962), pp. 52 ff. Rabbi Zalman Sorotzkin, On placing the *bimah* in the middle of the synagogue

[Maimonides states in *Hilchot Tefilah* 11:3: "The *bimah* is placed in the middle of the building in order that everybody should hear the reader of the Torah or the man who admonishes the people when they are on the *bimah*." Karo, in his commentary, in *Kesef Mishneh*, ibid., says, among other things, that the placing of the *bimah* in the middle is not a requirement but depends on time and place. In those days (of Maimonides), when the synagogues were very big, the *bimah* had to be placed in the middle so that everybody could hear, but in our time the synagogues are small and everybody can hear (no matter where the *bimah* is), and it is more beautiful to have the *bimah* on a side than in the middle. . . .

When the *Chatam Sofer* was asked (*Orach Chayim* 28) whether the *bimah* may be placed on the side, he replied: "The person who does this transgresses an explicit statement of the Talmud found in B. *Sukkah* 51. . . ." Although we can judge favorably those who have already acted differently in a small synagogue, this must not be done a priori. This most definitely applies to an old synagogue which is being rebuilt. No changes are allowed in this case. . . . In his will he admonishes us not to change any custom concerning the synagogue. . . .]

All this concerns the Halachah. However, because of the "fence," we must wage an open war against the least change in our synagogue, because any change in the structure leads to many other changes. They will proceed from external changes to internal changes: to changes in the liturgy, to the deletion of mentioning Zion and Jerusalem, of the sacrificial cult from the "prayerbook," as do the reformers. . . .

When the great (Orthodox) rabbis saw, after the time of *Chatam Sofer*, the accomplishments of the "progressive sect," who started out by moving the *bimah* from the center of the synagogue . . . they assembled in 5626 (1866) (*Chatam Sofer* wrote his responsum in 1830) and introduced important measures regarding the synagogue and *bet hamidrash*, viz., that one must not make any changes, neither on the external structure (prohibiting the tower) nor internally (the *bimah* can only be in the middle); to maintain a proper partition between the women's and men's sections; not to change the wardrobe of the cantor and members of the choir to make them look like priests and their servants; and other important measures (see *Lev Ha'ivri*, pt. 2, p. 63, of the Jerusalem 1924 ed.).

These measures were signed by great Hungarian rabbis and a few from Galicia. These ordinances, which were called *pesak din*, "legal decisions," were signed also by Rabbi Chayim of Zancz and Rabbi Yitschak Isaac of Zhidachov. . . .

Furthermore, since the main intention of the "progressive ones" (reformers) is to resemble the gentiles; that their temples resemble the houses of worship of other nations, the rabbi, the cantor, and the choir-members resemble the priests and their servants . . . they are transgressing Deuteronomy 12:30, 31. . . . The sages of Hungary enumerated in this matter eight prohibitions and two positive commandments (violated by the reformers). Why should we argue with the reformers? . . .

The plague regarding the "choir *shuls*" (reform temples) has not spread to Eastern Europe thanks to the alertness of the great rabbis there of that generation. When the sinners of our people planned to build such a (modern) synagogue in Kovno, i.e., a synagogue with a cupola and a *Magen David* on top of it, Rabbi Isaac Elchanan, the leading rabbi of that city, warned them that if they did not remove the *Magen David* from the roof, he would leave the town instantly and would never return . . . whereupon they removed the *Magen David*. . . .

Re the question: Is it permitted to attend a synagogue in which the *bimah* is on the side to be the tenth man of the *minyan?* The decision of the Hungarian rabbis implies that one has to pray alone, not hearing the *Kaddish*, the *Kedushah*, and the reading of the Torah (which require a *minyan*). Even on Yom Kippur he must pray by himself if there is no other *minyan.* . . . I traveled through many countries, especially Russia, Lithuania, and Poland, and saw that the pious Jews, and even the ordinary Jews, refrained from entering such a (modern) synagogue, even though they did not sin in changing the customs and especially the prayers as they now do in the United States. . . .

In the United States every "rabbi" builds a (prohibited) altar for himself. He permits what is explicitly prohibited in the Torah because he does not believe in the divine origin of the Torah. Matters deteriorated to the point that some of them replaced the Sabbath by Sunday to resemble the Christians. In some places they cook on Yom Kippur in one room of the temple, and the rabbi (spelled: ראבײ) announces from the pulpit: "Everybody who is hungry should come and eat on Yom Kippur." They come to the temple in cars and cabs on the Sabbath and Yom Kippur to "pray," and the "rabbi" and priest exchange their pulpits: the rabbi preaches in the Christian church and the priest in the temple. All this results because of the desire to resemble the gentiles (which started with not having the *bimah* in the middle). Mixed marriages are numerous, and the number of apostates is frightening. Even the reformers are scared because of the number of renegades, and seek counsel to stem this, but they cannot do it. . . . Had the great men of Israel seen what is now happening in the temples of the reformers (and even among the Conservatives, in whose synagogues the partition between men and women was abolished; the cantor prays facing the people to please them, and

not God)—they would have rent their garments and torn
the hair of their heads and beards, as did Ezra in his time; and
would have proclaimed a curse and excommunication against
the first step of reform, that is, to move the *bimah* from
the middle of the synagogue in order to make it resemble the
gentiles' houses of worship. Perhaps thus they would have
saved hundreds of thousands of Jews from mixing with the
gentiles and assimilation. This "decree" (keeping the *bimah* in
the middle of the synagogue) certainly would have been acceptable to the Jews everywhere, with the possible exception of
those who shed the yoke of the Torah and commandments, who
deserted the community of Israel.

The question of the person asking whether it is permitted to
enter, pray, and join the *minyan* in a synagogue that has the
bimah on the side implies that he did not find only this fault,
while all the other customs and prayers were all right. In a
case like this pious men may pray there. . . .

The art of the evil inclination (*yetser hara*) is that today he
tells people to do this, and tomorrow to do that, till he says
to them "worship idols," and they do it (*B. Shabbat* 105b) . . .
The *yetser hara* starts everywhere within his power with the
building of the *bimah* next to the holy ark. Next day he says
that the partition between men and women must fall. . . .

If you truthfully observe the rule that the Jewish custom is
like the Torah, you have to place the *bimah* in the middle of
the synagogue . . . because this is a foundation of our faith. . . .

Vol. 5 (1962), pp. 60 ff. Rabbi Mordechai Hakohen, On placing the *bimah* in the center of the synagogue
On the question that again was recently put on the agenda: Is
it prohibited or permitted to place the *bimah* in the center of
the synagogue? . . . This question has been discussed for generations in connection with the spirit of the transgressions

allowing the Reform movement in Germany and Hungary to shake up the House of Israel. The reformers intermingled with gentiles, learned from their deeds, and strove to imitate their laws at home and outside. They are especially obstinate in matters of the synagogue. . . . Many rabbis in former times prohibited one to change the location of the *bimah* because this would be the acceptance of a gentile law; because Jewish custom is like the Torah; and because anything new is prohibited by the Torah. . . . Though the law under discussion had been decided by the great sages of the past so far as its application is concerned, a theoretical discussion is still permitted. . . .

The following sages prohibit it (moving the *bimah* from the center of the synagogue to its side): [Mordechai Hakohen first cites *Sedeh Chemed:* There was a synagogue with the *bimah* in its center. When this synagogue was demolished in order to enlarge it, they planned to move the *bimah* to the end of the building to make it more beautiful and to have more space (for worshippers). *Chatam Sofer* was asked about it (*Orach Chayim* 28) and he prohibited the change.

After listing a considerable number of rabbis opposing the change, Rabbi Mordechai even cites archaeological evidence. On the Greek island of Delos, a synagogue from the time of the Second Temple was excavated, and the place of the *bimah* in its center was recognizable.

The following sages permit it:

The foremost rabbi permitting it is Joseph Karo, who says in his commentary *Kesef Mishneh* on Maimonides' *Mishneh Torah, Hilchot Tefilah* 11:3: "The placing of the *bimah* in the center is no requirement. Everything depends on time and place. In former times, when the synagogues were very big, the *bimah* had to be put in the center so everybody could hear. However in our time, since our synagogues are small and everybody can hear (no matter where the *bimah* is), it is more beautiful to have the *bimah* on one side than in the center."

Many of the great sages of later times follow Karo in permitting to have the *bimah* in an area of the synagogue outside of its center.

After citing several authorities and discussing their views, Rabbi Mordechai points out that Karo's view shows that there were synagogues in his time having their *bimah* at the end of the building.] This was also the case with old and new synagogues in Italy, and in the remaining synagogues of Spain, e.g., Cordova, about seven hundred years old; Toledo (about the same time) . . . in Livorno. In the great majority of the Italian synagogues the *bimah* was at the end of the structure, on the west side, opposite the holy ark. This being the case, why did the great sages of later times disagree with the former authorities, rejecting Karo's opinion, and put up a fierce struggle to allow the *bimah* only in the center? They did this only against the reformers . . . who labored to change not merely this one detail but sought to utterly destroy the foundations of our faith. . . . Since they wanted to strangle the old Jewish spirit by referring to the great sage Karo, the outstanding pious rabbis saw it their duty to make a fence . . . by not permitting the least change lest the sinners come and increase the transgressions. . . .

Maimonides explains (*Hilchot Lulav* 7:23), "They used to go around the altar with the lulav every day . . . and it has already been a universal Jewish custom to place the ark in the center of the synagogue and to go around it every day as they did with the altar in its remembrance." Thus it is explained in Saadya's *siddur*, p. 238, and at length in *Otsar Hageonim* on *Sukkah*, p. 60, in the name of Rabbi Yitschak Ghiat, who quotes *geonim*.

[After a lengthy discussion, Rabbi Mordechai tries to resolve the puzzling fact that some authorities hold that the *bimah* must be in the center of the synagogue, while others, just as pious, permit to have it near the wall, at the end of the synagogue. He makes the conjecture that in Babylonia and other foreign countries the synagogues had been built outside the cities (*B. Eruvin* 21a, *B. Kiddushin* 73b), but in the Land of Israel within the city (*B. Berachot* 8a, *B. Sotah* 22a). If this is so, it is plausible that in foreign countries they did not keep the Torah scrolls in the synagogue but in a safe place outside the synagogue.] They had been brought to the synagogue on the days when they were to be used, and were placed in the ark. . . . The ark was placed upon the *bimah*. The latter was built in the center to enable everyone to hear the reader. . . . However, in places where the scrolls were kept in the synagogue, in the holy ark, the *bimah* was built, or placed, on the western side of the synagogue. . . .

[After this far-fetched conjecture, Mordechai adds final advice which is unrelated to the entire discussion:]

In our time, we mainly have to protest, and even submit to martyrdom, in order that a proper partition be erected in the synagogue between men and women, since this is a law of the Torah in everybody's opinion.

Vol. 5 (1962), p. 321

Question: Is it permitted to say a new prayer which a (liberal) rabbi introduced?

Answer: This is prohibited.

Ibid., p. 330

Question: Is an Orthodox (female) teacher permitted to teach in a Conservative school?

Answer: If this teacher also teaches in a *kasher* (=Orthodox) school, then this is definitely prohibited because the students of the Orthodox school will say that it is also proper to study in a Conservative school. The reason: Both have the same teacher. This may result in great calamity. However, even without this reason it is prohibited to teach in their building even if they say all the prayers as ordained by tradition. . . . On the other hand, if they change the prayers even only a little, teaching them, even in another building, is prohibited. However, if the Conservative children come to an Orthodox school and want to study there in accordance with the strict tradition, then they may be taught Torah. Perhaps they will grow up to be observant Orthodox Jews.

Ibid., p. 330
Question: May a circumciser go to a home where the Sabbath is being desecrated?

Answer: According to the strict law he is prohibited from going to a place where the Sabbath or other laws are transgressed. Nonetheless, he is still obligated to go there and circumcise the child if no other *mohel* is available. However, immediately after he has performed his religious duty he should turn his back and leave.

Vol. 7 (1964) p. 399 Section *Sha'ar Halachah*, ed. Rabbi Moshe Stern.
Question: Is a wedding performed by a Reform rabbi (he is one of those who do not believe in the Torah at all, unbelievers and heretics) valid?

Answer: The marriage is totally invalid unless *kasher* witnesses were present. Every intercourse performed in reliance on the marriage ceremony conducted by the Reform rabbi is null and void (i.e., is like the cohabitation of unmarried persons). [The source for this decision is Responsa *Igrot Moshe*, *Even Ha'ezer* 76, 77. See there in chap. 74 the discussion concerning the marriage performed by a government official; and in chap. 75 about a marriage by nonobservant Jews performed by a gentile court, where the author discusses the above point too, and is very lenient.]

Vol. 8 (1965), pp. 281–92 Summaries of long responsa by Rabbi Moshe Stern, editor of *Sha'ar Halachah*.

P. 281 Question: May a Jewish teacher teach gentiles the Hebrew script or the Hebrew language in their schools?

Answer: It is proper to refrain from doing this.

Ibid., p. 284 Question: Is it permitted to have the wedding in the *bet hamidrash*, the circumstances being the following:

Prior to the wedding, women and virgins dance. After the wedding, at the banquet, men sit on one side, women on the other side with uncovered heads. Furthermore, after the wedding men and women dance separately, except for the family.

Answer: A wedding in a *bet hamidrash* is prohibited even if the bride and groom are orphans. The guests may get drunk at a banquet, even at a *se'udat mitzvah*, a religious banquet, or even at a wedding banquet for orphans. Therefore, a wedding may not be held in a *bet hamidrash*.

Ibid., p. 289 Question: If there are not ten men in the synagogue who observe the Sabbath, is it better to pray at home without a *minyan*, in order to avoid praying with desecrators of the Sabbath?

Answer: It is better to pray at home without a *minyan*.

Ibid., pp. 289–90 Question: If a deceased person has no sons, *may* his daughters, or *must* they, go to the synagogue and say *Kaddish* for their deceased parents?

Answer: This is not permitted, for if they are allowed, people might err and believe that women could also be members of the *minyan*.

Ibid., p. 291 Question: May a man who publicly desecrates the Sabbath be considered a member of the *minyan*; and is there a distinction between a Jew desecrating the Sabbath for the sake of convenience and for spite (*lehach'is*)?

Answer: They must not be included in the *minyan*, irrespective of their reason for desecrating the Sabbath.

Ibid., p. 291 Question: May a transgressor be called to the Torah?

Answer: No, under no circumstances. The congregation should make a rule that sinners are not to be called to the Torah.

Ibid., p. 291 Question: May a man who desecrates the Sabbath publicly be a member of the *minyan?* Should we distinguish in this matter between a man who desecrates the Sabbath just for his convenience (lit. "to satisfy his appetite or desire," a terminology originating with the transgression of the laws of *kashrut*) and one who transgresses the Sabbath in order to vex observant Jews? [For example, there is a halachic and theological difference in the case of a man who eats pork in order to satisfy his appetite, having a desire for it, and the man who does so in order to demonstrate his defiance of the law and vex his law-abiding fellow Jews. The latter transgressor is halachically and theologically a worse sinner than the first one.]

Answer: We must not even admit to the *minyan* of ten men a man who merely desecrates the Sabbath just for his convenience. This even refers to people who never learned about the strict laws of the Sabbath and who may even attend the synagogue on the Sabbath.

Ibid., p. 291 Question: May transgressors be called to the Torah?

Answer: One who desecrates the Sabbath, even if he does it

just for convenience, must not be called to the Torah. It is
within the power of the congregation to introduce a ruling
that no desecrator of the law be called to the Torah.

Ibid., pp. 291–92 Question: If an observant Jew requests that
his nonobservant sons say no *Kaddish* for him, should they
heed the request?

Answer: No, such a "will" has no validity. A father may
warn his sons, however, that if they do not repent, he would
ask them not to say *Kaddish* for him. Such a warning may have
a beneficial effect.

Vol. 9 (1966), pp. 361 ff. Rabbi Ephraim Grienblatt, on Bat
Mitzvah
[Rabbi Grienblatt discusses a new custom—a festival meal
given at the time when a girl reaches the age of twelve years
and one day, that is, the age at which a girl becomes obligated
to fulfill the religious commandments as does a boy at the age
of thirteen years.

The first question Rabbi Grienblatt discusses is whether the
banquet given at this time is considered a *se'udat mitzvah*, a
meal having a religious character, like the banquet given for a
Bar Mitzvah boy by the Ashkenazim.

Before answering the question, Rabbi Grienblatt points out
that the father is duty-bound to teach his daughter the commandments that concern her. Accordingly, we should strive to
arrange a *se'udat mitzvah* for our daughters just as we do for our
sons. However, according to Solomon Luria, the banquet arranged for the boy is a *se'udat mitzvah* only if he gives a
religious talk on the occasion of the banquet. On the other
hand, since a girl cannot be expected to give a religious discourse, the banquet would not be a *se'udat mitzvah*, unless we
permit a man to give a lecture in her behalf.

Next, Rabbi Grienblatt cites passages from the Responsa *Igrot Moshe* (*Orach Chayim* 2, 97). According to this responsum, a banquet given the girl upon her attaining Bat Mitzvah age is not a *se'udat mitzvah* because there is no actual difference between her religious life before and after reaching this age (she does not lay *tefilin*, does not become a member of the *minyan*, etc.). However, according to another authority, cited in *Magen Avraham, Orach Chayim* 225, n. 4 (and whom he cannot identify), it is a *mitzvah* to make a banquet on the day of the Bar Mitzvah just as on the day of the wedding. This indicates that a religious banquet also should be made for girls (the wedding feast is a *se'udat mitzvah* for both bride and groom).

Interesting is a compromise view cited by Rabbi Grienblatt (*Sefer Ben Ish Chai* 17, *Re'eh*): The girl should not be given a banquet, but should rejoice on that day anyway, put on a new dress and recite the benediction *shehecheyanu*, and get ready to accept the yoke of the commandments.

Among further views both pro and con, noteworthy is the notion that the Bat Mitzvah celebration must not be held in the synagogue because this would be an imitation of the gentiles and the "wicked of Israel" (reformers, Conservatives).

Rabbi Yechiel Weinberg (*Pardes, Nisan* 1963) is inclined to permit the Bat Mitzvah celebration provided it is not held in the synagogue, but rather in a private home or in a hall adjacent to the synagogue. He also makes a further condition: The rabbi must lecture the girl admonishing her to observe, from this day on, the commandments. Ultimately, the intention of the people who want to introduce this ceremony is decisive. Do they want to do this for the sake of performing a *mitzvah*, or do they intend to imitate the "heretics" (reformers)?

Rabbi Weinberg's conclusion is: Wherever the custom of

the Bat Mitzvah celebration has been practiced, it may be continued. However, it is better not to introduce this custom in places where it has not been practiced in the past. If it is observed, it must be done in a private home, not in the synagogue. Interesting is his suggestion that it is not worthwhile to put up a fight if the majority of a congregation wishes to introduce the custom. It is important that the custom strengthens the spirit of the Torah and the noble qualities in the hearts of the daughters of Israel.]

Vol. 10 (1967), pp. 288–317

[Rabbi Chanoch Sondel Grossberg gives summaries of a variety of religious aspects of the medical profession, pertaining to the patient, sickness, and treatment. Of particular interest for us is his discussion of the Liberal-Reform physician vis-à-vis the Orthodox physician and Orthodox patient.

Ibid., p. 299 A sick person, even if not seriously ill, may go on a Sabbath to a physician who desecrates the Sabbath though he knows that he will describe on paper the details of the sickness and will also write a prescription.

Even if there is an Orthodox physician in town, a Jewish patient may go to a nonobservant Jewish physician or to a gentile physician, if they are superior. The Orthodox Jewish patient may obey all the instructions of a Liberal-Reform physician.

An Orthodox physician should write the shortest possible prescription on the Sabbath. For example, if he would have to write *tish'im* (ninety) he should write, instead, *me'ah* (hundred), which has two letters less.

It is permitted to call a doctor on a Sabbath, even if he would have to drive a car.

An Orthodox physician is permitted to replace the receiver on the telephone so he could use the telephone in a case of emergency.

Ibid., p. 313 Sterilization of a woman whose life would be endangered by pregnancy is prohibited.

Ibid., pp. 313–14 If a pregnant woman contracted German measles and the physician says that the embryo is in danger, abortion, except during the first forty days of pregnancy, is prohibited. We are not permitted to kill an embryo just because he might be ailing after born.

Ibid., pp. 314–16 If a woman cannot conceive by intercourse, artificial insemination is permitted after ten years of marriage, and by using the semen of the husband. Some Orthodox rabbis also permit the use of another man's semen.

Vol. 10 (1967), p. 321
Responsum summarized by Rabbi Moshe Stern
Question: Is a *get*, Jewish divorce, necessary if the couple were married only in a civil ceremony?

[Answer: The marriage is valid according to Jewish law. If he signed a document to the effect that she is his wife, then this is considered a valid marriage effected by a document. The basis for this ruling is a Tosafot in *B. Yevamot* 31b.]

Vol. 13, (1970), p. 300
Responsum summarized by Rabbi Z. D. Slonim
Question: Is a rabbi who is teaching both Ashkenazim and Sefardim permitted to render decisions (in matters of religion) to members of each of these groups in accordance with its custom? If done, would this not constitute a transgression of the injunction: "ye shall not cut yourselves" (Deut. 14:1), which means, according to traditional interpretation: "Do not split up into separate groups."

Answer: The proper course is to decide for the Sefardim in accordance with the Sefardic ruling, following the customs and decisions of Joseph Karo (author of the *Shulchan Aruch*). On the other hand, for the Ashkenazim decisions should be rendered following Moses Isserles (who added the Ashkenazic practices and customs to the *Shulchan Aruch*). This is the opinion apparent in *Sha'ar Ephraim* 12. It does not constitute a transgression of the prohibition of Deuteronomy 14:1, as explained in *Sifte Kohen* (by Shabbatai Kohen), *Yoreh De'ah* 242, etc. The talmudic proof is found at the end of *B. Yevamot*, first chap. Here it is stated that the above law of Deuteronomy would not be transgressed if there were two congregations in a town, as long as the *bet din*, Jewish court, there would have but one head. Each of the two congregations may legitimately claim that it follows the custom of its ancestors.

Vol. 13 (1970), p. 314

Responsum summarized by J. J. Hershkowitz

Question: Is it permissible to use the pill in order to prevent conception in a case where the physicians advise the mother to use the pill due to the fact that frequent births weaken her?

Answer: In many instances physicians advise women to use the pill for no real reason at all, since they do not appreciate the importance of a blessed and upright generation. The parents are desirous to accept their advice in order only to improve their living standards. If they would be wise, they would understand that all the treasures of the world do not equal the value of the fruit of their womb.

However, in an instance of danger this is the best advice (i.e., the pill is the best means) for preventing conception (see also *Chelkat Jacob*, pt. 2, chaps. 11–14). The pill may also be permitted in an instance of urgent need, though her life is not in definite danger but rather in possible danger (ibid., chap. 12; see also *Noam*, vol. 6, p. 272).

SELECTIONS FROM משפטי עזיאל
Mishpete Uziel
[Judgments of Uziel]
Responsa by Rabbi Benzion Uziel (1881–1923)
Part Two

"Artificial Insemination" (Tel-Aviv, 1935) Responsum 19, pp. 46 ff.

[The problem of artificial insemination entails many considerations:

1. Is a woman impregnated by artificial insemination prohibited to a *kohen* (priest) for being a *zonah* (see Lev. 21:7)?
2. Is such a woman prohibited to her husband?
3. Is her child a *mamzer*, "bastard," if the donor of the semen is a close relative with whom a sexual relationship would constitute incest?
4. Is the child considered to be the child of the donor of the semen?
5. Is a woman impregnated by artificial insemination prohibited to marry for a certain period of time, as is the case for a normally impregnated woman or a woman who is nursing a child?

After a detailed examination of every point in the light of traditional sources, Rabbi Uziel arrives at the following conclusions.

337

(The answers do not follow the questions numerically. We keep Rabbi Uziel's order.)]

1. A woman impregnated by artificial insemination is not a *zonah* and is not prohibited from living with her husband since she did not engage in a prohibited intercourse.

2. The child is not a *mamzer*, even if the donor is a close relative or a *mamzer*, since she did not engage in a prohibited intercourse.

3. A woman is not believed when she says that she was accidentally impregnated while taking a bath in a tub in which a man, not her husband, had previously taken a bath. (Such an accidental impregnation is equated by Rabbi Uziel and other rabbis with artificial insemination.) Therefore, she is not permitted to live with her husband, or to free her child from the blemish of bastardy. However, her claim suffices to the extent that her child is only considered a doubtful *mamzer*, not a definite *mamzer*.

4. A child resulting from accidental impregnation in a bathtub (or artificial insemination) is not considered the child of the man whose semen was in the tub (or of the donor), neither with respect to inheritance nor in freeing the woman from the requirement of levirate marriage or *chalitzah* (the ceremony of rejecting the levirate marriage; see Deut. 25:5–10). However, according to some halachists (Judah Rosanes, author of *Mishneh Lamelech*, and Moses of Brisk, author of *Chelkat Mechokek*), the child is that of the donor in every respect. This means that if the donor is a *mamzer*, the child is a *mamzer* and prohibited from marrying a *kasher* (unblemished) Jew.

5. A woman impregnated by artificial insemination is prohibited from marrying until the time has passed which is prescribed for a naturally impregnated woman. (According to traditional law, a woman cannot marry as long as she is still nursing a child, which she has to do for two years; see

Shulchan Aruch, Even Ha'ezer, 13:11. The reason for this law is that a woman who marries while still nursing a child will concentrate on sex, which in turn may result in the spoilage of her milk. This will kill the child.)

[Rabbi Uziel's final remark is noteworthy:]

I wrote this with my limited comprehension in regard to clarifying this law. So far as its application is concerned, this law belongs to the category of laws about which it is said: "This is the law, but it should not be communicated for practical purposes." That is, it should not be applied (see *Eruvin* 7a; *Betsah* 28b; *Shulchan Aruch, Orach Chayim* 509:2). I wrote what seemed right to me in accordance with my limited understanding.

[Rabbi Uziel's is only one of the many responsa written on artificial insemination. Among later responsa on this topic are:

Noam, vol. 1 (1958), pp. 111–66: responsa by several rabbis. Ibid., vol. 6 (1963), pp. 195–99: responsum by Rabbi Benjamin Fuehrer. *Igrot Moshe, Even Ha'ezer* by Rabbi Moses Feinstein (New York, 1961), pp. 12–13. This is only a small selection of the responsa written on the above topic.

Responsa in English on artifical insemination have been written by Rabbi Solomon B. Freehof and Dr. Alexander Guttmann, both in *Yearbook of the Central Conference of American Rabbis*, vol. 62 (1953), the former on pp. 123–25, the latter on pp. 125–28.]

SELECTIONS FROM אגרות משה
Igrot Moshe (Even Ha'ezer)
[Letters of Moses]
by Rabbi Moshe Feinstein

Concerning a woman married by a Reform rabbi (responsum 76 [pp. 177–78], 12 Marcheshvan 5717 [Oct. 17, 1956], addressed to Rabbi Nachum Draizin)

The case under discussion concerns a woman who was married to a man by a Reform rabbi and where all the men present at the wedding were wicked people, who desecrate the Sabbath and transgress all the commandments of the Torah. The wedding meal consisted of prohibited food which was eaten by everyone present. Now, after some time has passed, the husband has left her, and it is not possible to secure a Jewish bill of divorce from him. Is it possible to permit her to marry someone else since her marriage was not performed in accordance with the law of the Torah?

Answer: In my humble opinion, the marriage performed by the Reform rabbi is invalid if clear evidence can be produced to the effect that no *kasher* (pious, Orthodox) witnesses were present who saw the groom giving her the ring and heard him recite the formula: "Be thou consecrated unto me, etc." According to *Chatam Sofer*, responsum 100 (Even Ha'ezer), if there had been two *kasher* witnesses who stood at a distance and were not able to see whether or not a *kasher* and expert rabbi who officiated had invited relatives to serve as witnesses to the wedding ceremony, this marriage is still fully valid. Although they neither saw nor heard the process of the marriage ceremony, it is not necessary to repeat the ceremony since the *kasher* people present know by estimation, which is comparable to public knowledge, that since the ceremony was performed by a *kasher* and expert rabbi, she was therefore properly married. However, it is clear and obvious that we do not apply the principle of *anan sahade* ... , "We are witnesses . . . ," (i.e., the principle that public knowledge has the same weight as the testimony of witnesses who testify to the proper performance of the ceremony if the ceremony was performed by a "wicked" reformer). The reason for this is that a Reform rabbi performs some kind of act which he invented and says that it was a marriage ceremony. . . . Therefore, it is obvious that the people who did not see and hear the Reform rabbi's ceremony, though they know that he did something which he calls a marriage ceremony, are not acceptable as witnesses to testify that there was a proper Jewish ceremony according to the Torah. This is the case even if it happens that he performed the ceremony in accordance with the law. However, in the case under discussion, this is not to be considered at all because there were no *kasher* witnesses present. Therefore, it is obvious, considering the above marriage ceremony, that she is not married and we need not have any scruples.

However, we have to judge the matter from the viewpoint that they lived together as man and wife, that is, if they lived in a place where *kasher* Jews live. In this case we have to consider the talmudic principles: "The witnesses to privacy are accepted as witnesses to intercourse" (*B. Kiddushin* 65b; i.e., the witnesses who saw the couple entering a place alone, like a room or apartment, and staying there long enough for con-

summating the marriage, are accepted as witnesses to intercourse, the act of consummating the marriage); and "A man
would not perform lewd intercourse, therefore he performs it
for the sake of marriage" (*B. Ketuvot* 73a). However, it is
obvious that we assume that he subsequently performed the
intercourse for the sake of marriage only if he knew that the
marriage ceremony was invalid, as explained in *B. Ketuvot* 73b:
"A man knows that the betrothal (i.e., the act of acquiring the
woman as wife) is not valid if the object of betrothal was worth
less than a *perutah*; therefore, he performs the (first) intercourse for the sake of a valid betrothal. On the other hand,
according to the view that a man does not know that a betrothal
is invalid if the object was worth less than a *perutah*, we say:
"When this man performs the intercourse, he does so in reliance
on the validity of the preceding betrothal" (in which case the
first intercourse is not performed as an act of betrothal, i.e.,
there is no valid marriage). . . .

It is clear that those who go to a Reform rabbi mistakenly
believe that the ceremony was valid and therefore perform
the intercourse in reliance on the preceding ceremony, which
was not valid.

We definitely do not say with regard to these people, who
transgress all the prohibitions of the Torah, that they would
not perform lewd intercourse (see the opinion of Isaac ben
Sheshet accepted by M. Isserles in chap. 26, and Karo,
149:6). . . .

Accordingly, the decision is that the above woman needs
no bill of divorce and is permitted to remarry.

Concerning a woman who was married in a Reform temple
(responsum 77 [pp. 178–80], no date given, addressed to Rabbi
Meir Bogner of Washington)
[The matter concerns a woman who was married in a Reform

temple, and it is known that there was not even one person present at the ceremony who would be considered a *kasher* witness. She and her husband lived together for several weeks in a gentile neighborhood. It is not known, however, whether *kasher* witnesses actually saw them living together. She now claims that because of his wild (abnormal) conduct (lit. "customs") the marriage was not consummated. She possesses a physician's written statement, which she had to show to the civil courts in order that they annul the marriage, stating that she is still a virgin. Her husband is an irreligious person, wantonly transgressing the laws of the Torah and desecrating the Sabbath. He was urged to give her a *get* (Jewish divorce), and (her relatives) were willing to pay him a large sum of money, but he refuses to comply.

She is now an *agunah* (and cannot remarry). Rabbi Feinstein was asked whether permitting her to remarry was possible since the marriage was not performed in accordance with the laws of the Torah.]

The answer:

According to *Chatam Sofer, Even Ha'ezer*, resp. 100, a marriage, even if no *kasher* witnesses were present at the wedding, may possibly still be valid for the following reasons: It is possible that *kasher* witnesses saw the couple enter the temple to be married there, or they saw them leave it as a married couple. However, this naturally refers to an instance in which the officiating rabbi was an expert in matters of marriage and reputedly was a Godfearing (i.e., Orthodox) man, who did not know that the witness whom he joined (as the second witness) was a relative (i.e., a person disqualified as witness). Our case, however, is quite different, since the marriage was performed by a reformer (*sic*) who, besides not being an expert in matters of marriage, does not care at all for the laws of the Torah. Most of the reformers do not perform the marriage ceremony in accordance with the law; therefore, we cannot say that the *kasher* persons who saw the couple enter or leave the temple knew (by conjecture) that the ceremony was performed in accordance with the law and can be considered as witnesses due to the legal principle *anan sahade* (p. 341). The reason for this negative opinion is that even if a marriage ceremony took place, we have a number of particulars that invalidate a marriage if not performed properly. Examples: The ring may have been hers prior to the wedding; or, he may have given it to her before the wedding as a mere gift, meaning that now, at the ceremony, he gives her nothing.

We have to be especially apprehensive that the ceremony may not have been performed properly, which requires that the "man acquire the woman." Many of the reformers merely exchange rings, and she also pronounces a formula. They likewise do a lot of other nonsense which they learned from the gentiles. It is also known that every one of them invents new (ways, customs). Therefore, even if in our case the ceremony were performed properly, . . . the marriage has no validity because there were no witnesses.

[In the next paragraph, Rabbi Feinstein discusses the question whether the common (public) knowledge of her marriage should be considered as validating the marriage. Citing halachic authorities, he rejects this consideration because this common (public) knowledge originated with the ceremony performed by a reformer.

Since the marriage ceremony had no validity, and only they (the couple) believed, erroneously, that it had validity, their living together as man and wife does not validate the marriage. According to the halachic sources cited, the consummation of the marriage may, under certain circumstances, result in a valid marriage, provided it was not done in the belief that the ceremony was valid. This, however, does not apply to the case before us, since the great majority of Americans know nothing about it. Therefore, even if one person happens to know that the ceremony was not valid, this has no effect since most of the people do not know about it and, therefore, the rule *anan sahade* (see above) does not apply here. This means, we do not assume that the couple consummated the marriage in order that it take the place of the marriage ceremony because they knew that the marriage ceremony had no validity.

Next, Rabbi Feinstein discusses the testimony of the physicians who claim that she was still a virgin. He rules that in the case before us, we accept their statement. Even those who maintain the general opinion that we must not rely on the testimony of physicians who are religiously unfit (not *kasher*) and who testify before the court, reason in this case that the physicians would be punished in case their testimony be false and therefore would not lie. They would be afraid also of the husband claiming that their testimony was false. The principle of *anan sahade* applies only if there was a normal intercourse resulting in loss of virginity, as is the case in the majority of instances. Yet, since it is known that there was no normal intercourse or no intercourse at all, as she claims, there was nothing that could be considered as an act of marriage. Afterwards Rabbi Feinstein, citing various sources, shows that there could not have been even a partial intercourse, which may be assumed when a man and a woman are together for even a short time. In this particular case, they had time for many complete acts of intercourse. Consequently, the principle of *anan sahade* does not apply, and there was, therefore, no marriage at all. Even if the physicians would lie, *anan sahade* could not be applied, since most or all people believe their testimony, it is plausible to maintain that they are afraid to lie.

Furthermore, it is unlikely that two *kasher* witnesses saw them living together as man and wife, since they lived together for only a few weeks and moreover in a gentile neighborhood. Therefore, we do not have to worry that there might have been witnesses as long as we have no knowledge about them.

After citing further sources to confirm the above view, Rabbi Feinstein requires that we (know) identify every person who was present at the wedding and establish their disqualification through *kasher* witnesses. This procedure is not necessary for individuals whose stores are open on the Sabbath or for factory workers, in which cases the transgression is obvious and well known in a particular town. The requirement of soliciting testimony is necessary only with respect to people who do not work at the present time, even though they are known as transgressors of the law. It is controversial whether this testimony has to be given in their (i.e., persons to be investigated) presence or not. Rabbi Feinstein quotes several sources pro and con, and discusses them. His conclusion is:

In principle, the witnesses ought to testify, in our case, in the presence of the men present at the ceremony. However, since this is not possible, we must be lenient in a case of *igun*, like ours, where she may be denied permission to remarry by accepting the more stringent principle. Therefore, we may question the witnesses even in the absence of the persons concerned. After you have clarified the fact that no *kasher* witnesses were present at the wedding who saw that the marriage was performed in accordance with the law, she may be given permission to remarry for the reasons stated above.]

THE LANGER CASE

פסק הדין בעניין האח והאחות

Pesak Hadin Be'inyan Ha-ach Veha-achot

[The Legal Decision in the Case of the Brother and Sister]

Responsa by Shlomo Goren, Ashkenazic Chief Rabbi of Israel and President of the Rabbinic Court in Jerusalem

Discussing the most celebrated halachic controversy in Israel's recent history, Chief Rabbi Shlomo Goren, in the above responsum of 200 pages emphasizes that he based his decision that the Langer brother and sister are not *mamzerim*, bastards, on pure Halachah, without concealing his honest halachic conviction. In other words, he did not consider the humane aspect and should not have been accused, therefore, of having been influenced by Liberal or Reform tendencies. He then proceeds by presenting the four principal legal points on which he based the decision. The halachic details are not within the scope of our objective in this book and shall not be discussed here.

One of the nine judges who constituted Rabbi Goren's court said that the decision of the Jerusalem Great Court, which declared the Langer brother and sister to be *mamzerim*, was a halachic disgrace.

Rabbi Goren points out in the interview that he did not

reveal the names of the nine judges in order to protect their lives and honor in face of the many vicious threats.

Rabbi Goren calls the vehement attack waged on him by his (Orthodox) colleagues, among them Rabbi Shach a moral and religious scandal. Even more outspoken is his criticism of Rabbi M. Porush, a member of the Knesset. The late Chief Rabbi Kook, whom Rabbi Porush likewise attacked, and whose effigy he shot and burned, said that the sufferings of Job were nothing in comparison with his (Rabbi Kook's) sufferings resulting from the hateful calumnies and threats. Rabbi Goren admits in an interview (הדואר Hadoar, Dec. 8, 1972, pp. 74–75) that he needs, and is getting, police protection against his fanatical halachic adversaries, just as was necessary for Rabbi Kook. (significant details of the case are given by A. Guttmann, "The Role of Equity in the History of the Halakhah" in *Justice, Justice Shalt Thou Pursue* (New York, 1975).

Selected Bibliography

Adler, Abraham Isaac. *Die siebenundsiebzig sogenannten Rabbiner und die Rabbinerversammlung (in Braunschweig)*. Mannheim, 1845.

Altmann, Alexander, ed. *Studies in Nineteenth-Century Intellectual History*. Cambridge, Mass., 1964.

Aszod Judah. Responsa: תשובות מהרי"א : יהודה יעלה 2 vols. Lemberg, 1873; Pressburg, 1880; New York, 1965.

Baeck, Leo. *Das Wesen des Judentums*. 4th ed. Frankfurt/Main, 1926 (Engl. trans. *The Essence of Judaism* [New York, 1948].)

Bäck, Samuel. *Das Synhedrion unter Napoleon dem Ersten*. Prague, 1879.

Bamberger, Bernard J. "Continuity and Discontinuity in Reform Judaism." *CCAR Journal*, January 1966.

Bamberger, Fritz. "Die geistige Gestalt Moses Mendelssohns." *MGWJ* 73 (1929).

Beiträge zur Geschichte der deutschen Juden: M. Philippson Festschrift. Leipzig, 1916.

Bemporad, Jack. "Rabbinic Attitudes Towards the *Union Prayer Book*." *CCAR Journal*, October 1967.

Ben Menachem, N. פיתבי רבי יהודה אסאד *Sinai* 62 (1968): 5–6.

Benet, Mordechai. Responsa: שו"ת פרשת מרדכי M. Sziget, 1889.
———. הר המור Vienna, 1862.

Berathungen der vom 14. bis 16. April 1846 in Berlin versamnelten Deputierten der Genossenschaft für Reform Judethum. Berlin, 1846.

Berlin, Naphtali Tsevi Yehuda. שו"ת משיב דבר. Warsaw, 1894.

Bernfeld, Simon. תולדות הריפורמציון הדתית בישראל Cracow, 1900.

Bettan, Israel. "Early Reform in Contemporaneous Responsa." *HUCA Jubilee Volume.* Special, 1925.

Blank, Irwin M. "Confirmation as a Conversion Experience." *CCAR Journal,* June 1968.

Blau, Joseph L., ed. *Reform Judaism: A Historical Perspective.* New York, 1973.

Bornstein, Lewis R. "Halachic Problems of Reform Judaism . . ." Unpublished thesis, Hebrew Union College–Cincinnati, 1972.

Borowitz, Eugene B. *The Mask Jews Wear: The Self-Deceptions of American Jewry.* New York, 1973.

Breisch, Mordechai Jacob. Responsa: ס' חלקת יעקב London, 1959.

Bresselau, Meir Israel. חרב נקמת נקם ברית Dessau, 1819.

Brown, Jonathan M. *Modern Challenges to Halakhah.* Chicago, 1969.

Chamiel, Chayim. החת"ם סופר על הריפורמה, על העברית ועל גורל ישראל בין העמים. *Sinai* 54, issue 3 (1964).

Charlap, Ephraim Eliezer Zevi Hirsch. ספר עטרת צבי Warsaw, 1897.

Chorin, Aaron. אגרת אלאסף Prague, 1826.

Chyet, Stanley F., ed. *Lives and Voices.* Philadelphia, 1972.

Cohon, Samuel S., *Judaism: A Way of Life.* Cincinnati, 1948.

Creizenach, Michael. *Schulchan Aruch oder Enzyklopädische Darstellung des mosaischen Gesetzes.* 4 vols. Frankfurt am Main, 1833–40.

Cronbach, Abraham. "The Sprout That Grew." *American Jewish Archives,* April 1975.

Davis, Moshe. *The Emergence of Conservative Judaism: The Historical School in 19th Century America.* Philadelphia, 1963.

Eger, Akiba. Responsa: שו"ת ר' עקיבא איגר Warsaw, 1834; מהדורא תנינא Vienna, 1889.

———, et. al. אגרות סופרים. Vienna and Budapest, 1929.

Eisenstadt, Meir ben Yehuda Leb. Responsa: שו"ת אמרי אש Lemberg, 1852; Ungvár, 1864.

Elbogen, Ismar. *Der jüdische Gottesdienst in seiner geschichtlichen Entwicklung.* 2d ed. Frankfurt/Main, 1924.

————. "Neuorientierung unserer Wissenschaft." *MGWJ* 62 (1918).

Eleh Divre Haberit. אלה דברי הברית Responsa by Orthodox rabbis. Altona, 1819.

Epstein, H. Fischel. Responsa: תשובת שלמה ס' 2 vols. St. Louis, 1913–41; 2d ed. Chicago, 1948.

Erster Bericht der Genossenschaft für Reform im Judentum abgestellt von deren Bevollmächtigten. Berlin, 1845.

Ettlinger, Jacob. בנין ציון ;ב"צ החדשות Wilno, 1878.

Feinstein, Moses. אגרות משה , אבן העזר 4 vols. New York, 1959–63.

Felsenthal, Bernhard. *Kol Kore Bamidbar, Ueber jüdische Reform. Ein Wort an die Freunde derselben.* Chicago, 1859.

Fishman, J. L. ערים ואמהות בישראל Jerusalem, 1948.

Fleckeles, Eleazar. Responsa: שו"ת מהר"אף ,תשובה מאהבה 3 vols. Prague, 1809–21.

Freehof, Solomon B. *Reform Jewish Practice and Its Rabbinic Background.* 2 vols. Cincinnati, 1944–52.

————. "Reform Judaism and the Halacha." In *Central Conference of American Rabbis Yearbook*, vol. 56. Philadelphia, 1947. Reprinted in *Reform Judaism, A Historical Perspective*, edited by Joseph L. Blau. New York, 1973.

————. *The Responsa Literature.* Philadelphia, 1955.

"Gates of Prayer . . ." (Essays by Lawrence A. Hoffman, Harvey J. Fields, Abraham J. Klausner, Samuel M. Silver, and Robert I. Kahn). *CCAR Journal*, Spring 1973.

Geiger, Abraham, *Nachgelassene Schriften.* 5 vols. Berlin, 1875–78.

Gellman, A. Leon. על פשעי הריפורמה Jerusalem, 1957.

Glueck, Nelson. "The Role of the Hebrew Union College in Jerusalem." *CCAR Journal*, October 1963.

Goldstein, Albert S., "Should We Give a Get?" *CCAR Journal*, June 1967.

Gordis, Robert. *A Faith for Moderns.* New York, 1960.

Goren, Shlomo, פסק הדין בענין האח והאחות Jerusalem, 1973.

————. Interview in *Hadoar*, December 8, 1972, pp. 74–75. הקיצוניים לא יקימו קהילות נפרדות reported by J. Kamai.

Gottschalk, Alfred. *Your Future as a Rabbi: A Calling That Counts.* New York, 1967.

Graetz, Heinrich, *The Structure of Jewish History and Other Essays*. Translated, edited, and introduced by Ismar Schorsch. New York, 1975.

Graupe, Heinz Mosche, *Die Entstehung des Modernen Judentums. Geistesgeschichte der deutschen Juden 1650–1942*. Hamburg, 1969. (Bibliography pp. 376–80.)

Greenwald, Leopold (Yekutiel Yehuda). אוצר נחמד Columbus, 1942.

———. לפלגות ישראל באונגריא Deva, 1929.

———. לתולדות הריפורמציון הדתית בגרמניא ובאונגריא Columbus, 1948.

Guttmann, Joseph, comp. *The Synagogue: Studies in Origins, Archaeology and Architecture*. New York, 1975.

Guttmann, Alexander. "The Moral Law as Halacha in Reform Judaism." In *CCAR Yearbook*, vol. 68. Chicago, 1958. Reprinted in *Reform Judaism: A Historical Perspective*, edited by Joseph L. Blau. New York, 1973.

———. *Studies in Rabbinic Judaism*. New York, 1976.

Guttmann, Michael. *Das Judentum und seine Umwelt*. Berlin, 1927.

———. "Die Stellung Mendelssohns zur Christlichen Umwelt." *MGWJ* 74, 1930.

Hamburger, Ernst. "One Hundred Years of Emancipation." *Leo Baeck Institute Year Book* 14. London, Jerusalem, and New York, 1969.

Hamburger, Wolfgang. "The Hebrew Union College." *Festschrift zum 80. Geburtstag von Leo Baeck*. London, 1953.

Herzog, Isaac. Responsa: שו"ת היכל יצחק, אבן העזר Part 1: Jerusalem, 1960; Pt. II: Jerusalem, 1967.

Hirsch, Richard G. "Social Values in Judaism and Their Realization in the Reform Movement." *CCAR Journal*, October 1971.

Hirsch, Samson Raphael (Pseudonym: Ben Usiel). *Neunzehn Briefe über Judentum*. Altona, 1836. In English: *The Nineteen Letters of Ben Uziel*, translated by B. Drachman. New York, 1942. In Hebrew: אגרות צפון Tel Aviv, 1948.

Holdheim, Samuel. *Ueber die Autonomie der Rabbiner und das Prinzip der jüdischen Ehe*. Schwerin, 1843.

———. *Die Religionsprinzipien des reformierten Judentums*. Berlin, 1847.

————. *Geschichte der Entstehung und Entwickelung der jüdischen Reformgemeinde in Berlin*. Berlin, 1857.

Horowitz, David M. "The Use of Halacha Dealing with Marriage in the Reform Movement . . ." Unpublished thesis, Hebrew Union College–Cincinnati, 1969.

Kabakov, Jacob. תגובות עבריות לריפורמה באמריקה (Hebrew Reactions to reform in America). *Hadoar*, April 5, 1974.

Kalish, Moritz. *Berlins Jüdische Reformatoren*. Berlin, 1845.

Kaplan, Mordechai M. *Judaism without Supernaturalism: The Only Alternative to Orthodoxy and Secularism*. New York, 1958.

Karff, Samuel E. "Judaism, Reform and Radical Reform." *CCAR Journal*, April 1968.

————, ed. *Hebrew Union College–Jewish Institute of Religion At One Hundred Years*. Cincinnati, 1976.

————. "The Rabbinic 'Idea of the Holy'" Unpublished D.H.L. dissertation. Hebrew Union College–Cincinnati, 1961.

Katz, Eliezer. החת"ם סופד Jerusalem, 1960.

Katz, Robert L. "David Caro's Analysis of the Rabbi's Role." *CCAR Journal*, April 1966.

Kaufman, J. H. יהדות רפורמה ללא משפט קדום in בתפוצות הגולה 4, no. 3. (Jerusalem, 1962).

Kluger, Solomon. האלף לך שלמה Jerusalem, 1968.

Korn, B. W., ed. *Retrospect and Prospect: Essays . . . CCAR 1889–1964*. New York, 1965.

Kravitz, Leonard S. "The Problem of the Prayer." *CCAR Journal*, October 1965.

Landman, Leo. *Jewish Law in the Diaspora*. Philadelphia, 1968.

Lehren, Zevi Hirsch, and Prins, A. A., eds. תורת הקנאות Amsterdam, 1845.

Levinsohn, Isaak Baer. מגלה עפה Carney, 1904.

Libermann, Eliezer. אור נגה Dessau, 1818.

Lichtenstein, Hillel. Responsa: תשובות בית הילל Szatmár, 1908.

Lipa, Chayim David (Yafeh). ששה מכתבים המפיצים אור Kassa, 1866.

Löw, Leopold. *Gesammelte Schriften*. 5 vols. Szeged, 1889–1900.

Löwenstamm, Abraham. Responsa: צרור החיים 2d ed. Sa.–Ujhely, 1868.

[Mahalumot...] מהלמות לגו כסילים, בגימטריא: גייגר (אויב) וכת דיליה:

(two letters by orthodox rabbis on the Synod in Augsburg, 1871). Leipzig, 1871.

Marcus, Jacob R. *Memoirs of American Jews, 1775–1865.* Philadelphia, 1955–56.

———. *Reform Movements in Judaism.* New York, 1963.

———, ed. *Essays in American Jewish History.* Cincinnati: American Jewish Archives, 1958.

Martin, Bernard. *Prayer in Judaism.* New York, 1968.

———. "Can Jewish Worship Be Restored?" *CCAR Journal*, April 1965.

———. *A History of Judaism.* Vol. 2, *Europe and the New World.* New York, 1974.

Mendelssohn, Moses, *Ritualgesetze der Juden . . .* Berlin, 1778.

Mevorach, B. נפוליון ותקופתו, רשימות ועדויות עבריות של בני הדור Jerusalem, 1968.

Meyer, Michael A. *The Origins of the Modern Jew.* Detroit, 1967. (Bibliography pp. 220–43).

———. "A Centennial History," Part I of *Hebrew Union College– Jewish Institute of Religion At—One Hundred Years*, ed. Samuel E. Karff. Cincinnati, 1976.

Mihaly, Eugene. "A Guide for Writers of Reform Liturgy." *CCAR Journal*, April 1965.

———. "Reform Judaism and Halacha: The Contemporary Relevance of the *Mishneh Torah* of Maimonides." *CCAR Yearbook* 64 (1954).

Millgram, Abraham A. *Jewish Worship.* Philadelphia, 1971. (Bibliography pp. 633–48.)

Neumann, Paul. *Die Reform des Judentums zu Berlin (Aufforderung zur Taufe).* Berlin 1846.

[Nogah Hatsedek] נוגה הצדק (four responsa by reform rabbis). Dessau, 1818.

שו"ת בשמים ראש Ascribed to R. Asher and later rabbinical authorities. Berlin, 1793; Cracow, 1881.

Oppler, P. F.; Ostertag, R. D.; Levy, H.; and Zedner, I., eds. *Zeitgemässe Organisation der gottesdientstlichen Gebräuche in Unruhstadt (Karger).* Unruhstadt, 1843.

Panet, Chayim Bezalel. Responsa: שו"ת דרך יבחר Munkács, 1894.

Petuchowski, Jakob J. *Prayerbook Reform in Europe: The Liturgy of European Liberal and Reform Judaism*. New York, 1968. (Bibliography, pp. 393–99.)

———. "Karaite Tendencies in an Early Reform Haggadah." *HUCA* 31 (1960).

Plaut, W. Gunther. *The Rise of Reform Judaism*. New York, 1963. (Bibliography, pp. 266–74.)

———. "The Sabbath and the Reform Movement." In *Reform Judaism: A Historical Perspective*, edited by Joseph L. Blau. New York, 1973.

Philipson, David. *The Reform Movement in Judaism*. Rev. ed. New York, 1931.

Protocolle der dritten Versammlung zu Breslau 13–24 Juli, 1846. Breslau, 1847.

Protocolle der ersten Rabbiner–Versammlung zu Braunschweig, 12–19 Juni 1844. Braunschweig, 1844.

Protocolle und Aktenstücke der zweiten Rabbinerversammlung 15–28 Juli 1845 in Frankfurt/Main. Frankfurt, 1845.

Reform Judaism. Essays by Hebrew Union College Alumni. Cincinnati, 1949.

Reines, Alvin J. "Reform Judaism." In *Meet the American Jew*, edited by Belden Menkus, Nashville, 1963.

Rotenstreich, N. "עם עובד", תל אביב, המחשבה היהודית בעת החדשה Tel-Aviv, 1945–49/50.

Rubinstein, B. בישראל . . . המערכה לתקון הדת Ph.D. dissertation, Jerusalem, 1958.

Rülf, S. F., ed. *Paul Lazarus Gedenkbuch: Beiträge zur Würdigung der letzten Rabbinergeneration in Deutschland*. Jerusalem, 1961.

Samet, Moshe Shraga. הלכה ורפורמה (ההלכה מול הבעיות המציאות בראשית העידן המודרני) [Halachah and reform—the confrontation of Halachah and actuality at the beginning of the modern era.]

Sandmel, Samuel. "The Clew to Survival," *CCAR Yearbook*, 1953. *A Jewish Understanding of the New Testament*, Cincinnati, 1956.

Schick (Sik), Moshe. Responsa: שו"ת מהר"ם שיק 4 vols. Vols. 1 and 2: Munkács 1880–81; Vols. 3 and 4; Lemberg, 1884.

Schlesinger, Akiba Josef. בית יוסף חדש Cracow, 1886.

———. לב העברי [Commentary on the will of Moshe Sofer]. Ungvár, 1864.

Schreiber, Abraham Samuel Benjamin (Ketav Sofer). Responsa: שו"ת כתב סופר 4 vols. Vols. 1–3, Pressburg, 1873–88. Vol. 4, Drohobycz, 1894.

Schreiber, Emanuel. *Reformed Jews and Its Pioneers.* Spokane, 1892.

Schreiber (Sofer, *Chatam Sofer*) Mosheh. Responsa: חתם סופר 6 parts. Pressburg, 1841–64. 7th part with notes by R. Simon. Munkács, 1919.

———. דרשות 3 vols. Cluj, 1929–39.

Schwarz, J. ס' זכרון למשה ה"/חתם סופר". New York, 1938.

Schwartzman, Sylvan D. *Reform Judaism Then and Now.* New York, 1971. (Bibliography pp. 229–32.)

Seligman, Caesar. *Geschichte der jüdischen Reformbewegung.* Frankfurt am Main, 1922.

Shohet, Azriel. *Beginnings of the Haskalah Among German Jewry.* עם חלופי תקופות. ראשית ההשכלה ביהדות גרמניה Jerusalem, 1960.

Silberman, Lou H. "The Theologian's Task." In *Reform Judaism: A Historical Perspective*, edited by Joseph L. Blau. New York, 1973.

Silver, Daniel J., comp. *Judaism and Ethics.* N.Y. 1970.

Spicehandler, Ezra. "Joshua Heschel Schorr: Maskil and Eastern European Reformist." *HUCA* 31 (1960).

Spitzer, Binyamin Shlomo Zalman. ספר תקון שלמה Vienna, 1892.

Stern, Selma. *Der Preussische Staat und die Juden.* 4 vols. Tübingen, 1962.

Strauss, H. A., and Grossman, K. R., eds. *Gegenwart im Rückblick.* Heidelberg, 1970.

Tal, Uriel. יהדות ונצרות ב"רייך השני" [Christians and Jews in the "Second Reich" (1870–1914)]. Jerusalem, 1969.

Tama, D. *Transactions of the Parisian Sanhedrin.* London, 1807.

Tiktin, Solomon. *Darlegung des Sachverhältnisses in seiner hiesigen Rabbinats Angelegenheit.* Breslau, 1842.

Tovya, Chayim, of Linik. Responsa: שו"ת דברי חיים Pietrikow, 1903.

Urbach, E. E. חז"ל, פרק אמונות ודעות [The sages: their concepts and beliefs]. Jerusalem, 1969.

Wallach, Luitpold. *Liberty and Letters: The Thoughts of Leopold Zunz.* London, 1959.

Zierelsohn, M. Chayim. Responsa: מערכי לב Chisinau, 1932.

Zilberg, A. B. Responsa: שו"ת משנת בנימין New York, 1948.

Zunz, Leopold. *Zur Geschichte und Literatur.* Berlin, 1845.

Zutra, Abraham. מלחמות ה' 3 vols. Hannover, 1836–63.

Zweiter Bericht der Genossenschaft für Reform Judentum abgestellt von deren Bevollmächtigten. Berlin, 1846.

Periodicals, Journals, Yearbooks

American Jewish Archives (Hebrew Union College–Jewish Institute of Religion, Cincinnati, Ohio).

American Jewish Historical Quarterly (American Jewish Historical Society, Waltham, Mass.).

Bitsaron: The Hebrew Monthly of America בצרון. ירחון למדע, לספרות ולבעיות הזמן (New York, N. Y.).

Central Conference of American Rabbis Journal (New York, N. Y.).

Central Conference of American Rabbis Yearbook (New York, N. Y.).

Conservative Judaism (New York, N. Y.)

Die Allgemeine Zeitung des Judentums (Leipzig, 1837–1922).

Ha'arets, Ma'ariv. מעריב, הארץ (Israeli daily newspapers).

Hadoar. הדאר (Histadruth Ivrith of America, New York, N.Y.).

Hatsofeh, Quartalis Hebraica. הצופה לחכמת ישראל (Budapest, 1911–31. Index Jerusalem 1973).

He'atid. העתיד. מאסף ספרותי – מדעי לברור עניני היהדות והיהודים. (Berlin, 1908–14).

Hebrew Union College Annual (Cincinnati, Ohio).

Hechaluts. החלוץ. מאמרי בקורת מחכמי הדור Lemberg (1852–89).

Historia Judaica (New York, N. Y., 1938–61).

Jewish Quarterly Review (Philadelphia, Pa.),

Jewish Social Studies (New York, N. Y.).

Jüdische Zeitschrift für Wissenschaft und Leben (Breslau, 1862–75.).

Kenesset Yisrael, כנסת ישראל. ספר שנתי לתורה ולתעודה. (Year-book, Warsaw, 1866).

Kiryat Sefer קרית ספר. רבעון לביבליוגרפיה של בית הספר הלאומי והאוניברסיטאי בירושלים (Bibliographical quarterly of the Jewish National and University Library, Jerusalem).

Leo Baeck Year Book (Leo Baeck Institute, London, Jerusalem, New York).

Magyar Zsidó Szemle (Budapest).

Monatsschrift für Geschichte und Wissenschaft des Judentums. (Breslau 1851–1939 [printed in Frankfurt am Main]; last vol. reprinted in Tübingen, 1963).

Noam: A Forum for the Clarification of Contemporary Halakhic Problems. נועם. שנתון לבירור בעיות בהלכה. (yearbook Torah Shelemah Institute in Jerusalem).

Otsar Hachayim, Zeitschrift für die Wissenschaft des Judentums. אוצר חיים, מאסף לתורת ישראל ולדברי ימי חייו Seini, 1925–1938.

Reconstructionist (New York, N. Y.).

Shalhevet שלהבת (Israeli newspaper).

Shomer Tsiyon Hane'eman שומר ציון הנאמן (Altona, 1846–55).

Sinai. סיני. ירחון לתורה למדע ולספרות. (monthly periodical published by Mosad Harav Kook, in Jerusalem).

Tarbits. תרביץ. רבעון למדעי היהדות. (quarterly for Jewish Studies. Jerusalem).

Tradition. (Rabbinical Council of America, New York, N. Y.).

Wissenschaftliche Zeitschrift für jüdische Theologie (Frankfurt am Main, 1835–47).

Zeitschrift für die religiösen Interessen des Judenthums. (Berlin. 1844–46).

Zeitschrift für die Wissenschaft des Judenthums. (Berlin, 1822).

Indices

/